AF364482

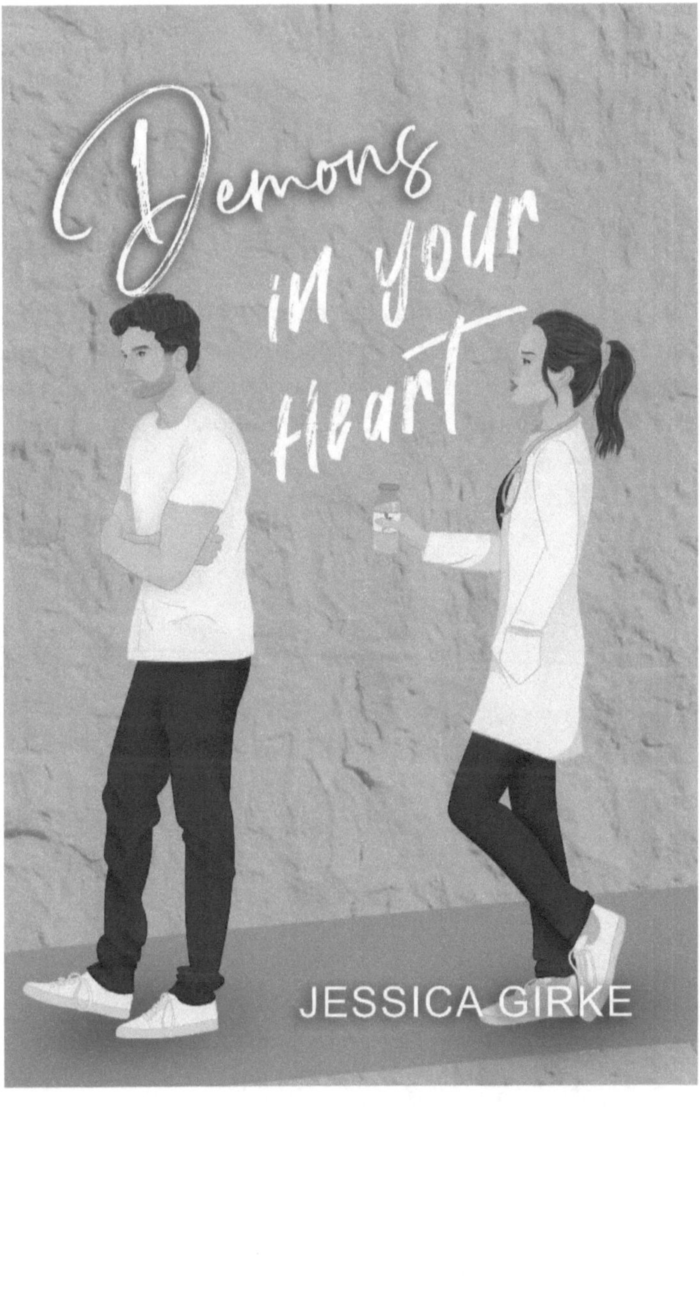

Demons in your Heart

JESSICA GIRKE

First edition

Cover Design by Joelina Falk
Editing by Becky Clapham

*"We all deserve second chances,
but not for the same mistake."*
*- Thabiso Owethu Xabanisa*

*To everyone who needs someone
to pull them out of their rabbit hole.
This one is for you.
You are not alone.
Keep fighting!*

<u>Content Warnings:</u>
Emotional trauma (grief, death, torture)
PTSD
Anxiety and panic attacks
Physical and mental violence
Detailed descriptions of accidents and injuries
Blood
Toxic behavior from parents
Self-hurt

# By your side

**June 2nd, 2022**

Lynn Summers, former lead doctor at the CIA headquarters, was sitting on the large queen-sized bed in her bedroom, her brown hair hanging damp around her face. The drenched knee-length black dress that she was wearing had soaked the sheets underneath her.

She didn't care.

Her gaze was fixed on the shining silver bracelet in her hands. It was a simple one with only a little heart pendant on it that contained two letters as an inscription:

A & L

Her sister Ann had given it to her when Lynn finished med school and had finally started to live her dream working as a doctor. Ann had told her that "with this bracelet she was always by her side, no matter how stressful life would be," but because Lynn's job required her to be in the OR so much, she never wore it.

Until last week when her whole world was turned upside down.

Ann was killed.

By terrorists.

Aiman az-Zawahiri had kidnapped Ann in May and tortured her for weeks until Lynn was able to provide him with some useful information about the CIA's terrorism task force. He was insanely obsessed with the idea of U.S. Agents or the military coming after him and tried everything to prevent his own death. Even kidnapping an innocent woman to get information.

To have a chance to save her sister's life, Lynn was forced to betray the man she had fallen in love with, Nate "Butch" Sheppard; CIA Agent and former Navy SEAL. He and Az-Zawahiri had a complicated past, as the Iraqi had kidnapped and tortured Nate in 2011 – leaving him with PTSD and severe nightmares that held him hostage to his own past ever since.

Lynn's mind wandered to the handsome man with the ocean blue eyes. She remembered the hurt and anger behind them the moment he realized her betrayal, turning them into a stormy ocean.

But when Lynn hit rock bottom, this man came and gave her a chance. A chance she didn't deserve and never expected to get. She'd repeated his words in her mind over and over during the past few days:

*"You didn't lose me, Lynn. I'm hurt. I really am. Your betrayal feels like a million needles inside my heart and you know how much I hate needles. But whatever this is between us is something special. It took me a while to figure it out but my heart skips a beat every time I hear you laugh, and my skin feels like*

*it's burning every time you touch me. You and I. This is special. And I don't want to give that up yet."*

And he really tried, more than Lynn expected him to. More than she deserved.

Today, at Ann's funeral, Nate had been by her side the entire time, even when Lynn was about to collapse at her sister's grave.

Her parents didn't take the message of Ann's death and the funeral very well. Her mother Thea cried the entire time, refusing to talk to Lynn and give her the comfort and embrace that the doctor needed. It was a difficult situation, even more difficult than the time her father, Jensen, had been in the ICU after catching Covid. He suffered from COPD, so his case was a severe one.

Although Ann lived further away from home than Lynn, she had been the one who kept everyone together, organizing frequent gatherings with the whole family like Easter brunch or Christmas dinners. She had also helped her parents with all the practicalities like insurance and taxes. She was a workaholic as well but had a more flexible working schedule so she could help more spontaneously. It was mostly via FaceTime though, as New York City was still a 90-minute flight from Washington.

Ann was the starlight of the family.

Thea and Jensen were proud of Lynn as well. Very proud. But they weren't as close as they used to be. Lynn had to cancel a lot of meet-ups with her parents due to her job. She was dedicated and her job was her priority, leaving her parents angry and alone way too often. Thea always told her to maintain friendships and not to live for her job.

"You only have one life, Lynn," was the mantra she repeated over and over again.

But her job made Lynn happy. It was what she wanted, what she dreamed of, and starting at the CIA was the height of that dream. Normally she didn't care if her parents disagreed with her life choices, but today things had gotten out of hand.

The starlight of the family was dead.

Lynn was now the only daughter remaining.

Nate thought about how lost Lynn had looked standing in front of Ann's grave, far away from her parents. Too far. He felt his heart ache for her and he tried to comfort her as much as he could.

Hold her. Support her. Be there for her.

His mind had never been so chaotic and confused. He'd heard a lot of songs about "Head versus Heart", but he'd never truly understood this line until now.

Now, when his mind was scolding him to not trust Lynn, to not let her be in his life, his heart was defending her. Because he loved her. Because he'd never felt so good around someone. Being with her felt easy, felt right, felt like it was the only thing he needed to survive. Her presence, her holding his hand, her kissing him. When he was with her, he felt like he was on an all-time high and that all his demons were silenced.

Gone.

The feeling overpowered the voice of doubt the moment he stood next to the doctor with his hand on the small of her back, in front of Ann's grave.

Nate remembered Lynn crying, loud sobs coming out of her mouth, and he remembered how her parents suddenly came close, standing next to Lynn in front of Ann's still open grave. How they carefully let the white roses in their hands fall down into the grave and onto Ann's coffin.

Thea was standing right next to Lynn, carefully taking her hand for the first time in hours, giving her some kind of comfort while sharing the same grief. Nate remembered how Lynn's eyes eventually teared up and how she reached for his hand to steady herself. He was happy for her. Happy that her parents finally gave her the contact she'd been so desperately craving the entire day.

He had been by her side but it was pretty obvious that she needed her parents. He hadn't known Ann at all and so he wasn't able to share the same kind of grief with Lynn.

"I'm so sorry," Lynn had mumbled over and over again to her parents. Louder, quieter, sometimes even swallowed by her sobs.

"I am too, sweetie," Thea had replied, her head hanging low and her eyes fixed on the coffin but she squeezed her daughter's hand slightly.

"This is all your fault," Nate heard Jensen mumble under his breath. He didn't know if Lynn had heard it too as she was still apologizing constantly.

"This is all your fault," the older man repeated.

Lynn's body stiffened and she stopped repeating the words. Painfully slowly her head turned towards her father, her lips parted, and her brows knit together.

"Jensen," Thea said in a straight voice. She was the only physical shield between Lynn and her husband while she tried to prevent the situation from escalating.

"No, sweetheart. It's her fault that Ann is dead. Our perfect little Ann and you know it too," Jensen hissed between his teeth.

His angry glare locked with Lynn and he shook his head and turned around to go back to the car. As if the world was grieving for the torn apart family, the heavens opened up and raindrops began to soak their clothes.

"I'm sorry, sweetie. He doesn't mean it. You know he's not good with emotions. He loves you," Thea mumbled before pulling Lynn into a tight hug.

Lynn didn't return it, her arms hung next to her body, shoulders tensed and stiff. She didn't cry, she didn't yell, she didn't argue. The moment Thea let go of the embrace, Lynn looked at her mother with certainty in her eyes before announcing,

"He's right. This *is* all my fault."

"Lynn!" Nate and Thea exclaimed in unison, neither willing to let Lynn blame herself for this.

There was only one person to blame and he'd already paid for it with his life.

"We love you, don't forget that," her mother said while grabbing Lynn's face with both of her hands and forcing her to look at her.

The doctor heard it but didn't respond, not even with a nod. Thea let go of Lynn's face and stepped away from her before she raised her gaze and looked at Nate.

"It was nice to meet you. Even in these very sad circumstances. Make sure that she's alright. You can call us... call me every time. I would love to meet you two again."

"I will. Thank you, Ma'am," Nate responded with a respectful nod.

Thea looked at her daughter once more before turning towards Ann's grave.

"I love you, Ann. I'll be back tomorrow," the older lady mumbled before finally leaving the graveyard towards the car where Jensen was already waiting.

"Lynn," Nate said carefully, but Lynn was completely lost in her own mind, her gaze fixed on the coffin below her so Nate was forced to simply stand by her side, holding her hand silently while the rain worked its way through their clothes until even their skin was soaked.

When the female doctor began to shake, Nate pulled her into his embrace and started to rub his hands up and down her back. He needed to get her home as soon as possible so that she didn't get an infection.

"Lynn..." he started again but was interrupted by her immediately. Her teeth were chattering, and she was hard to understand.

"I.. kn..ow... We.. We.. need t..to go h..ho..home."

"Yeah. Let's get you out of those clothes," Nate said and gently led her to the car that was waiting for them.

Oliver had organized a driver for Lynn so that she didn't have to drive back to the compound in her current mental state. The entire way back to the headquarters she was clutching the bracelet, her thumb carefully caressing over the small A that was engraved in it.

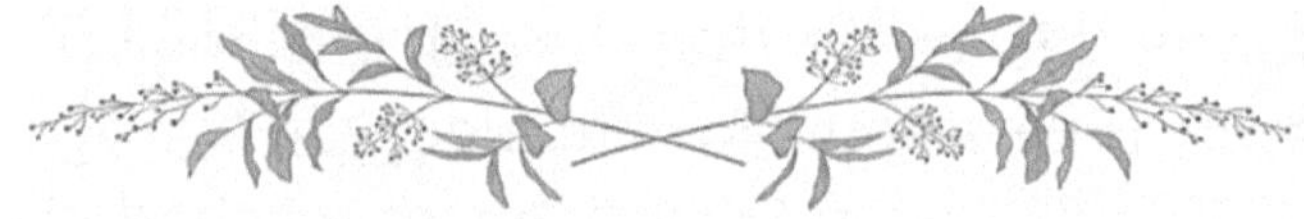

Now, an hour later, Lynn was still in the same wet clothes, still clutching the bracelet in her hand, but back at the CIA headquarters. Her phone buzzed constantly and she knew that it was her mom trying to call her, trying to speak about what had happened at Ann's grave. But she couldn't answer the phone because deep in her heart she knew that her dad was right.

Ann had died because of her.

Because she started this new job at the CIA.

Because she didn't tell the others about Az-Zawahiri's blackmail.

She was sure that if she had included Marta, Oliver and the others, they would have found Ann earlier and then her sister would still be alive.

A loud sob escaped her throat when Nate entered her room with a tray of food and a steaming hot chocolate. He now wore tight black sweatpants and a way-too-small black t-shirt that couldn't hide his muscular upper body. Even his nipples pierced through the thin fabric. But for once Lynn did not pay attention to the attractive physique of the man that had her heart.

Nate was still wearing his knee brace but he'd been able to walk without crutches for a few days now. His body was adjusting to the torn ACL pretty well. Only a small limp remained when he walked.

"You're still in that wet dress?" he asked, confused, while placing the tray on the bedside table and observing the doctor and the soaked bed beneath her.

Lynn didn't answer him but he could see her eyes fixed on the silver object in her hands while her thumb carefully caressed over the inscribed letters.

"Darling, you could get a cold, maybe even a lung infection. Come on. Let's get you out of that dress," Nate sighed, before stepping towards Lynn and reaching one hand towards her.

The doctor raised her head a little to look at him with puffy red eyes. He was giving her an assuring smile. This wasn't right. She'd hurt him. She'd betrayed him and he wasn't sure if he could ever trust her again. He'd said it to her a week ago, but still, there he was, standing right in front of her and smiling at her. Willing to help, willing to hold her until she felt better. She didn't deserve him.

Hell, she didn't even deserve to be alive.

It should have been her that was dead now, not her innocent sister Ann. It wasn't fair.

Nate looked at her with love in his eyes. He knew that he needed to follow his heart now, ignoring the voices of doubt. They'd have plenty of time to figure out their relationship, maybe even visit a therapist together. He wanted this to work. His heart wanted this to work. Lynn was the first person he'd really opened up to. The first person he'd ever felt was seeing the real Nate Sheppard.

The vulnerable one, the one who started to learn to accept himself and the world around him. She'd taught him how to smile, what it meant to care for somebody. She'd started to fill the emptiness in his heart with warmth, safety and love and, when her lips touched his own, it felt like this was exactly how it was meant to be: Nate and Lynn.

That was all he could think about at that moment, ignoring the rumbles in his mind warning him to never speak with the doctor again because she wasn't trustworthy.

Lynn grabbed his hand and he pulled her onto her feet. Her skin was way too cold under his touch, although she'd finally stopped shaking uncontrollably.

"Let's get you under the warm shower and then you can have some dinner, okay?" he suggested and Lynn nodded. A little sparkle appeared in her eyes when she realized that Nate really cared for her. That he was there, and that he would stay. Her lips curved just a little into a tiny smile.

They went into the attached bathroom and Nate carefully opened the zipper on the back of Lynn's dress before taking a few steps towards the shower to turn on the warm water. It was early June and the weather in Washington was still unusually cold. No early signs of summer, yet.

Then Nate turned around to Lynn again and saw that she hadn't even tried to get out of the dress. He sighed loudly.

"Darling, you have to help a little, okay? I can't do all the work for you," he said before stepping towards the door to leave the bathroom and give Lynn some privacy.

He was about to close the door behind him when he heard a barely audible "Nate" from the room. Nate stuck his head through the door to see how he could help her.

"Can you.. can you join me?" she asked with a pleading look.

Nate was surprised by her request as their relationship hadn't reached that point yet. They'd never seen each other naked before. Well, maybe Lynn had seen him naked during his surgery, but that didn't really count. Lynn noticed his hesitation, so she dropped her gaze to the floor and mumbled:

"Sorry, I know that would be weird."

Nate entered the room again and placed his hands on the outside of her upper arms.

"If you want me to join you, I'll join you. I just wasn't sure if it would make you feel uncomfortable seeing me naked. That's a huge step, Lynn." Nate chuckled a little, trying to cover his own insecurity and hesitation.

Lynn's chestnut eyes met his ocean blue ones again and she smiled.

"How could I be uncomfortable while seeing THIS." she said and pointed up and down his body.

The moment Lynn started to take off her dress, a knot appeared in Nate's chest and suddenly he wasn't comfortable. It was like they were crossing boundaries that shouldn't be crossed yet. Their situation was still way to fucked up to see each other naked.

"Sorry, Lynn. I can't," he stuttered and stormed out of the room, leaving a confused and sad Lynn behind.

She knew he was right. It was too early and it was a ridiculous idea. She despised herself for the stupid request, while she stripped out of the dress and stepped under the warm shower.

After fifteen minutes her skin was burning and she turned off the water, grabbed one of the big towels and wrapped her small frame in the fluffy material. At least she was so ashamed about the situation that she forgot about her grief for a few minutes.

With the towel still wrapped around her body she left the bathroom and jumped in surprise when she saw Nate sitting on the bed. He had changed the wet sheets while she was in the bathroom and she watched as he rolled a green grape between his thumb and index finger before throwing it in the air and catching it in his mouth.

"Nate!" she exclaimed and wrapped the towel even tighter around her body.

"Sorry. I... I don't know. I didn't want to just run away. You taught me to talk about my feelings, so I stayed," he answered and Lynn could literally see the mental battle in his brain through his eyes.

"No. I should be sorry. It was a stupid request. Way too early and definitely the wrong situation. I *am* sorry." Lynn said while she walked to her closet to grab some fresh clothes.

She headed back to the bathroom to change but left the door ajar to keep the conversation alive.

"Yeah. Way too early," he confirmed, but Lynn couldn't help hearing a little bit of sadness in his voice.

She closed the zipper on her jeans before leaving the bathroom again. Nate was still sitting on the bed next to the tray with food and the now probably-not-so-hot chocolate. The doctor placed her body next to his but made sure to leave a comfortable distance between them.

"Nate..." she started and Nate turned his head around to look at her with heavy eyes.

He was still confused. He wanted to join her in the shower, see her naked, hug her, kiss her and hell yes, maybe even have sex with her, but how could he do that? With the woman who'd betrayed him and his friends, working together with the man that destroyed his life.

"Mhm?" he answered simply, his internal battle still very present in the blue of his eyes.

They looked like a stormy ocean again and, as much as Lynn hated that she was the reason for this tempest, she had to admit that they'd never looked more beautiful. The blue of his eyes drew her into him and she never wanted to break their gaze again.

"Thanks for being by my side today. I'm not sure if I would've survived this without you. I know I don't deserve your kindness and your care. I know I hurt you and there's nothing I can do to undo that. I know. That's why it means the world to me that you've been there today. Thank you," she said and Nate could hear the adoration in her voice.

The doctor had raised her hand and wanted to place it on Nate's thigh but stopped in the middle of the movement. She'd already crossed boundaries today and didn't want to do it again. Nate saw her falter and quickly reached out his own hand, grabbed hers, and placed both of them on his thigh.

"Just because I'm still angry about what you did doesn't mean that I don't care about you, Lynn. This was a very hard day for you and of course I wanted to help and support you," Nate replied while he tenderly brushed his thumb over the warm skin on the back of Lynn's hand.

"Thank you. I don't deserve you, Nate," she whispered. They both stared down at their connected hands now, too shy, confused, and scared to look at each other. Nate didn't answer her as he wasn't sure if he would find the right words. All he did was continue to caress his thumb over Lynn's hand.

There was so much unresolved emotion between them. So much confusion, love, and hurt at the same time. Both of them wished things could be different or that they could travel back in time and prevent the betrayal from ever happening. But they had to face the truth and the one question that was heavily hanging between them:

Would they ever be able to love and trust each other again without doubts or fears?

# Rabbit Hole

**June 8th, 2022**

It was a few days after Ann's funeral and Nate and Lynn hadn't had much chance to speak. They were both too focused on themselves and surviving day to day to check in on one another. The doctor had to go back to the med-bay and treat patients together with the nurses Tia and Birdie. Although she wanted to see Nate, talk to him, and show him how much he meant to her, she remained distant. He was the one hurt and she didn't want to crush him with her presence.

Nate on the other hand, had fallen deep down the rabbit hole of his own mind. There was a consuming darkness inside his brain that sucked all the positive thoughts out of his body and only left the negative ones. His heart was powerless against the raging storm of negative thoughts inside his mind.

Nate raged, filled with anger about the betrayal and self-pity because life had been unfair to him yet again. Gone was the hope to figure things out with Lynn, the adoration for her, and the willingness to give her a chance.

Oliver was worried sick about his best friend, as he had locked himself inside his room for three full days, only coming out when the hunger was too strong to ignore and he needed to get some food.

That morning Lynn entered the communal kitchen to make herself some breakfast before her shift in the med-bay. Oliver and Marta were already sitting at the big dining table, enjoying their breakfast together.

"Good morning," Lynn said in their direction before walking towards the fridge.

She was craving porridge so she decided to make some with apples and cinnamon. She loved the scent of cinnamon as it always reminded her of Nate. Consciously or unconsciously she decided to have this breakfast on the day she missed him the most.

"Good morning, Lynn. How are you feeling?" Marta asked with a slight tremble of concern in her voice.

Marta had experienced a horrendous amount of grief before, after her husband and unborn child were murdered. She knew how devastating the feeling could be and that it was important to let the emotions flow in order to heal.

But ever since the funeral, Lynn had only focused on her job. They still had Toby around so it wasn't necessary for her to jump right back into the med-bay but the doctor insisted and told them she needed to be occupied.

"I'm good. How are you?" Lynn answered with a tiny smile on her face.

"Are you sure?" Marta continued, one of her eyebrows raised so high it got almost lost in her hairline.

Lynn sighed in response and, instead of answering her friend, she grabbed the almond milk out of the fridge and turned around towards the stove.

"Lynn. It's really important to grieve. I know it all feels empty inside of you but you need to feel these emotions.

You're a human being and we're all understanding. Your sister just died, you don't need to work again just yet. Take your time." Marta had risen from her chair and was now standing in the kitchen.

The doctor had her gaze fixed on the pot in front of her while she poured some rolled oats inside it. After adding the almond milk, she grabbed a spoon and waited for the milk to boil. All this time she ignored Marta, but then she turned around to her and whispered with a shimmer of tears in her eyes.

"I don't know how long I'm allowed to work anymore. You know, because I betrayed the CIA, so I want to enjoy it as long as I can. Also, it helps me distract myself. I don't want to be alone with my mind."

"Oh, Lynn." Marta engulfed her in a careful hug.

"Whatever happens, I know I deserve it. I fucked up. So I'm just waiting for the consequences."

"Director Burns is still negotiating with a few lawyers. We were all interrogated already but he's taking his time to decide, which is a good thing. He might be the Director of the CIA, but he's a human being, too. It'll be okay," Marta whispered in her ear, still holding her close.

Of course she'd been disappointed and hurt too. But she and Oliver had talked a lot about the situation and they both agreed that they'd have done the same in Lynn's position, so their anger had subsided pretty fast.

Would they have difficulty trusting Lynn again?

Sure.

But they still understood her decision.

Lynn freed herself from Marta's hug, smiled at the woman in front of her.

"Thank you. Having you as a friend means a lot to me. Especially after everything that happened."

"Of course, sweetie." Marta said, smiling as well.

Talking about the betrayal again was like tearing open the wound in Lynn's heart once more, so she closed her eyes for a second, took a deep breath, swallowed the lump in her throat, and turned around to Oliver.

"Have you heard from him?" She asked carefully.

"Who?" the blond man asked, but his face gave him away.

He was a former Navy SEAL and now a CIA Agent, but he wasn't able to keep a straight face towards her?

Lynn huffed and responded.

"Oliver... you know exactly who I'm talking about."

"No. I haven't heard from him. He's been in his room for the last three days. I haven't spoken to him and only saw him once by accident."

"What?" Lynn exclaimed with wide eyes, and her lips parted in shock.

"Yeah. I check on him twice a day to make sure he's still alive." Oliver chuckled a little, a coping mechanism for the concern about his best friend's mental state.

"He's in a pretty bad headspace at the moment," Marta added, and Lynn turned her head and looked at the other woman before her face fell.

"This is all my fault," she mumbled, but only Marta could hear it. She placed her hand on Lynn's upper arm.

"It's all going to be okay. He needs some time to sort out his feelings. He loves you and he's been by your side when you needed him. Now let him have some time to think about what's happened and how he wants to go on afterwards."

Lynn's eyes glimmered with tears when she looked at Marta again.

"I know," she whispered.

"It's gonna be okay. You love each other. That's all that matters. You'll work things out around that," Marta responded with an assuring smile on her lips.

The three were oblivious that the man with the ocean blue eyes was standing in the hallway with his back pressed against the wall. He was about to get some breakfast because he felt like his stomach had started to digest itself. It was almost painful, so Nate had decided to get a sandwich from the kitchen. He hadn't heard the full conversation, but it was enough to realize that Lynn was in the same devastating headspace as him.

The demons in his mind were so loud that he wasn't able to sleep, telling him reason after reason why he should never see Lynn again. Why he should shut her out of his life, and with every reason, every minute, every hour, his heart became weaker and weaker.

The only defender of Lynn.

Of their relationship.

Of their love.

When he was finally able to sleep, he was haunted by those chestnut-brown eyes in his dreams. These weren't nightmares. He dreamed about all the sweet moments between them. Their first hug, their cooking session, the little pillow fight, every time he had her in his arms while lying in either her or his bed. Every time her lips connected with his, a firework in his stomach exploded.

He re-lived all these moments in his dreams. It was the only thing that kept him alive and kept the flame inside his heart burning because even in the soul-destroying chaos of his mind, he knew; he loved her and he wanted a life with her.

"Nate's having his check-up appointment at 1:00pm. I'd appreciate it if you could make sure he shows up. I need to pull the stitches, check the wounds, and check his mobility to create his physical therapy plan." Nate could hear Lynn's voice coming out of the kitchen.

"I'll try my best," Oliver answered with a slight chuckle.

It seemed like the emotional conversation was over. Nate closed his eyes, took three deep breaths, and slowly entered the kitchen.

"I'll be there," he said towards Lynn before making his way to the fridge.

The doctor's eyes were wide, her jaw almost on the floor, and her eyes followed every movement of the man she was in love with.

"Nate..." she simply said, but her voice almost broke at the end.

Marta quickly exchanged gazes with Oliver, silently checking what to do now.

"Don't," he responded into the fridge while grabbing the cream cheese and ham.

He already had a pounding headache. He couldn't have this conversation now.

The small glimpse of hope in Lynn's eyes disappeared in a second before she nodded. Then she turned off the stove and turned towards Marta.

"You can have the oatmeal. I'm not hungry anymore."

With that being said, she hurried out of the room, leaving Oliver, Nate, and Marta behind without uttering another word.

Nate placed his plate next to the stove while peeking into the pot, apple and cinnamon oatmeal, his favorite.

"You want this?" He asked Marta, gaining a surprised grimace in return.

When Marta didn't answer he shrugged and poured the oatmeal into a bowl before leaving the kitchen again.

"You big, stubborn idiot!" Marta screamed after Nate.

"Sugar! You can't say that. You're still his boss," Oliver exclaimed, shocked, although he secretly loved his girlfriend for it.

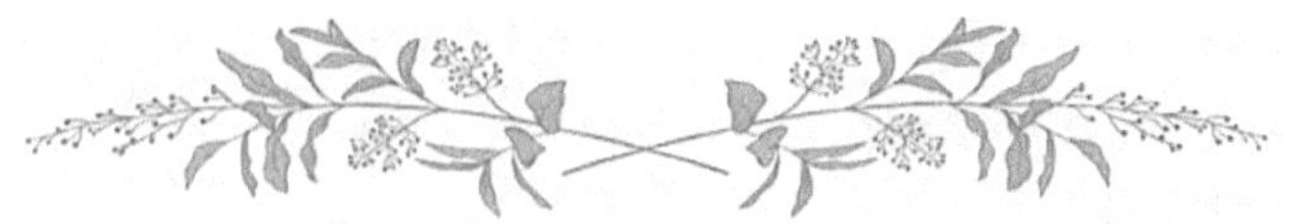

It was almost 01:20 pm and Lynn had stopped expecting Nate to arrive because he was never late. As she hadn't eaten her lunch yet she planned to head to the communal kitchen and get some food for her still emotionally exhausted body. Skipping breakfast this morning probably hadn't been the best idea.

When she was about to leave the med-bay through the automatic door she bumped into a tall and muscular body standing right on the other side.

"What the..." she exclaimed, astonished, before her eyes met the ocean blue ones of the man standing in front of her. Her gaze softened, and she whispered.

"Nate."

"I'm here for the check-up." he said with a quiet, emotionless, almost robotic voice.

Lynn saw the emptiness in his lifeless eyes and needed to swallow the lump in her throat. What had happened to him in the last few days?

"Sure. Come on in. Examination Room 1 please," she dictated and let him pass her to take the lead.

Nate took his seat on the examination table in the middle of the room while Lynn was closing the door behind her. She grabbed some surgical gloves and pointed at the backrest of the examination table. He had his legs hanging from the table but was now changing positions so she could reach his knee better. He was wearing tight workout shorts which managed to distract Lynn more than she would admit to someone. She placed her body on a swivel chair and rolled next to the examination table before asking,

"How's the knee? Any pain left?"

"Sometimes."

"Okay. I'm gonna take the knee brace off and then pull the stitches. Afterwards, I'll check your mobility."

"Sure."

His one syllable answers were driving her nuts but given the mental state he was in she was lucky that he was even saying anything.

"Wow, I thought you'd be a little more enthusiastic to improve in your recovery. If we continue like this, you'll be able to be out in the field in no time!" She smiled shyly at him, which he didn't return.

"Okay." He said, and avoided her gaze.

Lynn huffed in annoyance while she opened the straps on the knee brace and pulled it off his leg. Then she removed the dressings one last time and grabbed tweezers and surgical scissors to pull the remaining stitches.

She was so lost in her frustration that she didn't even realize how Nate flinched when she started to grab the first suture with the tweezers to cut it with the scissors. It took a sharp inhale from the man on the table for Lynn to turn her head and look in his direction. His lifeless eyes were filled with fear now as his PTSD brought back memories of his kidnapping and the countless tortures he'd had to endure.

Lynn not only halted her movement but leaned back, letting go of the suture.

"I'm sorry. I totally forgot about your fears," she said with guilt in her voice.

She watched him clench his jaws even tighter as he tried to prevent them from shaking. Both his hands were also clenched into fists. His general fragile state had empowered his fears, so much so that he couldn't even stand something as simple as pulling stitches. Lynn removed her gloves and placed one of her palms on his forearm. The warmth of the doctor's hand crawled its way up Nate's arm until it reached his mind, gently silencing the demons in his head.

He'd forgotten that Lynn's touch was like an antidote against the venom in his mind. His breathing steadied while they sat like that for a few minutes. When he was finally able to open his hands and jaw again, he mumbled a truthful "Thank you".

"Always," Lynn answered with an assuring smile on her lips.

She removed her hand from Nate's forearm, only for it to be caught by his strong hand half a second later.

He needed her touch now.

He needed her warmth, and he needed her love.

For the first time in days, he could see the light at the end of the tunnel. Like there was hope left. So he held her hand and pulled her closer. A little startled by his pulling, Lynn needed to stand from her chair and move in his direction until she was right by his side. She looked down at him and Nate lifted his head in her direction until their gazes met.

The sparks between them were shooting around like bolts of lightning.

Lynn lowered her upper body until she rested her forehead on his and automatically the two closed their eyes. It was an intimacy that both of them had missed over the last few days - after everything went south on that one night at the end of May.

For another minute nothing but their steady breaths and their hearts beating the same rhythm could be heard within the room before Lynn cleared her throat and leaned back, opening her eyes again. There was some depth behind the cerulean color of his eyes, which gave her some hints about his true mental state.

"I miss you, Nate," Lynn said with all the bravery she could gather.

Something flickered in his eyes, and a glimpse of sadness could be seen again.

"I miss you too, Lynn," he whispered in a husky voice. making the butterflies in her stomach go crazy again. She hadn't felt them in a while.

"Then why have you been avoiding me?" she painfully asked.

"I wasn't avoiding you. I was avoiding everyone. I was trapped inside my own mind." Nate sighed honestly.

He sounded scared and sad. He'd realized that what had happened to him over the last few days was dangerous and unhealthy and he really wanted to climb out of the rabbit hole.

"Are you feeling better now?"

"Much," he said while pulling her down towards him again to place a kiss on her nose.

Lynn practically melted under the soft touch of his lips. Until that moment, she hadn't realized how much she missed him. Cuddling with him and sleeping in his arms, it was like she was addicted to his touch. Before the blow of Lynn's betrayal they had been glued together at the hip. Very close all the time, almost dropping the l-word to each other while cuddling and kissing in bed every night. They'd been in a relationship, although neither of them had defined it verbally.

"Can I pull your stitches now?" she carefully asked, and Nate nodded.

Lynn slipped on fresh gloves and slid onto the swivel chair again to roll towards his knee. She turned her head to flash him another smile and quickly worked through the stitches to pull them all. It only took her 60 seconds until she exclaimed,

"All done!"

Nate let out the breath that he'd been holding during the procedure but he couldn't help himself and let his lips curl into a shy smile afterwards.

"Thanks, Doc," he said before sitting up and letting his legs hang from the table again.

He patiently waited for further instructions while Lynn tossed all the used equipment in the trash or into the ultrasound machine that disinfected the metal instruments after using them. Lynn swirled around in her chair and looked at Nate.

"We need to put your knee back in the brace, honey," she said, and Nate's face lit up the moment he heard the nickname.

"Sure. I totally forgot about it. What about the wounds? Do I need to put bandaids on top of them?" he asked.

"That depends on how you feel. You don't need it technically, but if the brace puts too much pressure on the incisions, then we can add some." Lynn answered while returning to the examination table.

Nate quickly grabbed the brace and pulled it over his knee to check if it hurt. He secured the straps and moved his knee a little.

"No, it's fine."

"That's great. I'll give you some anyway in case it hurts you later." Lynn responded and placed a little box with bandaids in his palm.

"Always concerned, huh?" Nate smirked at her.

"About you? Yeah, always," she answered with a twinkle in her eyes.

Afterwards, the conversation came to a halt. Several moments of silence passed between them while Nate watched his legs hang off the examination table. Lynn tilted her head a little and looked at him, confused.

"You're good to go. I need some time to work on the PT schedule. I'll send it to you as soon as I have it," she said with a smile.

She thought he'd waited for further instructions, but as the brunette man was bouncing his leg up and down nervously, she wasn't so sure about that anymore.

"Would... would you like to cook dinner with me today? I think I could use some solid food after the past few days. Oliver texted that he and Marta are going to watch a movie in the theater and I'd really like to have some company so I don't fall back into the darkness." His voice was low and husky, as if he were ashamed of what he was saying.

"I would love to cook with you, Nate," Lynn answered, her lips curling upward while she placed her hand on his shoulder.

He copied her smile as the warmth from Lynn's hand spread into every cell of his body. This was what he was looking for.

Love.

Happiness.

Peace.

And this woman was the only person who was able to give it to him. All he needed to do was give her a second chance.

# Trust

**June 8th, 2022**

Later that evening, Lynn changed into some tight blue jeans and a slightly oversized beige blouse with ruffles on the front and on the cuffs. She was nervous about having a casual evening with Nate for the first time since that eventful night.

Would they be able to just enjoy their time together and forget about what happened, even, for a short period of time?

With a small knot in her chest, Lynn left her room and made her way into the communal kitchen. When she walked through the doorframe she could already see Nate swirling through the kitchen while he placed a couple of pots on the stove. He was wearing tight, dark gray jeans, and a long-sleeved, navy-blue jersey shirt. The knee brace was still very present on his knee and, although he looked carefree in his movements, Lynn saw a little limp and hesitation in a few of them.

Lynn couldn't help but admire how the jeans emphasized his perfectly shaped butt. She quickly shook her head to get rid of the heat in her lower belly before reaching the counter.

"Hi Nate," she said and he spun around to face her.

His features brightened when he saw the doctor and his eyes wandered up and down her body for a second. Was Nate Sheppard checking her out?

"Hi, Lynn. Good to see you again," he smiled at her.

If Lynn hadn't been 100% sure that this was reality, she would have thought she was dreaming. Nate's mood had turned 180° since his check-up a few hours earlier. Nothing of the emptiness, sadness, and hurt was seen in his ocean blue eyes and Lynn wondered where it had gone. She knew from weeks of therapy sessions with him that sometimes his mind was a rollercoaster, but such a huge swing in emotions was rare, even for him.

"You're already busy making dinner?" She asked curiously, deciding that she would ignore the therapist's voice inside her mind for tonight and just enjoy spending time with the man she'd fallen in love with.

"Yeah, I started preparing everything. I googled some pasta recipes and this one sounded delicious. It's spaghetti with  tomato sauce and lots of feta cheese in it. The recipe said it was a viral recipe from Tuck Tuck or something like that. I went to the grocery store this afternoon to get the ingredients. I also got us some wine, if you don't mind."

"Tuck Tuck?" Lynn asked with furrowed brows, really trying to understand what the hell the man in front of her was talking about.

"Yeah, this weird app that all the teenagers use. The one with the short videos that make you feel like a dinosaur if you're older than twenty."

"Ohhhhh, you mean Tik Tok?" Lynn burst into laughter.

"Are you laughing at me, Lynn?" he asked with a little snicker in his voice.

Seeing Lynn laughing like that warmed his heart. Even if his ignorance was the reason for her laughter.

"I'm so sorry, but that was adorable!"

"That's not nice, darling!" Nate exclaimed and with a swift movement he grabbed the spatula and smacked it on Lynn's ass.

Lynn yelped in surprise. Both of them halted in their movements and stared at each other in shock. Nate's body had acted on autopilot and Lynn hadn't expected him to do something so playful.

The brunette man mumbled a quick "sorry" before he placed the spatula back next to the pot and moved towards the fridge to grab the feta cheese. Lynn took a few steps in his direction, stood right behind him, and pinched him on one of his butt cheeks.

"Heeeeeey!" He exclaimed, spinning around to face his attacker.

His face was now only inches away from Lynn's and his eyes flickered down to her pink lips. Lynn saw it and decided that kissing him right here, right now, would cross boundaries, so she stepped back.

"We're even now!" She chuckled.

The rest of their cooking was very uneventful. While eating in silence the two of them gazed at each other and from time to time they let their toes brush over each other's foot. It was like they were lovestruck teenagers again.

"You wanna watch the third Star Wars movie?" Nate asked, after they had placed their bowls in the dishwasher and cleaned the kitchen together.

"Actually..." Lynn started, and a frown was seen on Nate's face.

He was sure he wouldn't like what was coming.

"I love this. You and me and all of this. It feels like our nights before the... before I... you know. And I want that back. I want to just enjoy my time with you without worrying if you still mistrust me or hate me. But the only way to be able to continue exploring our relationship is to talk about the past. We need to talk about it to be able to find closure."

Lynn hated herself for that. She just wanted to enjoy their evening without overthinking it too much. She wanted to kiss him and cuddle with him while watching a movie. But the therapist inside her knew that they needed to face those demons together before they'd be able to heal. It was something Nate was familiar with and Lynn felt awful for adding yet another demon to his shoulders.

Nate's face dropped, his smile gone. He knew she was right and that just ignoring their problems wouldn't help but he'd really enjoyed their evening so far and he'd hoped to have one peaceful night with the woman he loved in his arms.

"I know," he responded, the sadness in his eyes visible when he looked at her.

He could see sadness in her chestnut eyes too and knew that it must have taken a lot of courage to say what she said instead of just watching a movie with him.

"Let's head to my room for a bit more privacy, okay? In case Oliver and Marta return earlier than expected," she suggested and Nate nodded in response.

They grabbed their glasses of wine and walked out of the kitchen in silence.

In Lynn's room, they took their usual places on her couch and just looked at each other without saying a word. The doctor didn't know where to start. Their situation was way too complicated and too fucked up. Finally, she cleared her throat, gulped down the rest of the wine in her glass, and started.

"Can you tell me what hurt you the most when you found out I worked with az-Zawahiri to save my sister?"

Her question caught him off guard as he hadn't expected her to jump straight to the point. He closed his eyes and tried to calm the storm of emotions inside his mind to figure out which one was the strongest and which wound needed the most time to heal. Unconsciously, his hand grabbed one of Lynn's and suddenly the storm became manageable. He had a clearer view of the things going on in his head and heart.

"It's not that you worked with a terrorist. I would've done the same if someone had kidnapped one of my loved ones," he started, a frown appearing on his face.

His eyes were still closed, as he was able to focus on specific things better then. Lynn had observed that several times during their therapy sessions. She'd also observed that touching her always helped him calm himself and find the right answers.

"What hurt me most is that you didn't even consider telling me. I get that you were scared, especially after you realized that he was able to hack into the security cameras, but it's me we're talking about. Why didn't you trust me? There would've been a way to tell me about it," he opened his eyes and Lynn could see tears in them that were on the brink of falling.

"Nate..." Lynn's face softened and her own tears slipped down her cheeks.

"Lynn, I opened up to you. I told you about the terror I've been through. I showed you a glimpse of the hell I endured while being held captive and I trusted you with all this because I realized that you could help me. You were the reason I felt normal again. Not a monster. Just Nate Sheppard. I know that with you by my side I would be able to defeat the demons inside my mind and recover again. You gave me hope."

This was a huge step for Nate as even though he'd admitted all these emotions to himself a few weeks ago he'd never vocalized them. Too scared that it would not come true if he said all those things and jinxed it. He could see pity and sadness in Lynn's eyes but also so much love and adoration. He couldn't remember the last time someone looked at him like that.

"It felt like someone stabbed me right in my heart when I realized that you didn't trust me the same way that I trusted you. That you never even considered telling me about Ann. That you never thought that I could have helped you. That hurt the most."

Lynn's lips were parted but she wasn't able to put her own thoughts into words. All this time, she'd thought that the act itself had hurt him, that it was the same man who tortured him eleven years ago, but now she realized it was never the fact that she worked for az-Zawahiri. It was all about trust.

"I... I..." she started but needed to stop because her body was shocked by a wave of crying and her jaw trembled.

Nate watched her with pain in his heart but he knew that they had to face this situation now. It was necessary for their recovery process, Lynn had told him that herself when he was having his therapy sessions with her.

"I was so overwhelmed by the whole situation and so scared. What if az-Zawahiri found out I asked you for help? I didn't want to risk Ann's life because I didn't want to lose..." she couldn't end the sentence as another wave of sobs crashed over her body. She felt like someone had her in a chokehold, the ability to breathe failing with every passing second while at the same time the guilt bored itself into her heart like a sharp knife.

Nate saw her struggling and couldn't hold it in anymore so he pulled Lynn into a tight hug. Her tears were soaking his jersey and he could feel the cold wetness on his shoulder.

"Shhh. It's okay," he purred while gently stroking his fingertips through her thick brown hair.

They sat like that for a while, with him gently scratching his fingernails over her scalp, until her crying finally subsided. She moved her body out of his embrace.

"No, it's not okay. I should've trusted you with the situation. It was just so overwhelming," she said with a tear-stained face.

"I understand. Please promise me that in the future you'll never hesitate to tell me something. Promise me you'll never keep secrets from me again," he demanded with a pleading look in his eyes.

"I promise."

"You know, I really want this to work out. You have a special place in my heart, Lynn Summers, and I really want to explore whatever this is between us," Nate whispered and fixed his gaze on hers to watch the sparkles in them appear.

"I want that too, Nate."

Nate sighed. He knew he needed to be fully honest with her right now for this to work. All their emotions needed to be out in the open and shared between them so that they'd be able to create a jump-off point for their relationship.

"It won't be easy for me, Lynn, because of everything that happened to me. I've always had problems trusting people and your betrayal didn't make that any better. You told me that your heart was always honest with me but it's hard for me to believe that. It's hard for me to think about the moments we shared and not question if they were real or a lie."

"I know, Nate, and I don't expect everything to be magically solved after this conversation. That would be unrealistic, but I'll do everything I can to show you that I am trustworthy, that none of the moments between us were a lie. From today onwards I swear to you that I'll never lie to you again, that I'll always tell you everything that's going on in my life so you'll never doubt how much you mean to me," Lynn answered with passion and determination in her voice.

They were only words and time would tell if actions would follow them but, at that moment, Nate's lips curled into a wide smile and, after seeing him smile, Lynn couldn't stop herself from smiling too.

He'd given her a real chance.

A real chance to find out what was going on between them and if they would have a future together.

The weight on Nate's shoulders that had threatened to crush him was finally lifted.

Lynn had been right.

They'd needed to talk about this to settle their relationship. Her betrayal wasn't magically forgotten and they would face ups and downs over the coming months but they wanted to try. He wanted to give her a chance and she wanted to prove to him that he could trust her again. This was a good start.

"So do you wanna watch the third Star Wars movie now?" He chuckled.

"Oh yes, please," Lynn answered with a wide grin.

On their way to Nate's room their hands never left each other and when Nate jumped into his bed and patted the empty space next to him Lynn's heart did a backflip. She carefully slipped underneath his big blanket and rested her head on the pillow that he'd ordered especially for her a few weeks ago, when she was staying with him after the surgery.

They lay next to each other for half the movie before Lynn couldn't hold back her yawn anymore. Nate side-eyed her as she struggled to stay awake. Her eyelids kept dropping until she started up again and tried to keep her body awake. But she failed miserably and, after Nate had watched her sleeping features for five minutes and totally forgot about the movie, he turned off the television. He shifted onto his side to face Lynn and pulled her into his arms so that he was spooning her.

The doctor had been awakened by the sudden movement of her body but when she felt two arms wrapped around her waist she closed her eyes again. Nate placed a little peck on the back of her head and purred.

"Goodnight, Lynn."

She wanted to answer him but her body was already too tired so only a "Mhmmm" left her slightly parted lips. Nate chuckled softly before he let his own head rest on the downy pillow and hoped for a peaceful sleep.

# Lunch Date

**June 9th, 2022**

The next morning, Lynn felt Nate's warm breath against her neck, and she realized that the Agent was still hugging her from behind. She tried to turn her head to see if he was still asleep but she couldn't turn it far enough to actually see his features.

"Morning," he mumbled with a husky voice before he carefully placed a kiss on her neck that sent shivers down Lynn's spine.

"Morning," she answered,  a small purr escaping her throat.

In reaction to this sound, Nate placed a few more wet kisses along her neck.

The next second, Lynn turned around in his embrace so that they were now facing each other. Her eyes were still sleepy, but she had a smile on her lips.

"Did you sleep well?" she asked with a gentle voice.

"Oh yeah. First night in weeks that I didn't have a weird dream. Thanks for that." He chuckled a little.

Their faces were only inches apart and Nate felt like Lynn stared right through his eyes and into his soul. She scooted a little closer in his embrace and their lips were almost brushing over each other. Her chestnut eyes were still locked with his blue ones.

"You have beautiful eyes," she whispered, her breath warm on his pinkish lips, making a little blush appear on his cheeks.

"Yeah?" was the only thing he could manage to say.

"Yes. Like sapphires illuminated by the sunlight."

"Yours aren't too bad either," he answered with an unusual smirk on his face.

Lynn loved this side of him. He finally felt safe enough to let go of the walls around his heart. Nate could see something shimmering behind the dark brown color of Lynn's eyes and knew it was love. She loved him. Her eyes told him that this had never been a lie and that her feelings for him had been there the entire time. She wouldn't be able to fake this shimmer. This sparkle. The love.

In an instant, his lips captured her bottom lip in a loving kiss. Lynn wasn't shocked by his sudden movement, as she had felt the sexual tension between them building. When he let go of her bottom lip she took the initiative and kissed him back with the same love and passion as before. Their lips were like magnets as they found their way to each other over and over again in gentle but also intense kisses, only breaking apart to catch a breath.

Nate nipped at Lynn's lips while one of his hands traveled to her neck to hold her close. His thumb brushed over her skin and he could feel her heartbeat hammering beneath it. When his teeth let go of her lip she quickly let her tongue stroke over his bottom lip in appreciation.

In response Nate parted his lips a little and let Lynn's tongue slide into his mouth. When the tips of their tongues found each other, a firework exploded in his stomach. A feeling that he had almost forgotten after the devastating mindset of the last few days. The warmth crawling through his body from the gentle touches of Lynn's tongue on his felt like his whole body was on fire.

When they finally let go both of their lips were swollen but they couldn't care less. Lynn rested her forehead against Nate's and could feel his hand stroke up and down her spine.

"Let me take you on a proper date," Nate whispered with closed eyes, their foreheads still connected.

"What's on your mind?"

"Nothing fancy, to be honest. Going out for lunch and then just seeing where we end up. Maybe walk around Langley a bit." Nate answered with insecurity in his voice.

He'd had to gather all his courage to even ask her on a date, he hadn't thought about what to do. All he knew was that he wanted to spend as much time with her as possible. The whole dating thing was new to him. He hadn't dated since high school and that had been over twenty years ago. Did things change? Did girls still like to watch a movie in the theater while cuddling and secretly kissing in the dark? Was going to a restaurant acceptable, or was it not enough? Did she need a full entertainment experience? Did he need to buy flowers? Would he pay the bill at the restaurant, or was that rude and they needed to split it?

So many questions were running through his head that, for a second, he regretted asking her out.

He was totally going to screw this up.

"Nate?" Lynn asked with furrowed brows.

She had seen him trapped inside his own mind so she placed her hand on his cheek and drew some tender circles on his hot and slightly sweaty skin. He looked up to meet her eyes and she could see panic behind his ocean blue ones.

"What's going on in that beautiful head of yours?" she asked with a smile on her face before placing a sweet kiss on his forehead.

"I... I haven't dated in a long time. I don't want to bore you. I want to make it right and not screw this up." his words tumbled together, and Lynn realized that he was about to have a panic attack.

"Shh... you won't screw this up, honey. It's me and you, remember? Whatever we do will be perfect because I'm with you. That's my favorite place to be," she whispered before peppering his face with kisses.

She had missed being with him and moments like this were what kept her heart beating and helped  her see a light at the end of the tunnel. Just two people in love, not thinking about what had happened to them.

"Just me and you," he repeated, and the storm behind his eyes subsided. One side of his mouth curled upward.

"Let's look for a restaurant and then just see from there. We don't need to stress out about that. Let's just spend time together, get to know each other," Lynn said.

"It feels like I've known you my whole life. My new life, the life I actually want to live now," he responded before leaning in and placing a kiss on her nose.

It was his love language. His way of saying "I love you" without actually saying it, because everything between them blew up in the honeymoon phase, they never actually said the I-word to each other.

"And I'm happy to be a part of that life," Lynn answered, and finally they connected their lips with each other.

Nate's skin lit up, as if an electric shock were sent through his body. But unlike the torture back in 2011, he was looking forward to feeling these shocks every day.

"Sunday?" Lynn asked with a wide grin on her face.

"What?" Nate tilted his head a little in confusion.

"The date. Let's do it this Sunday. I have to take my phone with me, but there's nothing planned for that day in the med-bay."

"Oh wow. Yeah. Yeah, why not? Let's go on a date on Sunday," Nate laughed in response before his face fell once more.

"What is it, honey?" Lynn asked, concerned.

"Let's... let's keep this our little secret, okay? Until we're sure how we want to continue with our lives. I don't want anyone to judge us. I want to explore this and see if it could work on our own. Without unwelcome comments all the time," Nate mumbled, a loud sigh following his words.

"I agree. Just you and me. That's all that it needs anyway."

Nate nodded in agreement, a shy smile appearing on his lips again.

"Okay, then I'll head out to get some breakfast and then back to doing my job in the med-bay. Pick me up at noon on Sunday?" Lynn asked.

"Sure. I'll be there!" Nate promised before giving her another loving kiss on her lips.

"Nate?"

"Yeah?"

"I don't need flowers, chocolate, or anything. I just need you. Don't panic about the dos and don'ts of a date. I haven't dated in a long time, either. Let's explore this together and see what we like. There's no website that gives accurate advice for dating. This is about us."

"Did anybody tell you how amazing you are, Lynn Summers?" Nate grinned.

"Not today," Lynn chuckled.

"You are amazing!" And with that said, he gave her a final kiss before shooing her out of his room.

With a spring in his step, well at least in his good leg, Nate headed to the bathroom to take a shower while Lynn got herself some oatmeal for breakfast.

**June 12<sup>th</sup>, 2022**

That Lynn was panicking about what to wear for their date was the understatement of the year. It was a warm day in early June, around 71°F / 22°C, so she was rooting around in her closet for a summer dress. She hadn't worn one in ages as she had been working so much she hadn't even had time to go out. Even when she did go out she'd always preferred jeans and a t-shirt. But today was a special occasion and she decided to grab the beige summer dress with flower appliques on it that she had bought for a summer wedding but never worn.

The dress was ankle-length, allowing her to still wear her favorite white sneakers without tripping over the skirt. It had short sleeves so it covered her shoulders completely. With a deep v-neckline, Lynn was able to wear a tiny golden necklace that Toby had bought her for Christmas two years ago. It had a small pendant with the outline of a heart. Toby and she had always made fun of how hearts were usually drawn, as they were so different from an anatomically correct heart. So him buying her a heart-shaped necklace was like carrying their inside-joke with her all the time. One last check in the mirror after putting her hair back in a ponytail, and Lynn was good to go. She felt confident and pretty.

As if on cue a knock sounded on her door and, with a wide smile on her face, she stepped towards the door and opened it.

"Hi. Oh wow, you look amazing!" she exclaimed towards the man waiting for her.

He wore tight black jeans and a light gray long-sleeved button up shirt. She wondered if that wouldn't be too warm for him but, after the slight panic this morning, she understood that he wanted to look perfect for their date. She would have gone out with him even if he were wearing a t-shirt.

"Look at you. You look like a princess," Nate commented, blushing after the words left his mouth.

He wasn't really good with compliments. Giving or receiving.

"Oh, thank you," Lynn answered, her face almost cherry red.

They stood awkwardly before each other, not knowing what to do or say. So far, everything between them had been intuitive. The cuddling, the kissing, the spending time together. But now, as they were about to give themselves a label and try to figure out their future... it felt different. Tense. Awkward. Maybe it was because both of them hadn't officially dated in years.

"Let's get going!" Lynn mumbled, and Nate stepped aside so that she could leave her room.

He extended his elbow to her so that she could grab it, like the gentleman that he was but Lynn hesitated for a moment.

"What about Marta and Oliver? And the others?" she mumbled.

"Marta and Oliver are still in his room. They were out yesterday and, yeah... I heard them very clearly having sex a few minutes ago, so they're probably asleep again now."

Lynn almost choked on her breath after Nate's words and they both burst into laughter.

"Oh okay," she managed to breathe out in between her laughter.

"I don't care about other Agents. It's Sunday, so most of them aren't here anyway and the others are in labs or at the shooting range. Not nearby at least." Nate answered as they started walking along the hallway and towards the elevators.

Lynn still hesitated but when they were standing next to each other in the elevator she wrapped her hand around his bicep. It had grown over the last few weeks as he had to use it more while walking on crutches. Not that she would complain, though.

Silently, they marched out of headquarters and onto the parking lot. Nate had rented a car so that they would be able to reach the restaurant easily. It wasn't a long drive but instead of listening to the radio and singing along, Lynn started up a conversation.

"So, tell me something about you," she said with her head turned in his direction.

"What do you want to know?" he asked, confused, his own eyes fixed on the street in front of him.

"Everything. I've realized we talked a lot about your time as a SEAL in our therapy sessions but never anything else. Tell me about your childhood, your family, and all that stuff."

Nate was silent for a moment but realized that she was right. He knew more about her than she knew about him, the basics at least. She knew the hard stuff and she knew why he had all his trauma and how it influenced him but nothing else. How could they fall in love without actually knowing each other? This question made him get lost in his thoughts for a moment before realizing he should answer Lynn or she would probably be confused.

"I was born and raised in California, about an hour from Los Angeles. We weren't wealthy, so both my mom and my dad had to work full-time. My mom even had a second job on the weekends so we were able to go on vacations. They worked their tails off to give me a normal life," he explained.

He regretted starting their date with such a heavy topic but she'd wanted to know about him and that was his past.

"Oh wow. Your parents seem to be great people," she commented.

"Were. They were. My dad got cancer when I was a freshman in high school and died within a few months. Mom never really got over it but tried to keep up a brave face in front of me. I knew that she started drinking after my dad's death but she still managed to do two jobs and be a good mom. I don't know how she did it but I had food and clothes all the time. She never missed anything when it came to school and none of my teachers ever realized that she was an alcoholic. I'm grateful for that because I don't have any bad memories of her. I'm just sad that I wasn't able to help her back then." He sighed heavily, and Lynn's heart ached when she heard his story.

This man had been through so much in his life. Losing his father early, a mother that was addicted to alcohol because of that, and then his soul-crushing time in the SEALs. He had been traumatized over and over again in his life. When would this finally stop?

Her eyes shimmered with tears and she reached over to the driver's seat to place her palm on his thigh. He avoided looking at her, his eyes still fixed on the street in front of him, but he appreciated the gesture.

"I'm so sorry to hear that," she mumbled, and Nate nodded slightly before Lynn added "What happened to her?"

"When I was declared killed in action after the Pakistan mission she wasn't able to deal with even more grief. My aunt told me that the drinking became worse, and she wouldn't leave the house for days. Ultimately, her body gave up. Her liver wasn't able to deal with the amount of alcohol anymore. They transferred her to a rehab but she never managed to get back on her feet."

"Were you able to visit her in rehab?" she asked curiously.

"Yeah, once. After the coma, my body was so weak. It took me months to get approval from the doctor so that I could fly to California and see her. When I did, we actually just hugged each other for a few minutes and cried. Both of our bodies were so weak. I was still in a wheelchair and it was the first time I managed to stand on my own after the coma. I don't think I've ever cried so much in my entire life. We cried for Dad, for the life that was taken from us. It was very freeing and I think both of us knew that it was the last time we'd see each other. Since that day she hasn't been clear in her mind. I visit her from time to time but the alcohol destroyed her brain so much she doesn't even know who I am when I stand in front of her."

They had reached the parking spaces in front of the Japanese restaurant that Nate had picked. He knew how much Lynn loved sushi as it was "super delicious but still not as unhealthy as pizza". He turned the engine off and moved his upper body in her direction. Lynn saw the stains of tears on his cheeks. He had cried while telling her about his past. Her hand was still on his thigh, and he placed his large one on top of hers, intertwining their fingers. There was a sad smile on his lips. A smile of grief, nostalgia, but also happiness, because even after everything that had happened to him, he was here with a woman he knew he loved. A woman who changed his miserable life and gave him hope. Yes, she betrayed him, but she was still the light that enlightened his day and the rhythm that kept his heart beating.

"You've been through so much in your life, Nate. You are so strong. You never gave up and you fought. You've fought for the life you deserve, for happiness. I know sometimes I sound like a broken record, but I'm so proud of you," Lynn said with a smile on her face and tears in her eyes.

"All because of you," he whispered, leaning forward and giving her a quick kiss on the lips. Then he turned around and left the car. He rounded the car to open the door for her and help her out.

"I'm sorry that I started our date with such a depressing topic. I hope you still want sushi?" He mumbled with a blush on his face.

"Of course, honey. And I'm grateful that you told me your story. Now I understand you even better," Lynn responded.

Nate only nodded at her before they both stepped towards the entrance door of the restaurant. He grabbed the handle and held it open for her. He truly was a gentleman. Lynn smiled and entered, her gaze wandering around the small but endearing restaurant. A lot of tables were already filled and they patiently waited for someone to get them seated. A small blonde waitress with a big smile on her face walked towards them, an iPad in her hands.

"Hello. Do you have a reservation?" she asked kindly.

"Yes, for Sheppard." Nate answered.

The woman scrolled through her iPad, and her eyes lit up when she found the name on her list.

"There you are. Follow me please." And with that, she marched with quick steps into the restaurant.

They had a table on the wall right next to a large aquarium full of colorful fish. Nate was about to hold out the chair for

Lynn but she had already taken her seat so he took his own in front of her.

"Do you know the system?" the waitress asked with another smile on her face, alternating her gaze between Lynn and Nate.

"Uhm, no. Can you explain it to us?" Lynn answered.

"So, you get this iPad and can order your sushi with the app on it. Each of you can order five items per round. A new round is available every 15 minutes. It feels a bit like online shopping, only with food." The waitress laughed.

"Okay, got it. What about drinks?"

"You can order those on the iPad as well but if you already know what you want I'll bring it to you."

"I'd love a beer," Nate answered.

"Just sparkling water for me, please," Lynn said. The waitress smiled at them before leaving them alone. Nate looked at Lynn with slightly widened eyes.

"Is it okay for you if I have a beer?"

"Sure. Why not?"

"I don't know. Me telling you about my mom being an alcoholic but still ordering a beer. People can easily judge that," he mumbled, seeming embarrassed.

"First of all, I'm not someone to judge. I don't care, really. You're a grown-ass man and I'm not going to judge you for having a beer, no matter what happened to your mom. You are not your mom, so enjoy your beer. It can help you relax a little." She winked at him, making the strong Agent blush.

Then she grabbed the iPad and put the first five items on the list. Three different maki rolls as well as some satay chicken and edamame beans. She held the iPad towards

Nate, who grabbed it and scrolled through it with furrowed brows. A minute later, he had picked his first order as well, and they waited patiently for their food to come.

"Do you have any siblings?" Lynn asked again.

"No. My parents couldn't afford to have another child. Even with me, it was hard sometimes, financially, I mean."

"Oh yeah, I bet. There's a lot of stuff to pay for when you're in school."

"Yeah. I was on my High School Baseball Team. A shortstop. I've always had a good eye for moving objects, I guess. There were a lot of expenses associated with that. Clothes, fees and stuff like that. I don't even know exactly what. Back then, I never cared. Mom never let me know how much she struggled to pay for all these things. She had a day job and a night job to get it done. Until my coach realized it and my stuff was paid for by donations to the school." Nate smiled at her, but the smile didn't reach his eyes.

"Your mom was really dedicated to giving you a normal life. I have a lot of respect for that."

"She really was. I wasn't able to appreciate it back then but now I understand it. I bet even more when I'm a dad myself someday."

"So you want to have kids?" Lynn asked, her eyes lighting up while she imagined him with a baby in his arms.

Wait, where did that come from?

Her hormones were messing with her today.

"Yeah, I always wanted to be a dad but after the kidnapping I actually never thought I'd be able to. Mentally, I mean. I always wanted to be a role model for my kids but what kind of role model would I have been? A broken man with nightmares and panic attacks who wasn't able to move on with his life?" The sadness in his eyes appeared again, and Lynn needed to swallow the lump in her throat but before she was able to say something, Nate continued,

"But since I met you, my mental state has improved so much. I'm still not fully healed, obviously. That'll take forever I guess, but I started to realize that it's not unrealistic anymore and that I could be a dad someday."

A smile appeared on his lips. A real smile. He reached over the table to grab Lynn's hand and drew small circles on the top of her hand with his thumb.

Lynn fought hard to blink away the tears that had gathered in her eyes, but one betrayed her and slid down her cheeks.

"That's the biggest compliment I've ever got," she whispered in his direction, before giving him the widest smile possible.

"Oh darling. I plan to give you compliments every single day, so don't set your expectations too low," he chuckled.

"That sounds pretty good," Lynn whispered, giving Nate heart-eyes.

Before they could continue their conversation, a waitress came and placed their orders on the table between them. It was a mess of small plates and bowls, although most of them only had a few items on them. Nate grabbed his chopsticks and let his gaze wander around all the delicious food.

"This looks amazing," Lynn commented and snatched a maki roll with her own chopsticks.

"A little weird, isn't it?" he chuckled. Lynn looked at him with a raised eyebrow.

"What do you mean?"

"Well, sitting next to an aquarium and having sushi with fish in it. Feels a little weird." He continued.

Lynn stopped her movement. The salmon maki roll was only inches from her mouth. She looked at him with wide eyes before turning her head and watching the colorful fish twirl around the aquarium right next to them. She had a painful look in her eyes, and he could hear her whine.

"Naaaaatteeeeeee."

He started to laugh. Deep and loud. It had been a while since she had seen him laugh like that. His hand was on his stomach, his head had fallen back, and he made the most beautiful sounds. Lynn couldn't stop herself and started to laugh as well, the salmon maki still between her chopsticks.

"I'm sorry, darling. Enjoy your salmon," he breathed while trying to stop laughing.

Lynn looked at him with a fake pout on her face before she couldn't control her expression anymore. The look in her eyes was almost mischievous when she whispered,

"Watch me."

Almost in slow motion, Lynn placed the salmon maki roll in her mouth and started chewing on it. Her face showed an exaggerated expression of joy and happiness, and Nate started to laugh once again. After she was done, she said,

"This one was dead already. We shouldn't waste it. So it didn't die for nothing."

"If you say so," Nate commented and placed a maki roll in his own mouth.

For a while they ate in silence, enjoying their sushi together, before both of them were unable to eat even a single maki roll. Lynn leaned back in her seat, sighing loudly and placed her hands on her stomach.

"That was a lot of food. My stomach looks like I'm five months pregnant," she chuckled.

"And you still look beautiful," Nate commented with a smirk.

"Sweet-Talker"

"Only telling the truth," he winked.

"Of course you are," Lynn rolled her eyes at him but couldn't hide the little smile that came up after his compliment.

"So..." he started, suddenly appearing insecure again. Lynn's smile fell, and she looked at him with a mixture of concern and curiosity.

"I'd really like to pay for us but I don't want you to feel uncomfortable with that. Don't know if things changed about paying the bill as a man," he stuttered.

"I'm totally fine with you paying the bill. Don't think that you're trying to overpower me or that you think I'm not capable of paying my own bills. I just appreciate the gesture." Lynn smiled at him.

Nate's facial expression lightened and he shot her a smile as well before nodding. He gestured to a waitress and paid the bill, before they stood from their table and left the restaurant. While walking towards their car, Lynn grabbed Nate's hand and intertwined their fingers. She wanted to feel close to him before they returned to headquarters and went on with their lives. With their rollercoaster between love and betrayal.

"That was a very nice date, Nate," she whispered, leaning her head on his shoulder while they were walking almost in slow motion towards the navy-blue car.

"I enjoyed it, too. Even with the heavy topics. I feel like I can tell you everything, Lynn. About me, about my past. Hell, I even talk about my feelings with you, although I've never been an emotional person, not even as a child," he chuckled.

"I bet you were a stubborn teenager." Lynn laughed.

"The worst. Sneaking out in the evening to meet girls," he snickered.

"Ohhhhhh, you were *that* kind of teenager? I bet every girl was madly in love with you," Lynn laughed while opening the door on the passenger side.

Nate entered the driver's seat, still snickering.

"Oh no. I was a chubby teenager, despite my baseball career. We couldn't afford healthy food so mom mostly brought takeout on her way back from work. My life was the epitome of being in the friendzone." He sighed heavily while remembering the time as a teenager.

"Wow, really? And when did that change? Because now you look unreal with your picture-perfect body," Lynn answered while pointing up and down his body.

When she realized what she had said her cheeks turned cherry red and she avoided his gaze. Nate laughed again, placed his hand on her thigh, and started the engine.

"It all came when I became a soldier. I never really worked out before, only the stuff we did in High School, but I realized that the drill at the academy worked great for me. My body changed within a few months." He had his gaze fixed on the street again while driving them back home to the headquarters.

"You have my full respect. I was never one to workout, either. I'm just lucky with my genes, I guess, because I never really took care of my nutrition or fitness in general, and I'm happy with my body. Yeah, there's no six pack, and I don't have a thigh gap, but I feel happy and confident in my body, and I think that's the most important thing."

"Absolutely true, Lynn, but we should try working out together. Believe me, you never feel better than after a good, draining workout," Nate commented. They had almost reached the CIA by now.

"You sure? Because after working out with you and Oliver after my accident in spring, I felt so sore. I couldn't move for days. That was so frustrating," she whined.

Nate let out a loud laugh, remembering how the doctor complained all the time.

"It'll get better when you work out frequently, darling. You just need to start somewhere. I promise, I'll be nice to you."

"Okay. Maybe we can try that. As long as I can spend time with you, I'm okay with doing that in the gym as well."

"You won't regret it!" Nate said with a wide smile.

He had parked the car in front of headquarters. Their date was officially coming to an end and both of them were sad about it. It had been so nice to just talk and enjoy their shared time. Not thinking about terrorists, betrayals, work, or grief. Even smiling and laughing. Lynn hadn't realized how much she needed that until today. It felt like the large cracks in her heart were healing a little after their afternoon together. They locked their gazes on each other, neither of them saying a word. But they didn't need to anyway.

A smirk appeared on his face before he left the car, stepped around it, and opened the door on the passenger's side.

"Milady," he said, reaching out his hand to her.

Lynn giggled a little but followed his suggestion and grabbed his hand. Their fingers never left each other while they headed towards the elevator. When it opened and they stepped out of it, they finally let go of their hands just in case Oliver or Marta were to appear without warning. But they were walking so close that the backs of their hands brushed against each other.

Standing in front of Lynn's room, they looked at each other again, unsure how to end this perfect day. Nate cleared his throat and pointed with his thumb at his door to indicate that he was about to go to his room.

"Well, thank you for this wonderful afternoon, Lynn. I really enjoyed spending time with you," he said, shyly, like an insecure sixteen-year-old after his first date.

"I have to thank you, Nate. This was the best date I ever had!"

His features lightened when he looked at her with wide eyes.

"Really?" he whispered.

"Yes, really! I hope there'll be more but it's my turn next time. I already have something in mind. Deal?"

"Deal!" Nate chuckled and took a step towards her.

They awkwardly looked at each other with their bodies only inches apart, unsure if they should hug or kiss as a goodbye.

Lynn decided to step on her toes and give him a small peck on the cheek before she stepped back towards her door.

"Goodbye, Nate."

"Goodbye, darling." Nate smiled at her, turned around, and marched towards his door when he heard her melodic voice again.

"Nate?"

He turned around on his heels and looked at her beautiful face.

"Would you join me for the rest of the day? I mean, it's still way too early for bedtime, but we could watch a movie or something. I just don't want to be alone, you know." Lynn stumbled over her own words. Her voice was thick with insecurity, her cheeks blushed, and her gaze locked with the floor.

"I thought you would never ask!" Nate answered, quickly stepping towards her and capturing her lips in a passionate kiss. He wrapped one of his arms around her while opening the door with the other. Still kissing, they stumbled into her room, and Nate gave the door a kick with his heel to close it.

# Firework

**June 9th, 2022**

Their lips remained locked together while they stumbled into Lynn's room and towards her queen bed. Nate held her close, so close that she couldn't tell where her body ended and his began. Lynn's calves crashed against the frame of her bed and, when Nate didn't stop walking, she fell backwards onto it, Nate still on top of her.

He stopped his fall with his right hand on the mattress next to her head so that his muscular, tall body wouldn't bury her. His other hand pulled away from underneath her back and he placed it on her waist while his tongue slid into her mouth. The tip of his tongue gently touched hers before he began to suck on her bottom lip.

When they broke apart to catch a breath, he opened his eyes again and met her intense gaze. A sparkle appeared in her chestnut eyes. One that was more than just the love he'd seen before.

Lynn's eyes mirrored the growing desire in her body.

Had she thought about having sex with Nate before? Sure.

But after everything that had happened she was sure that it wouldn't happen soon, especially not on their first date. When she had asked him to join her in the shower, which had been for comfort rather than sex, he had fled. And she'd completely understood because it had been way too early.

Now it was only a few days later and he'd made the first step by kissing her fiercely and leading her directly towards her bed. She could feel the growing bulge in his crotch as an indicator that he was definitely ready for sex.

The doctor wasn't sure if she should stop him because they would definitely cross boundaries today, and maybe he would regret it afterwards. He was led by lust and desire and pretty sure he wasn't able to think clearly at this point.

Heart vs. head

Nate noticed that Lynn had zoned out for a few seconds and thought that it was hesitation.

"Something wrong?" he asked before placing a more gentle kiss on her nose.

"Are you sure you want to do this, Nate?" she asked with a facial expression he couldn't read.

Was it a mixture between concern, sadness, lust, and hope? A combination that made no sense for him and left him confused. He placed his other hand next to her head as well and propped his body up a little to put some distance between their faces. He inspected her face with furrowed brows before he carefully answered:

"I *am* sure, but we can wait if you don't feel ready for this. It's a lot for a first date."

"No. No. I want this. Gosh, you can't imagine how long I've been wanting this. I've lay in your arms so often and all I could think about was you touching me in the right places." Her pupils were slightly dilated and Lynn could feel her panties getting soaked just by imagining everything Nate could do to her.

"Then it's time to turn that dream into reality," he smirked and let his hand wander down her body until he reached her thigh.

Before he reached her inner thigh, Lynn cleared her throat. She was fighting very hard to ignore the voices in her head and let her body become a slave to her hormones and desire.

"But are you *really* sure? After everything that happened? I don't want you to regret it afterwards."

Nate groaned in response but then pressed his crotch against her thigh to let her feel his growing erection.

"Does that feel like I'm not sure?" He winked at her before lowering his head to capture her bottom lip with his teeth.

After sucking on it for a short moment, he gently nibbled along her jaw until he reached her ear. The moment his soft lips left her skin, it was burning. Lynn's panties were completely soaked by now and the heat in her lower belly rose. It had been a while since she had someone who made her feel like Nate did.

"I just wanted to double check," she breathed, struggling hard not to let a moan escape her throat while Nate sucked on her earlobe.

The spot right behind her earlobe was one of her sweet spots and his lips came closer and closer to it. She knew that she wouldn't be able to think properly from the moment he reached it with his ridiculously soft lips and right now she wasn't even sure why she needed to think at all.

All she could think about was Nate fucking her until her brain malfunctioned.

"Lynn..." another nibble on her earlobe. "... all I can think about now is that I want our bodies connected in the best possible way. I want to have sex with you, Lynn Summers," he whispered in her ear, making her shiver and causing goosebumps to appear on her arm. He used the dark voice with the slight tremble that she loved so much.

"Nate," she moaned, not able to respond in any other way.

She could feel his smile against her sensitive skin when he shifted his head a little to start kissing her neck.

"Let me fuck you, Lynn Summers. We can talk about everything else later."

The screaming therapy voice inside her head was instantly silenced when his lips reached her sweet spot. Instinctively, she ground her hips against him and another moan escaped her throat. The smile on her skin intensified when Nate kissed along her neck, leaving a trail of burning sensation. He reached her collarbone with his lips while his hand carefully slid between her legs, using his strength to spread them a little before he tried to get his hand underneath her dress. But she was wearing a floor-length dress and he fumbled a little too long, fighting against the fabric. Lynn, her eyes still closed and enjoying his lips on her neck, reached down and dragged the dress up. Finally, his hand reached her soaked panties and she could feel him place another kiss on her collarbone.

"Seems like you are sure, too," he murmured.

Lynn, a bubbling and needy mess by now, could only nod while she opened her eyes to observe him change his position a little. He carefully pulled her into a sitting position so that he could open the zipper on the back of her dress before he pulled the whole fabric over her head, leaving her only in her lace panties and bra. They weren't matching because she hadn't expected to end the date by him seeing her in underwear.

Nate leaned back a little to let his eyes wander up and down her body. He had seen her in a bra before, when she was injured and had to wear the sling, but it had always been a sports bra, which covered her breasts in a less sexual way than the nude-colored lace bra she was wearing now. He let his index finger caress over her clothed breast, feeling the hard nipple underneath. His gaze locked with hers and Lynn was surprised that his normally more cerulean eyes were almost navy because of his dilated pupils.

This man was radiating lust and desire from every cell of his body.

When his finger trailed down her little belly and reached the hem of her panties, Lynn inhaled sharply. Her brain was foggy and all she wanted was his cock buried deep inside of her.

Seeing him truly admire her body from head to toe made her feel very comfortable, something she hadn't felt with many men before, but she knew that Nate respected her and wanted her to feel good, so he would never do something that she didn't agree with.

"Can I take off your bra, darling?" He asked carefully when his blue eyes met hers again.

She nodded slightly and felt his one hand wandering towards her back to open the bra. With a smooth movement, he undid the clasp and let the straps slide down her arms. He grasped her one arm and slowly pulled it out of the strap before repeating the same with the other. The bra fell into her lap and she could see Nate licking his bottom lip in anticipation.

"You're so beautiful, Lynn. I've never seen someone as beautiful as you," he whispered in her direction, sparkles of love in his eyes.

Lynn lowered her upper body slowly onto the mattress again and Nate quickly stripped off his shirt. He then moved towards the end of the bed so that his head was at the level of her breasts. He looked up, awaiting her permission. When she nodded again and closed her eyes, he started to place kisses on the outside of her breasts. His mouth moved towards her nipple while his hand respectfully laid on her stomach. Lynn's heart was beating faster and faster and when his lips reached her nipple and carefully sucked on it, a moaned "Nate" echoed through the room.

Nate' cock twitched desperately. It had been a while for him too and he was sure he wouldn't last long today. But it was their first time and he wanted to make sure that it was perfect for both of them. Her hips ground against him again, indicating how needy she was.

He let go of her nipple and looked up at her.

"Please, Nate," she whispered while bucking her hips one more time.

"What do you need, Lynn? Talk to me."

"I need you deep inside me."

They looked at each other and Nate's heart skipped a beat. He loved this woman so much and all he wanted to do was make her happy and comfortable.

"At your command, darling," he answered before opening the knee brace to get it off his leg.

Then he opened the zipper of his jeans. He wiggled a little in bed before he was able to pull his jeans and briefs down to his ankles and kick them off into the room. His already hard length slapped against his toned abs and when Lynn saw the size of it, she took a deep breath.

"I won't do anything that's uncomfortable for you. If it hurts, let me know immediately but I know you can take it," he said and waited for a response. When she only nodded, he added, "words, Lynn. I need words."

"Understood, Sir."

An animalistic groan escaped Nate's throat and his cock leaked precum. She knew exactly what she was doing to drive him crazy. He grabbed the hem of her panties, and she bucked her hips so that he could pull them down her legs.

When both of them were naked, they quickly checked each other out again. Love and desire were present in both of their eyes.

Nate's hand wandered towards her core and his thumb reached her clit. He carefully started to circle it and watched her for a reaction. Lynn's eyes fluttered closed and an appreciative whimper left her lips.

His other hand gave his length a few pumps. He was already painfully hard by now and he knew that he needed release soon.

Lynn moaned again and Nate left her clit to gently enter one finger through her folds. She was already so wet by now, and he could feel her walls clench around him. Her hips shot upwards, encouraging him to move his finger inside of her.

He bent it a little and reached the spongy spot inside of her, making her almost scream his name again.

"Nate. I can't hold it any longer," she exclaimed.

Lynn hadn't expected that it would take him so little time to catapult her over the edge, but it had been a while, and Nate knew exactly how to stimulate her.

"Come for me, darling." He smirked.

Lynn arched her back while her orgasm crashed over her like a tsunami. Never in her life had a man given her such an intense orgasm just with his fingers. She couldn't wait to see what this man was capable of with his cock.

When she came down from her high, she opened her eyes and found Nate hovering over her. With a swift movement of his knee, he spread her legs wider before lining up his tip with her entrance. Nate raised his head again and looked at Lynn. Desire was still present in her expression but he could also see a glimpse of fear. His cock was big and he knew that it wasn't easy to take for some women.

"I know you can take it. But if it hurts too much, please let me know immediately, okay?" he spoke with a loving voice.

"Yes, honey. I will," she answered with a shy smile on her lips.

The corner of his mouth raised as well before he slowly and carefully entered her. Lynn hissed and held her breath while her walls adjusted to his immense size. She'd never had a man with such a big cock before and, to be honest, it hurt a lot. It took her a while after he bottomed out until she felt comfortable and let go of the breath she was holding.

At that moment, she knew that he was the missing puzzle piece in her life. Their bodies were meant for each other.

From that day forward she would never be able to have sex with anyone else.

"You're doing great, Lynn. Taking me so perfectly. I'm so proud of you, darling. You feel so tight around my cock. So perfect," he praised her after seeing her furrowing her brows.

Lynn opened her eyes and locked her gaze with him, giving him the silent signal that she was okay. Nate smiled at her, leaned his head down and playfully bit along her neck while he started slow and gentle thrusts. He pulled his cock almost completely out before bottoming out again. Although she already had an orgasm, Lynn could feel another one approaching very quickly. Nate felt so good inside of her, and the size of his cock was perfect to bring her ultimate pleasure.

"Oh God, Nate. This feels so good," she exclaimed. Smiling into her neck, Nate increased the pace of his thrusts. Suddenly, Lynn wrapped her legs around his waist and her heels digging into his back where she had crossed them. The new angle of their hips allowed him to get even deeper inside of her, making him moan louder. He shifted his head and captured her lips in a fierce kiss that was constantly disrupted by moans from both of them. Lynn buried her teeth deep into his bottom lip while she started to match his rhythm with her own hips, and Nate could taste blood in his mouth.

"Lynn, I'm coming. I can't hold it any longer," he groaned into her mouth.

"Come for me, honey. Fill me up," she answered him and the knot inside her belly tightened.

She wouldn't need long for another orgasm either. This man was driving her crazy.

After a few more sloppy thrusts, he spilled inside of her while moaning her name in the sexiest way her ears had ever heard. Just the sound of this was enough to bring her over the edge again, and she screamed his name into the room while her body burned with pleasure. A tingling sensation on every inch of her skin while she desperately tried to catch Nate's lips again. The Agent was panting slightly but he kissed her back with the same fire. His thrusts subsided, but he stayed inside of her a bit longer.

Lynn's legs were trembling from the strength she used to keep them wrapped around Nate's waist, and she slowly let them fall down on the bed again. Nate broke the kiss and looked her in the eyes.

"That was awesome," he whispered, kissing the brick of her nose.

Lynn raised her arm and placed the palm of her hand on his slightly sweaty face, brushing her thumb over the hot skin.

"It was perfect. You are perfect."

The words "I love you" were sitting on the tip of Nate's tongue, but he wasn't brave enough to say them out loud. He didn't want to ruin the moment now that they were finally starting to get back together again. The moment he realized that she really loved him the entire time and that none of that was a lie, he allowed himself to love her, too. Even when she had betrayed him.

His heart guided the way but it was his mind that he was concerned about.

It was still early in their reborn relationship. They had enough time to become more comfortable with each other and find the perfect moment to say it. Not now, when they were both drunk on their post-orgasm high.

"You're perfect too, Lynn Summers," Nate simply said and placed a last gentle kiss on her lips before he pulled out of her.

He let his body collapse next to her and saw Lynn turning on her side, her arm wrapped around his abdomen. She placed gentle pecks on his shoulder before she rested her head on his bare chest.

"*Now* are you comfortable enough to take a shower with me?" she snickered.

"Yeah. I think that would be okay." He winked at her before leaving the bed.

Lynn followed him closely but suddenly Nate turned around to face her. Lynn almost crashed into him when she felt his hands on both of her hips. A second later she was pulled into the air and instinctively wrapped her legs around his hips while she yelped in shock.

"What are you doooiiiiing..." she giggled as he struggled to get them into the bathroom, her body in front of him blocking a lot of his view. He was also still limping and the pressure on his not yet fully healed knee was immense. Of course he hadn't put the knee brace back on again. Lynn would lecture him later for that.

"Taking a shower with you," he answered when they finally reached their destination.

Nate wrapped his arm around Lynn, who still hung on him like a koala, and turned on the water in the shower with his other one.

Underneath her core, his length was already starting to get hard again. How was this man already ready for another round?

Nate carefully lowered Lynn back to the ground and rubbed his left knee a little with slightly furrowed brows. Lynn looked at him, concerned, and when he saw her face he immediately stopped. He knew that Lynn was probably not happy that he was walking around without the knee brace, but it just felt weird to be naked with it on. Also, he didn't want it to hurt Lynn while they had sex.

"Are you hurt?" she asked.

"No. It's alright. Maybe just a little too much weight on the knee."

"What does that mean? That I'm fat?!" She exclaimed with a shocked expression.

Nate looked at her and could feel his heartbeat very fast. This was exactly why he was never good in relationships, he had a talent for always saying the wrong things. He just looked at her, a battle inside his mind over what could possibly be the correct answer but before he could decide Lynn burst into laughter.

"You should see your face. Hilarious," she chuckled, and Nate finally realized that she was just messing with him.

"Think that's funny?" He answered, stepping in her direction.

"I can show you what I think is funny."

He grabbed her arm, pulled her close, and tickled her waist. Lynn tried to wiggle out of his grip but of course Nate's strength was too much for her. She laughed and squeaked until she was out of breath and he finally let her go only to pull her into a gentle but tight hug.

Lynn rested her head on his bare chest when their naked bodies connected in a different way. Neither of them thought about sex at that moment, they just enjoyed each other's company and intimacy.

Nate smelled the familiar peachy scent of Lynn and it smelled like home to him. This woman was his peace, his light, his guidance, and his home. He wanted to have her by his side for the rest of his life.

"Nate?" She mumbled into his chest.

"Mhm?"

"This. This is perfect. You and me. I like this. A lot."

"Me too, Lynn. Me too."

And with that being said a firework in both of their stomachs appeared, overpowering the usual butterflies. This was the start of something good. The man with the ocean blue eyes and the doctor felt that they finally had a real chance for a happy ending.

# *Consequences*

**June 10<sup>th</sup>, 2022**

Because they had fallen asleep so early, Lynn was awake in the middle of the night, realizing a heavy arm lay on her stomach. She was on her back, still naked. Nate was lying on his side, facing her. The leg with the knee brace was on top of the blanket while soft snoring noises came out of his mouth. After they had taken an uneventful shower, they headed straight back to bed. Lynn forced Nate to put on the knee brace again before they snuggled into each other. There hadn't been many words between them, just the two of them lying with their bodies entangled as best as possible. Enjoying the company and love between them.

The betrayal wasn't magically forgotten, but they had both decided to ignore it for a moment and discover whatever this was between them. Having sex on a first date wasn't exactly Lynn's style but, technically, they had been in a relationship before the betrayal as well. They just didn't put a label on it.

Another snore left Nate's lips and Lynn needed to hide her smile. It was more than adorable. Lynn wished she could reach her phone to capture the moment because Nate looked so peaceful, almost happy, with his lips curled upward.

"Staring is rude," he mumbled into his pillow before opening his eyes a little.

Lynn chuckled.

"How did you know?"

"I know when I'm being watched," he responded before slowly scooting closer to her so that he could rest his head on her chest, above her breast.

Lynn shifted her arm so that she could comb her fingers through his messy hair. It had grown over the past few weeks as he hadn't had time to go to a hairdresser to trim it down again. It had started to curl a little and Lynn couldn't stop watching it while her fingers brushed through it. She really loved it when he had it a little longer. Not too long, but right now it was perfect.

"You're staring again," he commented, his eyes closed.

Lynn could feel his even breath on her skin, leaving goosebumps all over her arm.

"Sorry, I can't stop looking at you. I feel like I'm on an all-time high right now."

His head shifted a little while he tried to catch her gaze. Then smirked at her and said,

"I can show you another high if you let me."

"As good as this sounds, my body needs some rest from last night before we do whatever you have in mind for me."

"Sure?" he asked, letting the arm on her stomach slowly wander down her body.

She grabbed his hand, halting its movement, and placed it above her hips again.

"Yes, I'm sure. As much as I'd love to have sex with you again, yesterday happened in the heat of the moment. We should still figure things out between us," she mumbled, regretting her words the moment they left her mouth.

Nate sighed, pushed himself off her chest, and laid with his back on the mattress, staring at the ceiling above.

Silence lingered between them, but not a comfortable one.

"I know," he whispered after a minute that felt like an eternity for Lynn.

"I'm sorry," the doctor said, tears gathering in her eyes.

Guilt bubbled up in her chest for betraying him and that she couldn't just enjoy the moment with the man she loved.

They were both lying on their backs, shoulders brushing while they avoided looking at each other.

"You don't have to be. You're right. I'm sorry that I kind of took advantage of you last night. I knew exactly how to work you so that you'd agree to have sex with me," he whispered.

Lynn shifted in her position, now lying on her side, facing him. She had pulled the blanket to her chin, covering her naked body.

"Look at me," she demanded with a soft tone in her voice.

Nate followed her demand and turned his head towards her. Her heart broke when she saw the tears glistering in his eyes. He was as confused as she was.

"Oh honey," she added, pulling one arm out of the blanket, and placing her palm on his cheek.

A few tears had escaped his eyes, leaving a wet strain along his face. Lynn gripped his face tight, brushing circles with her thumb over his still hot skin.

"I don't know what to do. What to feel. I'm just so confused." Nate sobbed.

She hadn't seen him cry like that before. Especially not because of her. Because she had hurt him. Lynn's heart was heavy. It was aching, and she felt like she would never be able to fix the damage she did to Nate a few weeks ago. When she decided not to talk to him about the blackmailing and her kidnapped sister.

"I'm so sorry." Lynn started to cry as well.

Her hand was shaking slightly but it never left his face. Never stopped drawing small circles.

"I know you are and I understand what you did. Really. I just can't silence the demons in my mind. They keep on telling me that you're not trustworthy. That I should kick you out of my life. But I don't want to. Because you're the best thing that ever happened to me." Nate's voice was quiet, tender, and raw. Everything at once. And it was dripping with confusion.

"I wish I could go back in time and talk to you. Let you know about Ann. But I can't."

"No, you can't."

Silence spread between them. Nate tried to turn his head away from her, and tried to break eye contact but her small hand was ridiculously strong on his cheek and she forced him to look her in the eyes. The chestnut eyes that contained so much love for him. He could see it.

"I love you," Nate whispered so quietly, that he wasn't sure if Lynn had heard him but when he saw her eyes well up with tears again, he knew she had.

"Nate," she breathed heavily in reaction to his confession.

"That is the reason I'm really trying. Lynn, I really am. I love you and I'm willing to give us a chance. But it's so hard. You need to be patient with me."

"I love you, too. You can't even believe how much. That's why I'm so sorry. I messed up and now you're suffering because of me. Never, ever in my life did I want to be the reason for your suffering. You have suffered enough in your life and me loading another demon onto your mind is probably the worst thing I've ever done in my life. I don't deserve your chance or your love but I'm so happy that it's there. I'm so relieved to hear those beautiful words out of your mouth."

Lynn was still crying, but she scooted closer to him, their faces only inches apart. Nate turned on his side so that he was facing her as well. He placed his hand on her waist, looking into her chestnut eyes with so much love behind his own.

"I want this to work. I want to figure things out. I want to be with you. Every single day," he whispered, a shy smile appearing on his lips. His warm breath on her face made goosebumps appear on Lynn's arms.

"I want this too, Nate. Whatever I need to do to show you how much I regret my behavior and that it will never happen again in the future, I'm willing to do. Because I love you."

Her voice was harsh from the silent crying and thick with emotions. And hope. There was so much hope in her voice.

"For now, I just want you to kiss me," Nate responded, the shy smile on his face changing into a little smirk.

Lynn chuckled a little and scooted even closer to him. Their bodies pulled toward each other like magnets. She was well aware that he was only in his briefs and that she was naked. Her foot tangled in between his legs, her breasts brushing over his chest, and her lips hovered over his.

"I love you," she whispered before closing the gap between them and giving Nate the most tender kiss they had ever shared.

He pulled her even closer while kissing her back with the same tenderness and love.

"Say it again," he mouthed on her lips.

"I love you." Lynn smiled into him, their lips slightly touching.

"I love you, too," Nate answered before catching her bottom lip in another, fiercer kiss.

The world around them disappeared because everything that mattered was the two of them, right here, right now.

When they broke apart once again, Nate started to laugh. A deep laugh that was coming right from his chest. His whole body was shaking from the laughter and it was so affecting that Lynn couldn't stop herself from laughing as well.

"Why are you laughing?" Lynn asked in between shallow breaths.

"This wasn't exactly how I imagined the first 'I love you'. Not exactly like in a romance book."

"Screw the romance books. It was perfect," Lynn answered before giving him a few wet kisses along his face.

Nate squinted his brows together so that his face looked like a funny grimace when Lynn placed a few more kisses along his nose, cheeks, temples and forehead.

"It really was," he now whispered, before turning on his back and pulling her in his arms so that she could place her head on his chest.

Lynn listened to his quickened heartbeat while he brushed his fingertips over her upper arm. The combination of safety, love, and his heartbeat lulled her back to sleep immediately. Nate placed a last kiss on her head and mumbled another "I love you" before he fell asleep again as well.

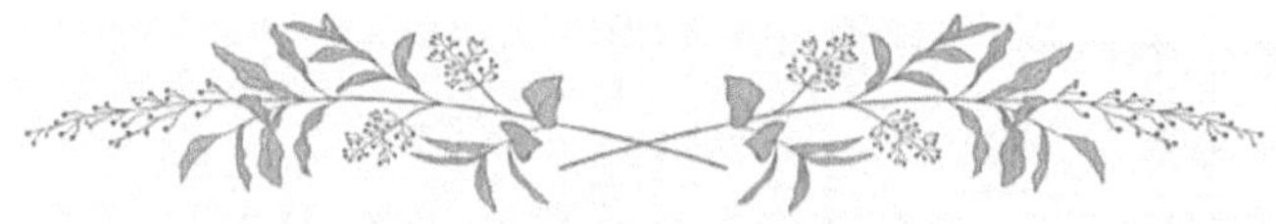

A few hours later, Lynn was carefully hustling Nate out of her room while she got dressed for her shift in the med-bay.

"See you later, darling," he whispered, gave her a last peck on her lips, and almost ran along the hallway, at least as fast as his still recovering knee allowed him.

Lynn shook her head, not happy about him putting too much pressure on the knee when they still hadn't talked about his physical therapy plan in detail.

But no matter what she did, she wasn't able to shake the smile from her face. She grabbed her phone and, out of instinct, went to send her sister Ann a message to let her know about this absolutely amazing first date with Nate. But when she opened the texts with her and saw them all empty, her heart stopped beating for a minute. She had deleted the entire chat with Ann because, in her rage and despair, she didn't want to see Az-Zawahiri's messages again. And the picture of Ann's lifeless body.

But now she realized that she had lost all the memories of their text conversations. Her eyes teared up again.

Quickly, she closed the empty chat with Ann and opened the one with her mother instead to tell her about the date but after the happenings at the funeral they hadn't been on speaking terms so she closed that chat as well, sighed, and decided to just forget about it and go to work. She let her mind wander back to Nate and their incredible date, not letting the intrusive thoughts take over her good mood.

After changing into her navy-blue scrubs, she left her room and stepped through the automatic door of the med-bay right next to it. Tia was sitting behind the counter, raising her head when she heard the door open and giving Lynn a small smile.

"Good morning," Lynn said with the widest possible grin on her face.

"Good morning, Lynn. Wow, you're in a brilliant mood. Don't like to be the one to ruin that, but Director Burns and Deputy Director Gómez are waiting for you in your office," Tia responded with a little bit of sadness washing over her face.

"Oh," Lynn mouthed.

Tia's words had sucked all the air out of her lungs. Her head began to spin, and she needed to close her eyes. The upcoming panic attack was near, and she reached out her arm to touch the wall next to her and steady her body. Because of the loud tinnitus in her ears, she didn't hear Tia's concerned voice. The nurse had sprinted from her place behind the counter and was now standing in front of Lynn, her hands placed on each side of Lynn's waist to steady her slightly shaking body.

"Lynn." Tia's voice became louder every time and finally Lynn opened her eyes again and looked into the dark brown, almost black eyes of the nurse.

"Yeah. Oh gosh, sorry. I'm okay. Just a little shock," Lynn stuttered.

"Looked more like a full blown panic attack to me." Tia sighed, brushing her palms over Lynn's upper arms to sooth her.

"You said they were in my office?"

"Yeah. Are you sure you're okay?" Tia's face was furrowed with concern and she gripped Lynn's arms even tighter.

"Yeah. Yeah, I'm good." Lynn gave her the fakest smile ever, but Tia couldn't force the doctor to stay, so she stepped aside and saw Lynn disappear through the door on the other side of the entrance.

The door to her office was ajar, giving her only a short moment to take a deep breath before entering the room with a fake smile again.

Director Burns and Marta had their backs to her, faces turned towards each other while they were chatting. When they heard Lynn enter the room, they spun around and watched the doctor step towards them.

"Director Burns, Marta." Lynn nodded at them before rounding her big desk and letting herself fall into the chair behind it.

"Doctor Summers." Burns smiled at her.

Why was he smiling? Was that a good sign?

"Lynn, good to see you. How are you doing?" Marta asked with the same weird smile on her face.

Lynn eyed her friend and tried to read behind the mask, but she couldn't.

"Depends on what we're talking about in the next few seconds," Lynn mumbled back at them, the fake smile washed off her face and she looked at them with concern flickering behind her chestnut eyes.

Marta let out a deep sigh, but the smile remained on her face.

Why was she smiling? Was that a good sign?

"Doctor Summers, we're here to talk to you about the legal consequences for your betrayal," Director Burns started and Lynn sighed in response.

Her eyes alternated between the Director and her friend, searching their features for any hints of the upcoming words.

"We had different lawyers working on your case and we asked everyone involved for their opinions. Not only on the situation itself, but also about working with you." Marta continued, giving Lynn another one of her smiles.

Normally Marta's smile was always so infectious that Lynn couldn't resist smiling herself, but currently she was so tense that she just wanted to punch out her friend's perfect teeth.

"I have to say, I'm impressed by how positive each one of your colleagues had talked about you. They all emphasized your passion for your work and your will to make things better for everyone. Also..." Director Burns started and tilted his head a little, while the smile disappeared from his face. "... they all told us they would have done the same in your position. Even Deputy Director Gómez."

Lynn's face fell a little and she looked at Marta and the Director with shock all over her face. They had all supported her?

"You've only been working for the CIA for a short time, but you managed to have all of them covering your back. That is really impressive, Doctor Summers."

"The lawyers considered the opinions of the others in their final decision." Marta added and Lynn's lips parted.

She didn't know if she had to say something, but Director Burns cleared his throat and continued.

"We all understood that you were blackmailed and didn't really have a choice other than working with the terrorist az-Zawahiri. Still, this is state treason, so there have to be legal consequences for you. Normally you would go to jail for that."

Burns decided to make a pause right after this sentence. Of course he did. It felt like he had Lynn's heart in his bare hand, only seconds away from crushing it. He looked at her, unable to hide the smile on his lips.

"But we were able to prevent you from going to jail." Marta bubbled into the Director's pause, earning herself an angry side-eye.

"Yes, Deputy Director Gómez is right. Instead you have to do 1,600 hours of community service here at the CIA headquarters. Means you're doing your regular job, but you won't get paid for it. Also you're under house arrest for the duration of the community service. You are not allowed to leave the compound. Your sentence starts immediately. Do you have any questions?"

Lynn stared at him with her jaw on the floor.

She didn't have to go to jail! And she was able to keep her job!

This felt like a dream. Was this a dream? Was she dreaming?

Lynn blinked a few times, unable to form words.

"Lynn, are you okay?" Marta asked with her head tilted and her eyebrows furrowed.

The doctor shook her head to bring her back to reality and answered.

"Yeah, yeah. I'm just... overwhelmed. I didn't expect it to be like that. Thank you. Really."

Director Burns smiled at her.

"I always try to keep the good ones," he said to her before standing up from his chair.

"If you have any questions, you can always call me. We'll figure things out." And with that being said he marched out of the room and was gone.

Lynn peered after him for a while before she let her gaze wander and looked into Marta's honey eyes. The Deputy Director had the widest grin on her face and stood from her chair to round the desk and give Lynn a hug.

"I don't deserve this," Lynn mumbled in Marta's shoulder, a few tears slipping out of her eyes, when she finally let go of the tension that had her whole body in a chokehold the last minutes.

"You made a mistake. We all do that sometimes. It's like Director Burns said, you were blackmailed and you didn't have a choice. You didn't betray us on purpose. That was a very important detail for the lawyers."

The two women let go of the hug but held each other close. Lynn's eyes were still glistening with tears and Marta's filled as well.

"Thank you. It's amazing to have friends like you," Lynn mumbled with a shy smile on her face.

"That's what friends are for." Marta smiled back at her.

Lynn couldn't stop smiling for the rest of the day. Even though 1,600 hours of unpaid work was a lot and she needed to check her finances to see if that would cause her any problems. But all of her friends and colleagues were on her side. Even Nate. The man she had hurt the most. They had all covered her back and wanted her to stay.

And that meant the world to Lynn.

# Therapy

**June 24<sup>th</sup>, 2022**

It had been two weeks since Lynn's job had been changed into community service. It didn't actually make much of a difference for her except that there was no payment coming into her bank account at the end of the month. She had checked her finances and everything looked okay so far. Without going out there was nothing to spend her money on anyways. All in all she was more than lucky and tried to show her gratitude to Marta and the others every day. She worked extra hard in the med-bay, made dinner for the others more often than usual and even baked cupcakes for the other Agents that weren't living in the compound.

It was her way of showing that she was grateful to still be there.

She was sure that some food and smiles weren't enough to get them to forgive her betrayal, but it was a start.

Lynn hadn't heard her alarm that morning and she needed to sprint into the med-bay without breakfast. Her stomach growled the entire time she was checking over some Agents before their upcoming mission. Thankfully she had about a half hour before her next patient. She needed to write the report for the Agents' team leader but, as she knew they wouldn't leave for the operation for another few days, she would be able to do it later.

"I'll get myself some breakfast in the kitchen. I'll be right back," she said towards Tia who was sitting on the counter in the entrance hall.

Lynn turned around and checked that nobody was in the waiting area that she had missed. After seeing that it was indeed empty, she left the room through the automatic doors and hurried along the hallway and into the kitchen.

Behind the kitchen island stood Nate, a black t-shirt with the CIA logo on the front, sweat dripping off his temples.

"Good morning, handsome," she smiled in his direction, letting him look up into her eyes.

He was currently preparing some bagels and had been totally focused on smearing butter across one of them. When he realized who was talking to him a beautiful smile appeared on his face and he responded.

"Good morning, darling. Didn't expect to see you."

"Yeah, I forgot my breakfast this morning and needed to get some food into my starving body," she chuckled but heard him click his tongue in disbelief.

"I didn't hear my alarm," she added with a strong urge to justify herself.

She had moved next to him and saw that he was in workout shorts. The knee brace was still around his knee and Lynn made a quick mental reminder to schedule him another check-up. He should be able to take it off soon.

"You can have one of my bagels," Nate offered, sliding the plate with the first finished bagel towards her. Lynn's eyes lit up when she saw the delicious breakfast.

"You sure?"

"Yes, darling. Take it, before I change my mind," he chuckled and Lynn didn't waste another second, grabbed the bagel and took a big bite.

"Mhhhhmmmm. Sas gud," Lynn commented, but Nate only raised an eyebrow at her because he didn't understand a word. Lynn giggled, swallowed the bite in her mouth and repeated,

"That's good."

"Made with love." Nate winked at her.

"Wait a minute? You originally made this for yourself, so don't try to sweet-talk me, mister." Lynn slapped her palm on Nate's upper arm with a loud chuckle.

"Hey!" He exclaimed and turned his head around to follow Lynn who moved to the other side of the island, placed her elbows on the counter and watched the brunette man curiously.

"Am I not allowed to add love to my own food?" He added, starting to prepare the second bagel that was still lying in front of him.

"Sure you are but it's unusual. Normally you only say that when you cook for someone you love."

"I am unusual." He winked at her.

Nate grabbed his own bagel with both hands and took the biggest possible bite with a loud hum of appreciation. After a few bites he said,

"I can taste the love. It's delicious."

"You're an idiot," Lynn laughed.

They ate their breakfast in silence, both of them still standing in the kitchen, gazes locked. There were no words needed while sparks flew between their ocean blue and chestnut eyes.

"I... I... have something today I wanted to invite you to," Nate stuttered, his brows knitting together in insecurity while his eyes slit away from Lynn's.

Immediate concern bubbled in Lynn's chest and she had a bad feeling about it. Nate was behaving strangely and the change in his emotions came too fast. She knew from months of being with him as his therapist, friend, and more, that this was never a good sign.

"What is it?" She almost whispered.

Her chest felt like someone had wrapped a rope around it and pulled it tighter with every second.

"I was thinking about another therapy session," Nate started, his voice low and full of insecurity.

The rope around Lynn's chest loosened and she let go of the breath she wasn't aware she was holding.

"Ohhhh! Of course." She smiled at him, relieved that he hadn't any serious or frightening news for her.

She took another bite of her bagel, licking the cream cheese from her fingers, that had managed to drop out of the bread.

Nate's eyes were fixed on her tongue, watching every move she made to lick her finger clean. Lynn hadn't realized it until she saw the blush on his cheeks. As slowly as possible, she took the finger in her mouth and released it with a loud plop.

Nate groaned in response, shook his head and grabbed his crotch to adjust whatever was happening beneath the shorts.

"That's not fair," he hissed, his hand still lingering on the growing bulge in his shorts.

"Maybe I can help you with your little problem after the therapy session." Lynn winked at him.

"Last time I checked it wasn't so little," Nate groaned, making Lynn almost choke on her next bite of bagel.

She coughed a few times, making Nate round the kitchen island and slap her upper back to help her.

"You're good?" he asked, trying to hide his laughter.

"Yeah, I'm fine. Just haven't expected you to be such a needy man."

"Depends on my company, darling." He placed a kiss on her cheek before grinding his half hard length into her thigh. Then he went back to the fridge and grabbed the family-sized container of orange juice to pour each of them a glass.

"I'd like to explore this side of you," she commented as she watched his biceps tense under the weight of the juice container.

"The making-breakfast-side?" he asked with another wink.

"The playful side," Lynn responded.

"I never knew I had this side in me, to be honest. But I like it."

"I like it, too."

Nate cleared his throat, obviously tiptoeing around the actual topic of their conversation; the therapy session. Lynn saw him taking two deep breaths, something he always did to keep his anxiety at bay.

"About the therapy session..." he started, looking at his feet uncomfortably.

She didn't interrupt him or help him out by finishing his sentence. He needed to be brave now and talk to her whatever was bothering him. That was part of his recovery process, too. He couldn't avoid uncomfortable and frightening situations for the rest of his life.

"... it's not a therapy session with you." He raised his head and looked at her.

"Oh." Lynn's face fell, although she tried to remain a neutral expression. But the hurt was visible in her eyes and the way the corners of her mouth were turned downwards.

"That's... that's okay. As long as you feel good, I'm fine with everything. I can understand that you don't trust me as a therapist anymore after what I did. And I wasn't your official therapist anyways. It's better if you talk to someone else." She gave him the most fake smile ever.

"No. It's not..." he started but she interrupted him.

"Hey, it's okay. I'm not mad. It's totally fine for me. I betrayed you, I took advantage of the trust you had in me, and used it against you. I wouldn't trust me either." A desperate chuckle left her throat, making Nate furrow his own face.

"No, Lynn. It's not that I'm having a new therapist. *We* are having a new therapist," he pressed out.

"We?" Lynn asked, confused. "What do you mean *we* have a new therapist?"

"I think we should do couples therapy. Maybe that could help us fix whatever is broken between us," he whispered.

She heard in the way his voice sounded that he had been scared to talk to her about it and that hurt her more than anything else. There had been times when he was open to her about everything. She was the one making him open up about everything he's been through for the first time in ten years. She had been his person of trust. His person of comfort.

But now he stood on the other side of the kitchen island, nervously stepping from one foot onto the other, avoiding her gaze and everything she could read out of his face was shame and guilt.

"Oh, yeah. Sure. Sure, we can do that," she mumbled, the gears in her brain working as hard as possible while she was trying to choose the next words.

"I... I just thought we were already on a good way, you know. Because of the date and the... the sex."

Her voice was so low, that Nate almost missed her talking because his heart was beating so loud and fast. He raised his arm, scratching the base of his neck and furrowed his face. He was also looking for the right words.

"We are. But I think as my therapy helped me so much, this could help us as well. I wanted to give it a try."

"Okay, yeah. Sorry, I was just taken by surprise. But of course we can do that. Someone like a mediator is always helpful." She now smiled at him again, honestly. She saw him exhale in relief before a shy smile danced around his lips as well.

"I'm happy you said that. Doctor Smith is coming this afternoon for a first session. Sorry that it's such short notice."

"WHAT?!" Lynn exclaimed, sighing deeply. "How long have you known?" she added.

"A week," he mumbled into his beard so she couldn't understand him.

"Nate."

"A week," he repeated, louder this time.

Lynn turned on her heels and groaned in frustration. She closed her eyes, her back facing Nate, and she took three deep breaths. Trying to calm the anger.

"Okay. When?" she asked, still turned away.

"5:30, I already checked with Tia and Birdie that you don't have any patients then."

Lynn turned around, now obviously angry.

"So you talked to Tia and Birdie about this but didn't think about telling *me*?" she spit at him, bashing both of her palms on the surface of the kitchen island. Nate jumped a little, surprised by the intense and harsh reaction of Lynn.

"I haven't told them that we have a therapy session. Just that I need you tonight and that they should block your calendar." Nate had his hands in front of his chest, trying to calm the situation with this gesture.

"Oh wow. You want applause for that?" Lynn huffed.

"Darling. I'm sorry I didn't tell you. I just couldn't find the right moment for it."

"What about right fucking after you made the appointment with Doctor Smith?" Lynn slammed her hands on the counter again.

"I know. I know. I'm sorry, okay? Should I call him and we postpone the session?"

"No. I'll be there." And with that being said Lynn turned around and left the communal kitchen to head back to the med-bay.

"Conference Room 2," Nate shouted after her, unsure if she had heard him or not. With a loud sigh he drank both his and Lynn's glasses of orange juice before heading down to the gym to do some of the physical therapy exercises Lynn made him do daily.

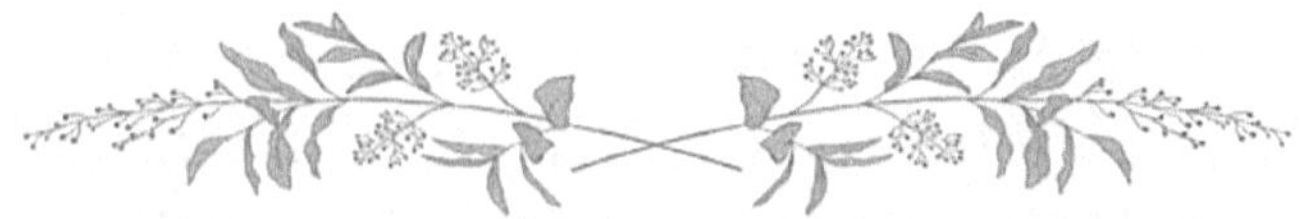

Lynn felt nervous the entire day, looking at her watch every thirty minutes to check when it was time for her to leave for the therapy session. At 5:15 she said goodbye to Tia and Birdie who only snickered in response. Obviously they both thought she was having a date with Nate.

The moment she stepped out of the door, she saw Nate leaning on the wall opposite her. He gave her a shy smile.

"Didn't know if you heard me. We need to go to conference room 2 in the front building," he said, pushing himself off the wall and standing right in front of her.

"Okay thank you. I need to change my clothes though."

"Sure. I'll see you there."

"Nate?" Lynn asked, her eyes looking at him with a pleading look.

"Can you wait for me? I wanna go together," she whispered.

"Of course, darling. Want me to wait here?" Nate smiled at her, happy that her anger was gone, and they were able to talk to each other without screaming.

"No, you can come with me. Nothing you haven't seen before," she chuckled, grabbed his hand and entered her room.

It was a silent signal of peace, their intertwined fingers spreading a warmth through both of their bodies.

Lynn stepped towards her closet, stripping out of her scrubs until she was standing in front of it in only panties and a nude lace bra. She quickly changed into a pair of jeans and a gray t-shirt, before turning to Nate, who had turned his back towards her. Maybe he was uncomfortable with seeing her only in her underwear. Or maybe he only wanted to be a gentleman.

Lynn approached him from behind, wrapped her arms around his waist, crossing them over his abs. Nate flinched a little, but remained his cool. He was still uncomfortable with someone touching him from behind without any notice.

"I'm sorry," she whispered before placing a few kisses on his shoulder blades.

"For what?"

"That I was a bitch earlier," she sighed, leaning her forehead against his back.

"You weren't a bitch," Nate commented.

He placed his arms above her hands and pulled her even closer enjoying the tender moment between them.

"Oh I was. Just... that you weren't brave enough to talk to me about the therapy session. That hurt me. That made me realize that things between us are not what they were before." Nate felt her deep exhale through the thin fabric of his t-shirt, making him shiver a little.

"I know."

"What happened to us, Nate?" Lynn sobbed and Nate felt his fabric getting damp with her tears.

He grabbed her hands, freed himself from her hug and turned around to face her. He placed his hands around her neck, carefully brushing his thumbs over her throat.

"I don't know. But we will fix it. I believe in us," he whispered before placing a long kiss on her forehead.

"I'm scared," Lynn whispered, the tears still falling.

"I am, too. But I wouldn't have called Doctor Smith if I didn't think our relationship could heal. We'll figure it out, Lynn. You and I." Nate placed a kiss between her eyebrows and another one on her nose, making Lynn giggle a little.

"You and I," she repeated before connecting her lips with his.

They had a long way ahead of them before Nate would be able to trust Lynn again, before they would find the ease and comfort in their relationship outside of dates and sex. They needed to find their dynamic again and they would only be able to do it with a lot of work, patience and time.

But they were both willing and optimistic.

With entangled hands they stepped into the conference room where Doctor Smith was already waiting. He had pushed the tables towards the walls and three chairs were standing in the middle of the room, two of them facing each other. Doctor Smith was a man in his late fifties, his gray hair long and in a ponytail. He smiled at the couple entering the room.

"Dr. Smith," Nate said before reaching out his hand to shake the therapist's.

"Mr. Sheppard. Nice to meet you."

"Thank you for coming over to have the session here. We really appreciate the flexibility." Nate smiled at him. The doctor then turned towards Lynn, reaching his hand out once again.

"And you must be Doctor Summers then."

"Yes. Nice to meet you."

"The pleasure is all mine. Take a seat over there." He pointed to the two chairs that were facing each other.

Of course. This was a couples session – it was all about the two of them.

Nate and Lynn took their seats in front of each other, too far away to be able to hold hands or even touch their feet against each other's. Lynn's weird gut feeling appeared again. She knew how important physical touch was for Nate.

"Mr. Sheppard already gave me a quick head's up about your situation, but I would like to hear from both of you, what you want me to do for you."

"We want to get the ease back in our relationship." Lynn started and Nate picked up the ball and continued,

"We know that we love each other, but with the betrayal my trust was destroyed. I want to trust her again, I want to live my life with her and we need some guidance to get that back."

Doctor Smith nodded at them, taking some notes on a clipboard in his hands.

"Mr. Sheppard, you say you want to live your life with Doctor Summers. What is currently holding you back from doing that?"

Nate looked at him, before turning his head towards Lynn. The doctor was already staring at him with expecting eyes, a lot of hope shimmering behind the chestnut brown of them.

"Communication is a very important thing for me. I want to share everything. No secrets, no mysteries. That is very important for me because of my past. I want to know that Lynn will always talk to me about everything that's going on in her life. The good and the bad things. I never want to think that she's maybe hiding something. I never want to hear again that she considered not telling me something."

"Okay, understood. But please Mr. Sheppard, talk to Doctor Summers directly. Not to me." Dr. Smith smiled at the two of them.

"I already promised you that I will always share what's going on in my life. Communication is important for me, too." Lynn responded in Nate's direction.

"I want us to be a team, darling. You and me. But for that I need to know that you trust me with everything. That I'm the first one you come to when something's up. That you'll never doubt that I can help you. Because we'll always find a way together." Nate's voice was more pleading, tears gathering in his eyes. He was more emotional than Lynn expected him to be.

"I want us to be a team, too. Share every moment, emotion, thought."

"What can you do in the future to prove to each other that you are a team? How exactly do you plan to gain trust and ease back?" Dr. Smith asked in the room.

The room was silent for a moment while both Lynn and Nate were thinking about the right answer. Nate was the first to open his mouth,

"I think time will tell. We'll try to spend time together, talk to each other as much as possible, and go on dates. Face different situations together."

"And continue the therapy sessions," Lynn added with a smile towards Nate.

They had a plan for the future, and they were sure about their feelings. This was a good jump off point for a healthy relationship. For happiness and for ease.

It would take time, but they were willing to spend it.

Together. As a team.

# Forest Picnic

**July 12th, 2022**

"Hey, do you have a minute?" Nate's head appeared in the door frame with a mischievous grin on his face.

Lynn was deep in her surgery reports, so she jumped a little in her chair before looking up and into ocean blue eyes.

"You scared me," she exclaimed, before bursting into laughter.

Nate entered her office and closed the door behind him, taking long steps towards her desk before placing both of his palms on it and leaning down. Lynn tilted her head a little, unsure what that stupid but cute grin on his face was supposed to mean.

"I'm sorry. I didn't mean to, darling. You look cute when you're totally lost in your own world."

"Cute, huh?" she smiled at him.

"Yeah, extra cute when you stick your tongue out in concentration. God, I love it when you do that." He pushed himself off the desk, rounded it and stood behind Lynn.

She still wasn't sure what he was up to, but she tried to relax and wait for him to finally say why he came to visit her in the middle of her shift. He placed his hands on her shoulders and started to give her a massage. Lynn hummed in appreciation and closed her eyes, while Nate worked his thumbs through the knots in the lower parts of her neck.

"You're working so much lately," he whispered towards her.

"I know. I have to. I don't want to disappoint Director Burns, the lawyers or even Marta. I'm very lucky with the sentence I got. I deserve to be in jail. But instead I'm still allowed to work here," she sighed.

"I know, darling, but you getting burnt out wouldn't help anybody. We need you here." He placed a few loving kisses on the back of her head, while still pressing his thumbs along her cervical spine.

"I know. It's just a lot to do at the moment. We're having the new Agents starting soon and I needed to give the medical approval for their hire. It was a direct order from Director Burns."

"Lynn Summers," Nate said with a flicker of anger in his voice, making Lynn open her eyes and turn her head as best as possible to look at the man standing behind her.

"What?" she asked, amused.

"Stop making excuses for working too much. I know you feel guilty and that's the only reason you're working twelve hours a day. You don't have to, darling. Nobody expects you to do that."

"But..." Lynn started but was interrupted immediately.

"No buts. I talked to Tia and Birdie and you don't have important cases this afternoon. So you're gonna have the afternoon off and you can spend it with a handsome man of your choice." Nate had leaned down to whisper in her ear.

"But have you..." she started, being interrupted again.

"Yes, I've talked to Marta and it's allowed. No problem, I checked it all for you." He smiled into the sensitive skin of her neck.

"You're the best," Lynn whispered with a wide grin.

Her sore muscles gave her the clear signal that taking the afternoon off was a brilliant idea to relax and clear her mind.

"I know," he said in between wet kisses on her neck.

Lynn purred in response, a slight moan almost slipping through her lips, but she caught it before it escaped her mouth.

"So who's gonna be the lucky and handsome man you spend your free afternoon with then?" Nate asked. His mouth was pressed on her ear, his breath hot and wet and a shiver trailed down her spine.

"Maybe I can get some shooting lessons from Oliver. Heard he's a good teacher," Lynn said between gritted teeth, trying desperately to suppress her laughter.

"What?" Nate exclaimed, his voice almost breaking at the end. He leaned back, his hands and mouth leaving Lynn's body, before he grabbed the chair she was sitting on and turned it around so that she was facing him.

Lynn tried to maintain her straight face, visibly amused about the shocked reaction of the man in front of her.

"You're serious?" Nate asked, his eyes glimmering with sadness, the smile gone.

Instead of answering him, Lynn stood from her chair and stepped towards him until their chests were almost pressed against each other. He tensed, unsure and confused about what she was about to do or say. Painfully slow Lynn raised her arms and wrapped them around his neck, leaning forward. Their lips only inches apart.

"Of course I'll spend my afternoon with the most handsome man on this base," she whispered before connecting her lips with his. He smiled into the kiss before kissing her back with tenderness and love.

"You mean me, right?" He chuckled in between the kisses.

"Of course I mean you, idiot," Lynn responded while playfully biting his nose. That stupid, little, perfect nose.

"Good. Just wanted to double check." Nate relaxed, placing a tender kiss on her nose, because he knew how much she loved it.

They held each other close, looking into each other's eyes while a comfortable silence filled the room. Their love for each other was communicated nonverbally.

"I may have an idea how to spend the afternoon!" Lynn exclaimed louder than she wanted, making Nate scrunch up his face in pain because of the too-loud sound in his ears.

"Oh, sorry," she giggled before placing more kisses along his face as an apology.

"What's your idea?" he asked.

"Let me surprise you. I gotta check something first and then pick you up from your room in an hour. Okay?"

Nate raised an eyebrow at her. Since his kidnapping, he didn't like surprises because during that time all the surprises he got were connected with torture and pain. But he'd never told her that before, so he couldn't blame her.

"I don't like surprises. But I trust you. I'll be waiting for you," he responded, a little flicker of insecurity in his eyes.

Tears brimmed in Lynn's while she grabbed his face tightly and gave Nate a last passionate kiss before turning away. Nate was quicker, grabbed her hand, spun her around and pressed her against his chest again. Tears had escaped her eyes, but she was still smiling. A combination that Nate didn't understand. Concern filled his heart and he forced Lynn to look at him.

"What's wrong?" he asked.

"Nothing. It's just..." she let out a stifled sob. "... you trust me. That means so much to me."

Nate hadn't realized that he'd used the word "trust" and now that he was thinking about it, he smiled at her.

"I do. I trust you," he whispered, placing another kiss on her nose before wishing away her tears with his thumb.

"I love you," she whispered, tears still slipping out of her eyes.

"I love you, too," he answered.

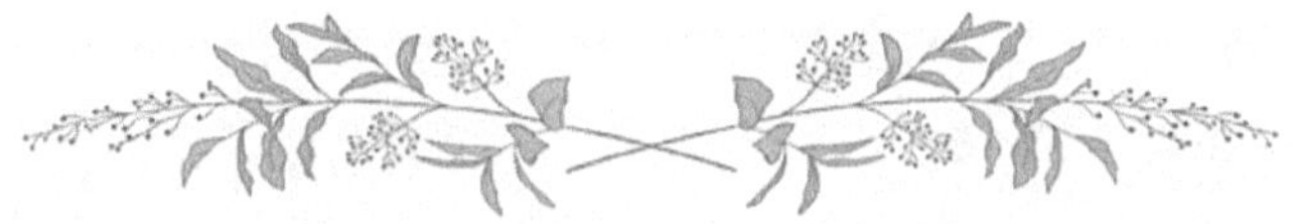

A loud knock sounded on Nate's door and he quickly jumped off his bed to open it. He was reading a book while patiently waiting for Lynn to come and pick him up for whatever surprise she had planned. He was nervous, had already had to change into a third shirt because he was sweating so much. The warm weather in the middle of July didn't make it any better.

This week he'd finally gotten rid of the knee brace so he was able to wear some dark shorts without any restrictions.

The scars on his knee were still visible but he knew that within a few months they would fade and would not be as prominent as they were right now.

With a few quick steps he walked to the door and opened it. Lynn was looking at him and her eyes lit up the moment they met his. She extracted her arm to show a basket full of food as well as a blanket.

"Surprise!"

"What kind of surprise is this?" Nate chuckled while observing the items in the basket.

"I thought we could have a picnic. Just the two of us and maybe some bees," she laughed before stepping aside so that Nate could leave his room and join her.

He copied her laughter, closed the door behind him, and reached out his arm for her to grab it. She entwined her fingers with his as they stepped towards the elevator. The moment they passed the communal kitchen they could hear someone whistle after them before a female and a male voice burst into laughter.

Oliver and Marta.

Nate's face was cherry red when he realized that they were whistling after them, but he stopped and shouted towards the open door:

"Get yourself a room and don't have sex in the communal kitchen!"

Silence followed before the two voices were whispering towards each other.

"Oh, don't think I can't hear you moan his name when you have sex right next to my room," he added and they could hear footsteps approaching before Oliver's head appeared in the doorframe.

"Don't tell anybody," he said with an angry pout on his face.

"Don't you think they all already know? There are hearts practically flying around you every time you're in the same room. Only blind idiots wouldn't see that," Lynn answered this time and they could see Oliver blush. A moment later Marta appeared behind him, her face as red as Oliver's.

"Is it that obvious?" she mumbled.

"Yes. Yes, it is." Lynn laughed.

"Shit!" Marta whined.

"What's the problem?" Nate asked, confused.

"I'm his boss. It's not allowed to have a relationship along the hierarchy," Marta sighed.

"We won't tell anyone. You can be whatever you are when you're around us. We support it." Lynn smiled at the pair in front of her.

"We..." Oliver started, turned his head towards Marta before looking back at Lynn with a smile. "...we've been in an official relationship for two months now. We just didn't announce it with everything that was going on." They looked at each other again with the biggest smile on their lips. Yeah, they were deeply in love.

"I'm happy for you." Lynn answered, giving both of them a careful hug before stepping next to Nate again. He nodded at the pair in front of them, unsure if he should hug them as well.

"I'm happy, too," he quickly added after Lynn gave him a demanding side-eye.

"Thank you," Marta mouthed towards them. She alternated her eyes between Nate's and Lynn's faces before she lowered her gaze and saw their intertwined fingers. Lynn followed her gaze, let go of Nate's hand quickly and stared at the floor, her cheeks flushing.

"I'm glad you're giving each other a chance," she commented.

It was a bit pathetic, because Lynn had visited her half an hour ago to ask if she was allowed to go into the attached forest or if that would be registered as "leaving headquarters" and would mean a break of the rules regarding her sentence. They'd had to call the technician that installed the tracking app on Lynn's smartwatch but finally she'd got confirmation that she was able to reach a few areas outside of the buildings as well. Of course she had told Marta about the picnic idea and that's why the Deputy Director was standing in front of them with a knowing grin on her face. Trying to hide the information she already had before this encounter.

"Yeah. We are, too," Nate answered, stepping from one leg on the other a few times.

Lynn knew that it was one of his habits when he was nervous, so she grabbed his hand again and cleared her throat.

"So, we gotta go. See you tomorrow!"

"Sure! We're out for dinner tonight, so don't be confused when you're alone when you return," Oliver answered, before he and Marta stepped back into the communal kitchen, whispering and giggling. *Like teenagers*, Lynn thought and shook her head.

Nate and she made their way out of the two buildings and were standing in front of the main entrance. Nate still didn't know where to go so he just simply followed Lynn, who made her way past the parking lot. When she turned her head to look at Nate, she saw him looking around nervously and confused. With a gentle squeeze of his hand, she tried to reassure him.

"We need to get onto Colonial Farm Rd and after a few steps there's a small path leading directly into the forest. We'll follow that for a while until there's a small grass field. That's our target," Lynn explained and Nate nodded.

"But are you allowed to go there?" he asked, concerned, nodding towards the watch on her left wrist that was tracking her movements.

"Yes, checked it with the technician. It's not as strict as I thought because I have a radius around headquarters that I'm allowed to enter. This field is within that radius," she explained with a puffed chest.

She was proud that she had figured that out and that she was able to enjoy some time with Nate outside of headquarters. Outside of their rooms.

"That's awesome. I've never been in the forest to be honest," he answered, his hand gripping hers tightly and she felt that his mind was drifting to all the various reasons why he never felt safe enough to leave headquarters to go for a walk.

She understood, even without him saying it out loud, so she gave his hand a squeeze to bring him back to reality. He turned his head in response and gave her a weak smile.

They reached the grass field five minutes later and while Nate was getting the blanket ready on the floor, Lynn was digging through the basket to prepare the snacks. Meatballs, sandwiches, and some mozzarella and tomato skewers.

"That looks delicious, darling," Nate commented, wetting his lower lip with his tongue.

"Yeah, I didn't want to starve if we're going to spend the entire afternoon here."

She stepped behind him, wrapped her arms around his abdomen before crossing her hands on his stomach. Her lips hovered over his shoulder blade, unable to reach his neck because of the difference in their heights. She placed a gentle kiss on his clothed shoulder before leaning her head into his back. Nate hummed in appreciation, letting his fingertips gently strike over her forearm. She was wearing a t-shirt too, so he could see and feel the goosebumps on her arms the moment she heard him moan slightly.

"I love when you make that sound," she whispered and pushed her body even closer into his. Carefully, he turned around within her embrace so that they were face to face. Her face was now buried in the fabric on his chest, her arms still wrapped around his middle while he wrapped his own around her shoulders, holding her as close as possible. He placed his chin on the top of her head, smiling like a love-drunk idiot.

Their bodies were practically merged together, hearts beating in the same rhythm, steady breathing hypnotizing them both. It was a magical moment.

Just Nate and Lynn.

"I love you." He had shifted his head to bury his nose in the peachy smelling hair of his favorite doctor. Placing a kiss on it to underline his statement.

"I love you more," she whispered in his chest, her voice muffled.

Nate's stomach started to grumble, destroying the moment between them. They untangled themselves and started to laugh.

"Gotta get some food in your stomach, big guy," Lynn chuckled, holding a sandwich in front of Nate's face. He smiled at her, grabbed the sandwich and took a big bite.

They sat down on the blanket and ate in silence, looking at each other with goofy smiles from time to time. Lynn scooted closer as soon as she had finished her last meatball, leaning her head against Nate's shoulder who was still eating a sandwich.

He wiggled his arm from underneath Lynn, wrapped it around her shoulders while holding the sandwich with his other hand. It was dangerously close to falling apart but he didn't care. He wanted to have Lynn close.

"Thank you for this," Lynn started and saw Nate turn his head in her direction.

"Well you prepared everything for the picnic. I should thank you!" He said between bites.

"Yes, but you organized for me to have the afternoon off. That was very thoughtful of you, so yeah. Thank you." She smiled into his shoulder before placing a kiss on it.

"Glad that you enjoy it. My cute little workaholic."

"I am not a workaholic," Lynn protested, her mouth open in a theatrically shocked expression.

"I said cuuuuuuuteeee," Nate responded before playfully nudging his shoulder into hers. Lynn started to laugh.

"Be thankful that you're adorable, or I'd be really offended right now."

"I'm adorable, huh?" He smirked at her.

Lynn could see some of the mayonnaise on the side of his mouth so she extended her finger to swipe it away. Nate saw it coming, wasn't sure what Lynn was about to do and ducked underneath her finger. She looked at him surprised, trying again to swipe it away in the second try but he ducked again.

Lynn stabbed her outstretched index finger in his shoulder and said between gritted teeth,

"I'm just trying to get the mayonnaise off your face, you idiot."

Nate looked at her, something between shock and a smirk on his face before he pressed his own finger in the rest of his sandwich and smeared mayonnaise onto Lynn's nose. The doctor shrunk back but couldn't avoid the attack.

"Yooouuuuuu…" she exhaled, pushing herself out of her sitting position and onto Nate.

The Agent was caught off guard, so he didn't have a chance to defend himself. He fell with his back on the blanket underneath him, Lynn lying on top of him. The sandwich had burst into pieces, but neither of them cared at that moment.

"You're such an idiot sometimes," she huffed before starting to tickle Nate's waist.

She wasn't sure if he was ticklish there as well, but she thought she would give it a try. Right after his knee surgery she had discovered that he was ticklish under his feet, so maybe he was ticklish at his waist as well.

Nate managed to swallow the bite in his mouth before he started to snort and giggle. He was way stronger than Lynn and if he really wanted her to stop, he knew he would easily have been able to overpower her. But he let her tickle him, suffering through the attack. Lynn lay on top of him, her hands never leaving his waist while Nate tried to squirm his body out of her grip. His abs started to hurt from all the giggling, snorting and laughing.

The moment Lynn noticed that his breaths had become more and more shallow, she stopped her attack and gave him some time to breathe. He couldn't stop laughing, even now after Lynn had stopped.

"Why are you still laughing?" Lynn asked, confused.

"Because even if that was the worst torture ever, I still love you because you're so adorable."

Lynn didn't answer. She just looked him in the eyes with tears gathering in her own.

"Darling, you gotta stop crying randomly. You're really confusing me," he sighed.

"Do you realize what you just said?" Lynn asked with a voice dripping with love.

"No...I..." Nate furrowed his brow while trying to remember the exact words he had said.

Suddenly his lips parted, and he looked at Lynn in shock.

"That your tickling was the worst torture ever," he whispered.

"Yes." Lynn smiled at him.

"Oh my god. That's the first time I thought about torture and didn't think about Iraq. Oh my god, Lynn. The first time!"

He practically screamed at her, before grabbing her face with both of his hands and plastering it with wet kisses.

Lynn squirmed in his grip, but she was so happy for him, so she let him do whatever he needed to do.

"I love you. I love you so fucking much," he said between kisses.

Suddenly he stopped, his hands still holding her face tightly. And then she could see it in his eyes: The love.

The pure and innocent, never ending love that this man held for her. And all she could do was smile at him.

They adjusted their positions a little as Lynn rolled off his body. He still lay on his back, Lynn wrapped in his arms, while she placed her head on his chest.

"You are the most adorable man I've ever dated," she whispered. With her ear pressed on his chest, she could hear his heartbeat quicken after her words.

"Wow," he answered.

"I wanna get to know everything about you, Nate. And when I say everything, I mean everything."

"Then give me some questions," he responded, carefully caressing his fingertips over Lynn's back.

"What's your favorite color?"

This wasn't exactly the question he had expected, but he answered it anyway.

"Yellow. Because yellow reminds me of the sun. The sun reminds me of summer and summer reminds me of you."

Lynn couldn't answer him. Tears dripped on Nate's chest, soaking the fabric of his shirt. She let out a silent sob, but of course Nate had heard it.

"You okay?" he asked, lifting and turning his head to look at her face, but he wasn't at the right angle.

"Yes... Yes. I... I've never had someone say something so nice to me. I'm not used to compliments."

Instead of answering her, Nate raised his head a little to place a loving kiss on Lynn's hairline.

"I love you," he whispered with a smile on his face.

"I love you, too," she sobbed in his chest, still not able to control her feelings.

They lay like that for a while, shooting some questions back and forth to get to know each other. They were mostly basic questions like taste in music, favorite movies, favorite dish, what was on the other's bucket list and stuff like that.

Because of everything they'd been through together, Lynn and Nate already had a deep connection. But they totally missed the beginning phase of a relationship where they get to know each other. They had started on a different level, but now caught up with everything that came to their minds.

It was already after 7 pm when they decided to go back to headquarters and watch another movie together. With intertwined hands and wide smiles on their faces, they entered Nate's room and practically jumped into his bed.

Nate pulled her close so that Lynn was lying in his arms while they watched a horror movie. It was his turn to choose a movie and he'd always loved a good movie with some splatter and jump scares in it. Mostly the paranormal ones with women climbing out of TV's or spooky looking nuns in mirrors. The ones where you know it's not realistic.

Because Nate's life had been like an action movie and thriller at the same time, he preferred to watch Science

Fiction, Fantasy or paranormal movies. It let him dive into a completely different world and forget about his reality for a moment.

"Why do we have to watch thiiiiiiiis?" Lynn screamed in terror after she practically jumped out of Nate's arms.

"Come on, it was my choice. And it's fun. All the adrenaline rushing through my veins," Nate laughed, before pulling her closer and placing a few kisses on her head.

"I hate horror movies because even if I know that something will scare me in a second, I still jump. I'm not made for watching this scary shit," Lynn sighed, turning around in Nate's arms and hiding her face in the fabric of his t-shirt.

"I'll be here to protect you if someone comes out of that TV," he chuckled, his eyes still fixed on the TV screen, where one of the characters was currently suffering a brutal death.

"Not helping!" Lynn's face was still buried in Nate's chest and she even pulled the blanket higher to place it over her head.

"You want to watch something else?" Nate asked, she could hear his amusement in his voice.

"No, it's fine."

"Okay is this one of the 'No it's fine's that is actually fine or one of those where you actually want me to turn off the movie but don't say it because you're too shy or you want me to suggest it. Women are complicated," he sighed deeply.

Lynn pulled her head out from under the blanket and looked at him with a furrowed brow.

"What?" she asked, confused.

"Yeah. You know I'm not good with this whole communicating thing and I don't want to ruin it because I can't read between your lines."

"Nate," Lynn said, propping herself up on one arm to look him in the face. He looked at her with insecurity in his eyes.

"You've really improved your communication skills and you can be proud of that. Also I always try to communicate honestly with you. That means when I say it's fine, then it is fine. No different meaning between the lines. Okay?" she added.

"Okay. That's good." Nate leaned forward and gave her a light kiss on her nose.

Lynn went back into her position next to him, head resting on his chest. The movie was still playing and she closed her eyes, just enjoying Nate's comforting scent of sandalwood and cinnamon and drifted off to sleep.

# Happy Birthday

**July 31st, 2022**

"Happy birthday to you, happy birthday to you, happy birthday my wonderful darling, happy birthday to you", Nate half sang half whispered in Lynn's ear early in the morning.

She was still sleeping, but of course his voice woke her. Oh, and maybe it was his hand between her legs that had a big impact on her waking up as well. Nate left wet kisses along her neck until he reached her collarbone.

"Nate," she giggled with her eyes still closed while his hand wandered dangerously near to her core.

"What? You don't like my singing voice?" Nate stopped kissing her, a fake pout in his lips.

"Yes... Yes. I... I'm just not used to someone being so nice to me," she stuttered a little.

"I know, darling, but it's my job to change that. Boyfriend's duty," he chuckled but stopped abruptly.

His eyes widened and he looked at Lynn in shock. The moment he was about to pull the blanket over his head to disappear in shame, Lynn said,

"What did you just say?"

Nate didn't answer and successfully hid his face underneath the blanket, mumbling something Lynn couldn't understand. She grabbed the hem of the blanket and pulled it down again, revealing Nate's cherry red face that he had scrunched together in a painful expression.

"What did you just say?" Lynn repeated and she couldn't hide the smile on her face.

"Boyfriend's duty," Nate repeated so low, she almost missed it.

Nate opened one of his scrunched eyes to look at Lynn, waiting for a reaction while his whole body was filled with fear.

"I like the sound of that." Lynn smiled at him.

In a second Nate's face relaxed, his eyes wide and one side of his mouth started to curl upward.

"Yeah?"

"Yes, honey. I'm not good with relationships so I don't know if and how to declare yourselves as boyfriend and girlfriend. Does that just happen, or do you talk about that? I wasn't brave enough to ask you," Lynn babbled, underlining her statement with wide gestures.

"Right? It was so much easier back in school when you just wrote a letter to ask if someone wants to be your girlfriend or boyfriend," Nate sighed before letting his head fall back into the soft pillow.

"I would have loved a letter." Lynn winked at him.

Nate's head was turned in her direction and she could see a smirk appear on his face before he jumped out of the bed and ran towards the desk on the other side of the wall.

"What are you doing?" Lynn laughed, watching him curiously.

"Wait!" he said, holding his outstretched palm towards her while he dug in the drawer.

While exclaiming a loud "Ha" he grabbed a mossy green notebook and placed it on the surface of his desk. Then he grabbed a black pen and started to write something on one of the sides of the notebook. It took him a while, before he ripped the page off the book and jumped back into the bed. Lynn couldn't stop laughing about the almost dorky and playful behavior of Nate. He placed the paper in her hand.

*Lynn Summers,*
*Most beautiful woman on this planet. My sunshine, the woman that makes me smile and laugh and feel happy. The woman that not only repaired my knee but also my mind. The only one that manages to silence my demons with a simple touch. When I'm with you, I don't have nightmares and now I am running out of cute things to write. You're already looking at me confused. So, Lynn Summers, do you want to be my girlfriend?*

*Yes*                          *No*

Lynn smiled like a maniac when she grabbed the black pen out of Nate's hand and circled "Yes" multiple times. Then she gave the paper back to Nate, who was smiling as wide as Lynn.

"Girlfriend," he whispered before leaning in to kiss her.

"Boyfriend," the doctor whispered back only a second before their lips collided.

Nate pulled her close, parted her legs with his knee and ground his hips against her. She could feel his hardening length underneath his boxers and the way he pressed it against her core, made her lower belly feel like it was on fire.

"Let me show you what I have in store for you as your boyfriend," he whispered in Lynn's ear with a rumbling gravel in his voice. She felt his voice vibrate through her whole body and ground her hips against his. Nate groaned in response, grabbed the hem of the oversized shirt that Lynn wore as pajamas, and pulled it over her head. She arched her back a little to help him get rid of the thin fabric and as soon as her bare upper body laid down on the mattress again, she could see Nate's blown pupils.

He was feral for her.

His hungry eyes wandered over her body, followed by his index finger that carefully stroked along every part of her. He was worshiping her, showing her how much he loved her body and that she was perfect for him.

It was the biggest compliment she'd ever received.

He took his time letting his fingers playfully twitch one of her nipples while he leaned his head towards her to place wet kisses along her jawline. Lynn had her eyes closed and enjoyed every careful touch of the man she loved more than anyone else. Nate's ridiculously soft lips followed her jawline until he reached her ear – knowing well that behind it was one of her sweet spots. He let his tongue slightly brush over her ear lobe until his lips sucked on said spot.

"Nate," Lynn moaned in response and wrapped one of her arms around his upper body to find a hold somewhere. But as he was only sleeping in his boxers, her hand didn't find anything other than his messy hair, pulling his head back a little and away from her ear.

Nate whined because of the hard pull, opened his eyes and looked at her. Lynn still had her eyes closed, her lips slightly parted and she looked like an angel in his eyes.

"How could I be so lucky to have someone as beautiful as you as my girlfriend," he whispered. Lynn opened her eyes, and her chestnut ones met his. Because of his blown pupils they looked almost completely dark with only a shiny icy blue ring around his pupils. It was beautiful.

He didn't let her answer, turning her on her back and placing himself above her, his hands on each side of her head. Lynn could feel him press his length against her core and she growled in impatience.

"Nate."

"What do you want, darling?" He smirked at her, underlining his question with another movement of his hips. He was already fully hard and he couldn't wait to rip his boxers off.

"Fuck me. No teasing, please. I need you," Lynn whispered, sparkles dancing behind her eyes when she smiled at him.

Nate lowered his upper body and connected his lips with hers in a fierce kiss. At the same time his hand wandered down her body and met the hem of her panties. He slipped it inside and roughly dragged one finger through her folds.

"Shit," Lynn inhaled sharply. She hadn't expected him to start right away, but as quickly as his fingers came, they left her again, making her feel empty.

"Just wanted to check how wet you are already," he growled, before pulling Lynn's panties down her legs.

"Always, when I'm with you." Her answer made a moan slip out of his mouth and the hand that had been on her core now stroked his cock through the fabric of his boxers.

"What are you doing to me, Lynn Summers?" he asked before sitting back on his ankles to get rid of his underwear. He slid both of his feet out and threw them behind him on the floor of the room.

"It's called love, Nate," she giggled, slightly moving her now naked body on the soft sheets of the bed.

He climbed back on top of her, parting her legs with one of his knees and hovered his lips right above hers. He knew exactly what he was doing, as he lowered his hips enough so that the tip of his cock put a little pressure on her clit.

"No teasing," she moaned but couldn't stop her eyes from rolling back in her head.

They'd had sex a few times after that first date and she never felt as good as she felt with him. Although Nate told her he hadn't really had sex in the past decade, he truly hadn't forgotten how to treat a woman. It hadn't taken him long to get back in shape.

"I love you, too," he whispered on her hot lips and waited for her silent permission to enter her.

Lynn bucked her hips a little, feeling more pressure of his dick on her clit. Nate smiled into her skin, lined up his cock with her entrance and slowly slid himself in. Her arms wrapped around his shoulders and her fingernails gripped into his skin. Lynn's brows were slightly furrowed while they both waited for her to adjust to his size. She'd probably never get used to the initial sting of his size.

A few heartbeats later Nate carefully started to pull his cock almost completely out before burying it deep inside of her again. He wanted to be as slow and gentle as possible until she was fully adjusted but it seemed like Lynn was feeling better than he thought, because she wrapped her legs around his waist and crossed her feet above his butt.

"So needy," he commented but she only dug her heels in even more. Nate growled, pushing himself even deeper inside of her. Her moans intensified and he knew he was hitting the right spot inside of her. His thrusts increased in speed while his mouth collided with hers once again. Their kiss was sloppy, wet, and full of fire. Their tongues danced with each other before Lynn dug her teeth in Nate's lower lip. He whined but could feel the knot in his stomach building faster and faster.

"Don't stop," Lynn begged, her heels digging deeper in his butt and he knew he would have some bruises there tomorrow.

Nate grabbed both of Lynn's hands, intertwined their fingers and placed them above her head.

With every thrust of his hips he reached the spongy spot inside of her, making Lynn tumble over the edge while screaming his name. The combination of his name out of her mouth, the pain of her heels on his butt and her beautiful expression as she rode out her orgasm, made him spill deep inside of her with a final thrust.

Nate was panting and he felt Lynn's legs shake around his waist. She opened her eyes and started to laugh while unwinding her legs and letting them fall to the mattress next to his broad body. Nate carefully pulled out of her and let himself fall next to her.

He raised an eyebrow on her but she only looked at him and laughed even louder, crunching her nose and making adorable sounds.

Nate couldn't hold back and started to laugh as well, although he didn't even understand why they were laughing.

"I can't believe..." she started with heavy breaths, her body still shaking from exhaustion "...I had to turn thirty to finally like my birthdays. It's not even 8am and this is already the best birthday of my life."

Nate turned towards her and placed a single kiss on her nose.

"From now on I'll make you like every birthday. I promise!"

"That sounds fantastic." She smiled at him.

"Let's have a shower." Nate slipped out of bed and reached his hand out towards Lynn.

"I don't think I can walk," Lynn answered, a slight touch of shame flickering in her eyes.

"No problem, darling. I've got you." Nate rounded the bed, placed one of his hands under her knees and the other under her upper back. With ease he lifted her from the sheets and carried her bridal style towards the bathroom.

Because it was Sunday, Lynn didn't have a regular shift in the med-bay and Nate had promised to make her some breakfast. They quickly changed into some comfortable clothes and left her room to head to the communal kitchen.

The moment they walked through the door, a loud "bang" could be heard and Lynn was covered in confetti. She practically jumped in the air, turned around to Nate and buried her face deep into his chest in fear. It vibrated while he laughed, putting his hands on her back and clapping it assuring.

"Turn around, darling," he said to her and Lynn did what she was told.

Her fear disappeared in a second when she looked into multiple smiling faces; Marta, Oliver, Toby, Jakob, Tia, Birdie, Peter and, to her big surprise, her mother Thea and her father Jensen. Her mouth opened and formed a perfect "o", but she wasn't able to say a word. Marta realized that she was overwhelmed and exclaimed, "surprise!"

She was standing next to Lynn, a weird looking cardboard cylinder still in her hands. Lynn looked around her and finally noticed that she and the floor beneath her were covered in confetti.

"Marta and Oliver made breakfast and called your friends and parents so that we can celebrate your special day," Nate explained, because all of them were still awkwardly standing around the room.

"Oh, that's actually a really nice idea. Thank you so much." Lynn smiled, shuffled on sore legs towards Marta and engulfed her in a hug.

"Happy birthday, sweetie," the Deputy Director said before placing a kiss on Lynn's cheek. After the two women separated, Lynn headed towards Oliver to give him a hug as well. The blond Agent chuckled.

"Happy birthday, Lynn. This was all Marta's idea, I just helped to get everything ready."

"That's important, too. Thank you, Oliver," Lynn answered, the smile on her face impossible to fade.

Lynn gave another hug to all her colleagues at the CIA as well as Toby before she swallowed the lump in her throat and stood in front of her mother. They had messaged a few times but it was more of a casual "hope you're okay" text that her mother sent from time to time but they hadn't actually spoken since the happenings at Ann's funeral.

"Mom," Lynn's voice almost broke at the end of the single word. She couldn't stop the tears from falling while she stood two feet in front of her mother. Nate had silently followed her through the room, thanking the others for coming while one of his hands lingered above the small of Lynn's back. Giving her the right mixture of support and freedom in this overwhelming situation. Now he was closer to her his hand pressed on the fabric that covered her upper body. He stabilized her in more ways than just the physical.

"Happy birthday, baby," Thea whispered before reaching out both her arms to give her daughter a tight hug. The two women were holding each other close, Lynn silently crying into her mom's shoulder, while Thea patted her back from time to time.

"I wish she would've been able to be here, Mom."

"Me too, baby. Me too. She would've been so proud of you for doing such a good job, saving the world with your work."

"I'm just their doctor, Mom. It's not me who's saving the world."

"You stitch them back together so they can go out there to save the world again. It's your work as well. Ann would be proud of you and I am too."

Nate rounded the pair and reached his hand out to Jensen, breaking the ice, making things easier for Lynn.

"Sir." Nate nodded.

Jensen hesitated for a moment but then shook Nate's hand with a quiet "Agent."

A second later Lynn appeared next to Nate, linking both of her hands around Nate's bicep. It was a very clear indicator that she wasn't willing to give her dad a hug. She hadn't forgiven him. He hadn't texted her once since his harmful words at the funeral and Lynn was pretty sure he'd meant every word of it.

Jensen tried to muffle a few coughs and Lynn rolled her eyes. She knew that was him trying to show her that he was still struggling with his COPD and it felt like a silent accusation; *"Look I am pretty ill you'd better forgive your poor father"*, but the pity strategy wouldn't work with her.

"Happy birthday, Lynn," he added after a few more coughs.

Lynn looked at him with a blank face, only nodding in response. Everyone felt the growing tension, so Marta's voice was a welcome distraction from the rumbling family drama.

"Breakfast is served, everybody please take a seat."

Lynn unwrapped her hands from Nate's arm, turned around, and made big steps towards the dinner table. Nate gave Jensen a weak smile before following after her.

The table was filled with delicious breakfast dishes; pancakes, waffles, French toast, a big bowl of oatmeal, and even hearty dishes like scrambled eggs and different variations of sandwiches. Lynn could identify one of them as Marta's special sandwich with cream cheese, ham, and salad.

"This looks amazing. When did you make all this?" Lynn asked surprised, her head turned towards Marta and Oliver.

"We were up pretty early. Couldn't sleep anyways..." Oliver answered, throwing a knowing glance between Nate and Lynn.

The doctor blushed immediately and scrunched her face in shame. Oliver and Marta burst into laughter and Toby followed after realizing what Oliver meant.

"Hey it's your birthday. You can celebrate it any way you want to," Toby commented. As he was sitting right in front of Lynn, she kicked her feet under the table and hit him on his shin. Toby whined before scowling at her. Lynn placed some French toast and a waffle on her plate, a smile on her face.

Nate was sitting on her right side, Marta to her left. They faced Toby and her parents, making the tension rise again. Thankfully they ate in silence, some small talk here and there. Lynn felt one of Nate's hands around her shoulders, resting on the top of her chair, and she tried to avoid leaning into him. Except for her parents, all of the people round the table knew about them dating again. After the weird encounter with Oliver and Marta on the day of their picnic they'd decided to let everyone know so that they didn't have to sneak around the building or look behind them before kissing each other. Of course the secrecy gave their relationship some sort of adrenaline rush, but with everything that had happened to them, they were just happy with some normal dating.

"That was an amazing breakfast," Thea said with a shy smile towards Marta and Oliver.

Marta shot Lynn's mom a smile back before all of them cleaned the table and stored the leftovers in food containers together. Afterwards, they scattered around the room talking to each other, laughing, and drinking different variations of coffee. After Lynn had told the story of how Nate tried her special vanilla latte macchiato the first time, Toby immediately demanded to get one as well and Tia and Birdie agreed. Marta and Oliver had tried it before, so they stayed with whatever was in their mugs.

Although it had been two weeks since Lynn and Nate had announced their relationship, Marta and Oliver were still too anxious to do the same. With the hierarchy within the Agency this could possibly cause some trouble and none of them wanted to change the team or even quit. Was it morally right to hide it? Probably not; but it was understandable.

Lynn caught the two lovebirds giggling with each other and secretly touching each other as often as they could. Oliver even had his right hand on Marta's thigh the entire breakfast, brushing his thumb over her jeans. They were adorable and it was a shame that they couldn't be open about it. At least they were able to be when they had couples nights with Nate and Lynn. This was something they discovered over the last few days, mostly cooking together or watching a movie.

One night even Tia and Birdie joined, which was a rare occasion. Although the two nurses stayed at the compound as well, they both had boyfriends outside the Agency. They had talked to Lynn about it because of course they wanted to leave the headquarters for dates and other stuff couples do. Lynn was totally understanding but ordered that one of them always had to be in the building in case of an emergency.

It was great to see them all so carefree this morning. Toby had become very good friends with Tia and Birdie when Lynn was hurt and not able to work. He had also been there after the betrayal came out and before Lynn was officially allowed to work again. Right after Ann's funeral.

Speaking of Ann. The emotional break between Lynn and her father was the only thing that stopped Lynn from exploding with happiness.

Everyone could feel the tension, shooting Lynn a pitiful smile then and now. Marta's idea to invite her parents was great and it would have been the perfect time to forget about what happened at the funeral. But it  turned out that it was still lingering between them, her mother Thea the only buffer between the two stubborn and hurt people.

Lynn was on her way to talk to Peter Davis, who was standing next to Oliver and Marta. She wanted to take him away, so that the two had some time to talk on their own and share some secret intimacy but her fast steps were interrupted by someone touching her shoulder from the side. She startled, before turning around and looking into the Chestnut eyes of her father.

"Lynn..." he started, his expression impossible to read.

The doctor looked at him with parted lips and the moment she was about to build the walls around herself again, she saw the warning glare from Nate behind her father's back. He stood there, alone, with only a mug of coffee in his hands, watching the situation and willing to intervene if needed. His glare said it all.

Give him a chance.

And that was what she did.

"Dad," she said.

It was the first time in months that she had said this word. A word that meant so much to her. So many conflicting emotions. From love to hate to insecurity. Guilt and Anger. This word contained all those memories she had locked away somewhere in her heart and now they threatened to come back to the surface.

"Can we talk for a minute?" Jensen asked, hope glistening in his eyes.

"Sure. Let's head somewhere more private. I'll show you my room," Lynn answered and turned around without waiting for his answer.

Jensen followed her without a word, leaving Thea and Nate behind. Both of them with eyebrows knitted together in worry.

They entered her room and Lynn collapsed on the couch in it.

Her therapy couch.

Her dad took his place next to her, shifting uncomfortably and looking for the right words to start this overdue conversation.

"I'm sorry," he finally said, looking at his daughter with tears in the corner of his eyes.

He was too proud to let them fall, but Lynn saw them and she knew that it meant a lot. Her father was like Ann; they never cried. No injury, not even the death of his own parents made him cry. Or his daughter. But here they were and he looked at her with tears very visible.

Lynn grabbed one of his large hands with hers and smiled at him.

"I'm sorry, too," she whispered, her own tears falling freely down her cheeks and onto her shirt, leaving dark wet circles on the fabric.

"You don't have to be. I talked to my therapist about the funeral and realized that I had no right to talk to you like that. What happened to Ann is not your fault and I don't want you to feel guilty for it. There is only one person to blame and he already got what he deserved," Jensen sighed.

"When you practically spit at me and wished that I was dead instead of Ann, that triggered all the guilt and shame inside me. If Nate hadn't been there to support me... I don't know if I would have ever made it out of that darkness," Lynn sobbed, quickly standing from the couch to search for some tissues.

Her father stood after her, reached out his hand and whispered a loving "come here" before engulfing her in a bear hug.

"It's not your fault. I was driven by grief and I can only apologize for the horrible things I said. This won't change anything because I can't take them back and I can't make it undone but I'm sorry and I hope someday you can forgive me," he whispered in her ear while holding her close.

She could feel his heart beating underneath his ribs. It was fast and it was strong.

"I didn't know how to behave around you today. Sorry for being a dick again. Seems like I need to learn a lot," Jensen sighed and then chuckled a little.

Lynn wiggled her upper body and he let her go from the hug.

"It's a good thing that you're seeing a therapist. That always helps," she commented with a smile on her face.

"Yeah, it really helped me to grieve and to understand that I'm a very complicated person sometimes. I'm very fortunate that your mother is still by my side because I don't deserve her after being such an asshole for the past few months," he chuckled again, but Lynn knew that it was only to cope with the fear of losing his wife.

She never expected her father to be that reflective and it surprised her in a positive way.

"When you love someone, you stay by their side. No matter how rough the path looks ahead of you," she commented, her mind slipping towards Nate and his beautiful smile that made her ears flush.

"Like you and this Agent, huh?" Her father winked at her.

"Nate. Yes. He's my... my boyfriend," Lynn answered with the widest grin on her face.

It was actually the first time he addressed Nate to someone as her boyfriend. And she liked the sound of it.

"That's amazing. He's a good guy," Jensen commented.

"How do you know?"

"The way he looks at you. The tiny smile on his lips when he watches you move around the room. Oh and I can practically see his eyes turn into hearts when you look back at him. This man is head over heels for you, sweetie."

Lynn looked at her father in surprise. Was it really that obvious that they loved each other? Nate Sheppard? The grumpy lone wolf now had heart eyes?

She had to smile again because she was so proud how far he had come. He wasn't fully healed, obviously, but he had made huge steps towards having a normal life. He joked and laughed with their friends, had breakfast and movie nights with people, and he was more and more able to express his feelings. That was a huge step. Lynn made a mental note to talk to him about her father's observations because she wanted to make sure that he also realized how proud she was and how proud he could be himself.

"And I'm head over heels for him," Lynn answered her father.

"And that's all that matters. I'm happy for you. But always use protection!"

"Daaaaaaaaaad..." Lynn whined before both of them burst into laughter.

Jensen pulled her into another hug and whispered "I love you, sweetie" in her ear.

The two headed back into the communal kitchen, freed from the demons in their hearts and with smiles on their faces.

Thea was currently teaching Nate one of Lynn's favorite dishes from back when she was a teenager and Nate had even made some notes on his smartphone.

"What are you plotting here?" Jensen asked, making the two turn around and face the intruder.

Thea shot alternating glares between her husband and daughter, trying to read their minds or  expressions.

"We're good, Mom." Lynn rolled her eyes.

"It's about damn time!" Thea exclaimed and grabbed both of her loved ones into a group hug.

Nate looked at them with a smirk on his face when suddenly Jensen grabbed his free arm and pulled him into the middle of the chaos. Nate was surrounded by faces and arms and didn't understand what the hell was going on.

"Welcome to the family, Son," Jensen chuckled before the three Summers' finally let go of the hug.

Lynn looked at her boyfriend with with a wide grin on her face and Thea said,

"You wanna be part of this family so you have to deal with the chaos that comes with it."

"Oh I think I can handle that. It's all worth it for this wonderful woman," Nate laughed and gave Lynn a kiss in front of her parents' eyes.

# Overseas Operation

**August 1st, 2022**

"Nate Sheppard you are officially cleared for missions again," Lynn said before giving the man that was sitting on the examination table a loving kiss.

"Yeah! Finally! Marta gonna be happy because the team is scheduled for another operation on Wednesday. We weren't sure if I'd be able to be part of the team, but now I am. Can't wait to get back in the field."

"But be careful. Not only because of the knee," Lynn looked at him with worry flickering in her chestnut eyes.

"Of course, darling. No matter what mission I'm on, I'll always come home." He grabbed her hand and placed tender kisses along her knuckles.

"To you," he added after seeing tears in the corners of her eyes.

"Good because I can't imagine a life without you," Lynn whispered, her lips curling into a shy smile.

"Hey, you're my first girlfriend in a very long time. I wanna enjoy that a little longer." Nate was trying to lighten the mood. His heart was full of love and his eyes shone bright with happiness.

"I'm okay with that," Lynn laughed, stepping back and grabbing her iPad to finalize the report.

She wanted to send it to Marta immediately so that she was able to consider Nate as available for the upcoming mission.

Nate waited on the table for Lynn to give him some final instructions but when she was deep into typing the report on her iPad he jumped off the table and gave her a quick kiss on the nose.

"I'll go to Marta's office and tell her the good news," he whispered before rushing out of the examination room.

Lynn only nodded, totally focused on the screen in front of her. A few minutes later Nate arrived in front of Marta's office, smiling at her assistant Blaire.

"Hi. Is she free? I need to talk to her."

"Agent Sheppard. Good to see you. Yes, you're lucky. Deputy Director Gómez just finished a meeting and now has a thirty minute gap in her calendar."

Blaire looked him in the eyes, a wide smile on her face. Nate nodded, turned around and knocked on the wooden door. A muffled "come in" could be heard from the inside and so he opened the door.

Marta sat on her desk with her eyes fixed on the screen in front of her. She had furrowed her eyebrows while Nate could see her eyes flicker across the screen as if she was reading something. Her lips were parted and she huffed a low "huh" while still reading. A few moments passed before she raised her gaze from the screen to look at the person that had entered the room.

"Oh Butch, do we have a meeting?" she asked, a mixture of confusion and panic in her voice while she made some hectic clicks with her computer mouse.

"No. No. I just had my final check-up with Lynn and wanted to tell you in person that I'm cleared for missions. Oliver said there's one coming up very soon and I can support the team with that."

Marta looked at him, her features widening while she processed what he had just told her.

"Oh, Butch that's great! So your knee is all healed then?"

"Yeah. As good as new. Lynn's currently typing the final check-up report to send to you, Oliver and HR but as I know time's ticking for the upcoming mission, I wanted to let you know in person."

"That's good. Well…" Marta cleared her throat "… you better talk to Oliver about the mission. He's in charge of it and he can give you a debriefing. They're headed out in two days."

"Okay, thank you!" Nate smiled at her and was about to leave the office when Marta cleared her throat loudly.

The brunet man turned around and looked at her. He knew this behavior from Lynn, when she wasn't sure if she should say something or just ignore whatever was bothering her.

"Yes, Marta?" he asked with a cheerful smile on his face.

"Other than the knee, you're good again?" she asked, her eyes showing regret the moment she finished the question.

"What do you mean?"

"You were in a pretty bad headspace over the last few months. I know you two are on good terms, official relationship and all that but is your mind okay with it all? Are you able to go on a mission again?"

Nate knew she was partly worried on a professional level but also because she was a good friend. And she was right. It had been a rough few months and he'd been in his rabbit hole a few times but things with him and Lynn were going great, he was happier than ever. He hadn't thought about the betrayal in a few days. It was all good.

"Yes, actually, my mind is better than ever."

"Good. I'll believe you without a professional report on that. We need you out there again. Also, I haven't seen you smiling like a love drunk idiot for nearly ten years. I don't know what Lynn does differently than the other therapists, but it's working," she laughed.

"I don't know either, but it's just amazing. She's the best thing that ever happened to me."

His mind drifted off to the brown-haired woman with the chestnut eyes.

"Maybe it's the sex that lightens your mood," Marta giggled.

"Pardon?" Nate looked at her with widened eyes.

"Thin walls, Butch..." Marta laughed even more.

"Oh my god..." Nate groaned and turned his back towards Marta.

His and Oliver's room were right next to each other and he even fled to Lynn's room when Marta and Oliver were too loud in the middle of the night but he'd never thought about the fact that they would be able to hear them, too.

His face had the color of radish by now and he buried it in both of his palms.

"I'm just gonna pretend we never had this conversation. Thanks for ruining my day, Marta," he huffed and quickly stepped out of the room without closing the door. Marta couldn't stop laughing and sent a text to Oliver to warn him.

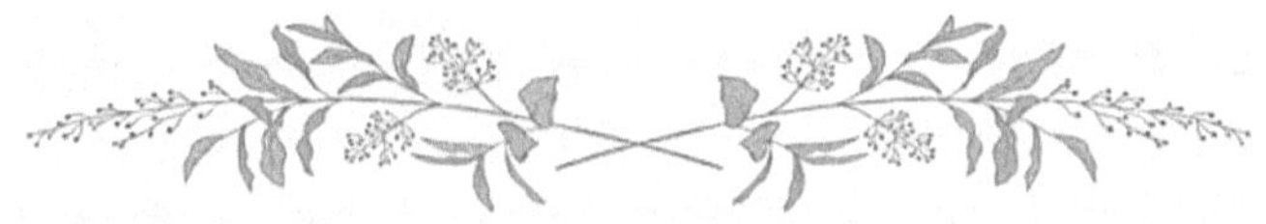

When Nate entered one of the offices their team could use to investigate and plan missions, he saw Oliver, Peter Davis, and an unknown young woman, leaning over a large map that covered almost the entire desk.

The door had been open, but he still knocked on the doorframe to let them know that he had entered. Still a gentleman.

Oliver's head was the first to turn around and Nate could see his eyes light up when he saw his best friend.

"Butch." He smiled at him.

"Need some support on the mission?" Nate asked while stepping towards the desk the others were gathered around.

"You're cleared?"

"Yes, Sir. Cleared and ready to head out on Wednesday!"

"That's amazing. We could really use someone with your experience. I was about to let Eliana come with us, because the more the merrier but she only joined the CIA two weeks ago and doesn't have any experience in operations abroad," Oliver explained and pointed to the woman standing with her back towards Nate. She was still observing the map in front of her until Oliver called her name then she turned around and stared at Nate with a neutral face. Nate raised an eyebrow at her, made two steps in her direction, and extended his arm.

"Nate Sheppard, but you can call me Butch."

"Eliana Richards and just for the record, I would've been able to do the operation with the team. I was the best Agent on my team at the FBI."

Nate could hear Peter huff and roll his eyes in response and now he was even more curious as to what was going on.

"FBI to CIA is a major difference but I'm sure you would've been great support."

Nate gave her a fake smile, feeling confused and a little insecure about the situation. He had been more comfortable around people over the past few months but something that Eliana radiated made him feel uncomfortable..

Eliana only gave him a fake smile in return but he could see something flicker in her eyes. She was still young, in her late 20s, and by her facial expression and sassy comment he realized she was still very much a greenhorn. An arrogant greenhorn that overestimated herself badly. All bark, no bite. Which was okay. A lot of Agents were like that. One day they would get grounded. Mostly involuntarily.

Nate respected FBI Agents a lot but what they did in the terrorism task force was much more than any of the FBI Agents he knew could ever dream about. It was risky, it was mentally and physically challenging, and only the best of the best got a spot on their team.

Many tried. Many failed.

Oliver had strict rules and to pass the tests he prepared was hard. Nate was sure even he would fail some of them but luckily he'd worked with Oliver for over a decade and they understood each other without words. Which was a great advantage out in the field.

"Eliana is the first one to pass all my tests in the past few months and Marta, Director Burns, and I decided to hire her. She did the regular on-boarding process for the first week and joined our team just a couple of days ago." Oliver explained after he had curiously watched the first interaction between their new team member and his best friend.

It was important for him to make sure the dynamic in the team was good and that they were able to work together no matter what happened during an operation. There was already a weird rivalry forming between the two younger Agents on his team and he was happy that he had Nate as a buffer between Peter and Eliana.

"That's great to hear. Welcome to the team," Nate said to the woman that was still standing in front of him, challenging his gaze with a stare.

After a few seconds of them just looking at each other, Eliana shrunk back and gave him another smile before turning around to Oliver and Peter again. Peter just looked at her and every cell of his face screamed hatred.

Nate wondered what had happened in the few days that Eliana had been on the team to piss off Peter to this extent. The boy was always friendly, easily followed orders, but still remained open-minded and flexible even in the heat of battle. He had a perfect instinct for when he needed to disobey Oliver's order in order to sustain the success of the mission. Like when he shot Az-Zawahiri to save Oliver's life.

Peter was like a rough diamond. He had it in himself but he was also very insecure, always needing Oliver to support him and tell him that he'd done a good job. He was a good

Agent and, in time, he would get the necessary confidence, Nate was sure about that.

It took a lot to piss someone like Peter off. Nate made a mental note to observe the two and he was sure Oliver expected him to do exactly that.

Oliver cleared his throat, pointed his finger on the map on the desk and asked,

"You're here for a debriefing or you wanna do that later?"

"Yeah, sure. Go on. Let me know the plan."

Nate stepped towards the desk, finding his place between Peter and Oliver and gave the young Agent a wink and a clap on the back. Peter whispered "good to have you back" before Oliver started his explanation.

"After Az-Zawahiri's death the Middle East feels like a ticking time bomb. Different terror organizations are trying to take control of the region but all of them are weak in comparison to Az-Zawahiri. He inherited Bin Laden's territory and managed to extend and defend it for a long time. Now this huge territory is split between the remaining factions but none of them actually hold the scepter for the whole region. Until a month ago, when one of them started to battle against the others, gathering sub-organizations of al-Qaeda under his command. His name is Mohammed Atef. He was mostly active in Afghanistan but seemed to change location because now he's very active in central Iraq. We observed his activities over a number of weeks and now they can't be ignored. The operation itself is very clear: enter the hide-out, find and eliminate Atef. His organization is growing so we expect a bunch of hostiles in this hide-out. Too many to handle alone. So we're getting  support from the SEALs."

Nate raised his eyes from the map of the hide-out towards Oliver.

"Who's in charge?" Nate asked carefully.

"They are. It was a long and hard discussion on the call and they don't care that we were the ones that found the hide-out. Liam was actually a great help with that. We wouldn't have been that successful at this early stage without him."

Nate nodded. He hadn't worked much with Liam Thomas but the little computer nerd with the glasses was actually a huge gain for the CIA.

"Anyone on the SEALs side that we know?"

"No, pal. All the comrades we know are way too old to be SEALs now. They changed to other companies I guess," Oliver laughed.

"Do they know we're former SEALs?"

"Yeah, they do."

Nate sighed, his eyes never leaving Oliver's. It was a conversation between the two of them, totally ignoring the fact that Peter and Eliana were with them in the room.

"How much do they know?" Nate asked, his lower lip started to tremble and there was pain in his stomach like someone had stabbed a burning hot knife in the pit of it. As if on cue, Peter started to move from the desk, giving the two older Agents the privacy they needed but Eliana was still standing at the desk, her gaze alternating between Nate and Oliver.

"Eliana, come on. Let them talk alone," Peter whispered to her.

"Why? We're part of the team as well so we should know what they're talking about," Eliana responded.

"Because it's not a topic we should hear about. It's something private," Peter explained, but Eliana remained standing where she was so Peter grabbed her by her arm and pulled her out of the room but not without listening to her tremendous amount of cussing.

After a few moments the room was silent again and Nate found himself drifting off in his own mind. It was the first time that he was confronted with the SEALs again and he knew that the operators on their side would do detailed research on all the members of the terrorism task force. That meant they would get to know his history, would get to know about the Pakistan mission, the kidnapping, the torture, his mental and physical state.

He'd never wanted to know how much the SEALs actually documented about his state. After being released from the hospital he went straight home to see his mom, worked on the rest of the rehabilitation from there, and then joined Oliver at the CIA. He'd never even called his former colleagues.

Nate never wanted to talk about that topic again.

But now he was confronted with this chapter of his past.

He took a deep breath, waiting for Oliver's answer.

"They know about Pakistan, the kidnapping and how we found you, and that you left the SEALs because of irreparable physical damage."

"Physical?" Nate's eyes widened.

"Yes. We needed to give them a reason as to why you wouldn't return to active duty and the doctors, therapists and me decided to go the easy way. And to be honest with all your injuries and the broken bones that were treated way too late, nobody actually expected you to be back to 100%."

Oliver let out a loud sigh, before regaining his composure and shot a tiny smile at his best friend.

"I didn't know about that. Thanks, Oliver."

"Of course."

After the short, vulnerable moment between them, Oliver explained to Nate when they would leave headquarters, where and how they would meet the SEALs, and how the cooperation between CIA and SEALs had been planned. He had already got a message from Marta, that she'd informed the military operator that Eliana was replaced by Nate. They were still waiting for the final approval but Nate should make sure to be ready on Wednesday morning.

After everything was cleared up, Oliver answered all of Nate's questions to make sure he knew exactly what to expect. Afterwards they both left the office to look for Peter and Eliana. It was already late so they found them in the communal kitchen, together with Lynn and Marta. Marta had prepared a huge pot of chili con carne for everyone and they enjoyed their dinner in company.

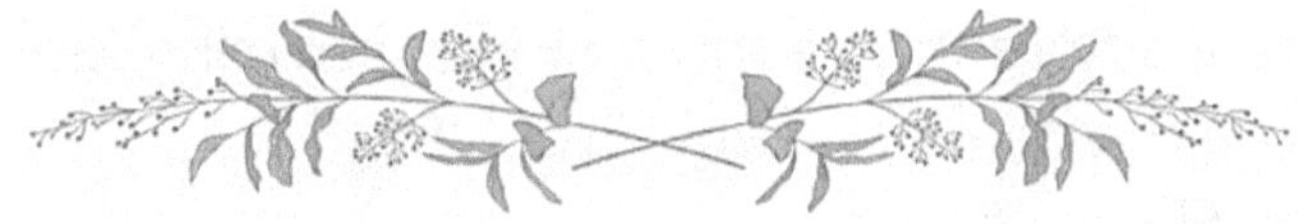

**August 3rd, 2022**

"Be careful, okay?" Lynn whispered before giving Nate a last kiss. They were standing in the communal kitchen, waiting for the terrorism task force to leave for the operation in Iraq.

"Always," Nate answered, giving her a kiss on her nose and grabbing his backpack.

Marta looked at Oliver with heart-eyes, but as they were surrounded by Eliana and Peter, they didn't kiss each other.

"Yeah, be careful," Marta said.

She looked between all three of her Agents, but her words were mostly meant for Oliver.

"I'm not gonna say some cute last words to you, Davis. Sorry. Need to find someone else for that," Eliana huffed and Peter gave her an annoyed look, before turning around to the others while mumbling "then just shut up" so quietly that only Eliana had heard it. Her face fell, she hadn't expected him to give a sassy response.

An hour later the three men were sitting in a military plane on their way to Iraq. They had met the SEALs at the airbase before leaving together. Nate and Oliver were feeling nostalgic as the whole situation reminded them of their shared past as SEALs themselves. They had been to that airbase plenty of times before, a feeling of excitement and nervousness filling their stomachs. No matter how many missions they did, those feelings never subsided. It was a similar feeling right now but the circumstances were completely different. The three SEALs that completed their team were Hyena, Gorilla and Crocodile.

Classic SEALs callsigns.

During the 21-hour flight to Iraq they had several conversations about the plan, checked the blueprints of the hide-out again and prepared their guns and other equipment like flashbangs and headgear.

The SEALs would go through the front entrance and the Agents would take the one on the side. The blueprints had revealed that the side entrance was mostly used for deliveries as it was close to the infirmary and a warehouse-like storage area. They had to be quick and quiet, making sure to catch Atef before he was able to flee.

After arriving at a secret base, they stored their bags in the barracks that were in the same area and prepared to head out to the hide-out in just under fifteen minutes. They didn't want to waste anymore time.

When they gathered around the vehicles that would transport them to the target, Nate observed with a smile that the SEALs were still using the M4 carbine rifles, even when they definitely had a more modern version.

He looked at his own AK-47, sighed and looked up to Oliver who shot him a questioning side-eye.

"I loved the M4's. They were light, reliable and easy to handle. So much better than the ones we use now." Nate shrugged his shoulders.

They couldn't see the SEALs' faces, but Nate was sure he detected a smile underneath Gorilla's ski mask after his comment.

The ride towards the hide-out was quiet, all of them in their own mind, trying to mentally prepare for the upcoming task. They didn't know what to expect as Liam wasn't able to hack into the cameras this time.

"Finally one of the terrorists upgraded their security system!" he'd shouted into the room, getting a warning from Marta that this was nothing he should be happy about. But Liam was just Liam.

It took them almost an hour and a half from the base to the hide-out but when they arrived Nate already had a bad feeling. They parked the vehicles outside, making sure that none of Atef's men were able to see them arrive, but when they left the transports all he could hear was silence. It was so quiet. Too quiet for the hide-out of a terrorist that was trying to gain control over the whole of Az-Zawahiri's former territory. He was fighting a war and for a war you needed people.

With some silent commands Hyena gathered them around him and whispered,

"The goal is to catch him alive. No shooting unless you have my permission. Understood?"

They all nodded and started to spread out towards the hide-out. The closer they came to it the worse Nate's gut feeling became.

"It's too quiet," he whispered towards Oliver and the blond nodded.

They had done so many operations together and knew how those were supposed to go.

They reached the side entrance, halted their movements, and waited for Oliver's signal to enter. Peter clenched his fingers around the AK-47 in his hands. The young Agent was still nervous on operations, especially after what happened last time, when he decided to kill Az-Zawahiri to protect Oliver. The lead Agent shot him a knowing look with a little nod, calming Peter's insecurity in an instant.

It was time for work mode.

As quietly as possible, Oliver opened the door, while Nate and Peter covered his back with their weapons ready to shoot.

They entered a small room with large metallic doors on each side. Nate entered first, closely followed by Peter, with Oliver bringing up the rear. The brunet man stepped in front of the door on their right, turned the knob, and pushed the door open. Like the blueprints had shown them, this was the warehouse area. But it was abandoned. Quiet. Empty.

With quick steps they rounded the shelves before Nate mouthed a "clear" towards his colleagues.

They left the room again and prepared to enter the other metallic door. It led them into a long hallway with multiple doors to both sides. They knew that behind three of these doors they could find offices, at least they looked like that on the blueprint.

Before they were able to open the first door, they heard Hyena talk over comms to them.

"So far everything is clear. Not a single hostile."

"Same here. We're about to check the offices before heading towards the med-bay and the attached holding cells to make sure," Oliver answered before signaling for Peter to open the first door.

The room had been an office once but was mostly abandoned, with a thick layer of dust over the desk, the computer screen, and the cabinets in the back.

"Clear," Peter whispered, who had stuck his head through the doorframe first.

The second office looked the same but the third one was used recently. A closed laptop was laying on a clean desk, two burner phones laying right next to it. On the wall behind the desk they found a pin board with dozens of photos on it. They showed different popular locations in Washington D.C and New York City like Times Square, Capitol Hill, The Lincoln Memorial, or Mount Vernon.

"What's this?" Nate asked with a raised eyebrow, taking a closer look at all the different pictures. Between them he found notes in Arabic.

"I have no idea, but this room was used recently," Peter commented while Oliver told the SEALs via comms what they had found.

"I'm on my way to inspect it myself. Don't touch anything," Hyena had answered, making Oliver roll his eyes and hiss.

"Who do they think we are? Kindergarten kids?"

"Oliver," Nate suddenly said, his eyes fixed with one of the handwritten notes.

"What is it?"

"My Arabic is a little rusty, but I know this word. *Qunbula*. This means bomb."

Oliver froze on the spot, a shiver running up his spine, before he slowly made his way to Nate and looked at the note himself.

The brunet man pointed to one of the words on the note. After years of working for the SEALs and now in the terrorism task force, they had learned a few words of Arabic and this was one of them. His heart stopped beating for a moment.

Did that mean Atef planned on bombing one of these places in Washington or New York? Or maybe even all of them?

Before he could tell Hyena about it, the SEAL entered the room, looking at three very shocked Agents.

"Atef planned some attacks. We need to find him as soon as possible!" Oliver shouted at him, seeing even the SEAL surprised at the discovery.

"Okay, hold on. I'm collecting and documenting the evidence here. McGreen, Sheppard and Davis, you're checking the med-bay and the holding cells to see if you can find any hostages. Crocodile and Gorilla are still checking the sleeping accommodation. They should be done soon." Hyena commanded.

The three CIA Agents looked at each other, held their rifles in front of them again, and went to the end of the hallway.

"I'll check the holding cells and you and Peter can go through the med-bay. That area looked bigger, so you can easily split up. They only have three holding cells, so I should be done at the same time as you two." Nate suggested but saw hesitation on Oliver's eyes.

The hands that were holding the AK-47 started to tremble a little, something that was unusual for Oliver.

"I don't know if I like that. Let's stay together." The blond responded, but Nate had only focused on the storm that appeared behind Oliver's green-blue eyes. What was wrong with him?

"I'll be fine, pal. No need to worry about me." Nate gave him a smile.

Oliver smiled back at him, but it didn't reach his eyes.

"Okay. Let me know if you find anything."

"Sure."

Nate opened the door to the holding cells, feeling Oliver's eyes bore into the back of his head. He wondered what was going on with his best friend. This was more than just unusual behavior, worry, or insecurity. Something was up but Nate couldn't put his finger on it yet.

The hallway was empty and dark, the lights didn't work, and it looked like they hadn't held a hostage here in a while. He passed a locked door and wondered what was behind it. He remembered from the blueprint that it had been a bigger room that didn't look like one of the cells, but he wasn't exactly sure.

So he passed the closed door and saw three open ones distributed over the hallway. One on the right and two on the left side. Their metallic doors had small, yellowed windows in them that made it impossible to look through but he didn't need to anyway as the doors weren't locked. Two of the three doors even stood ajar so that he was able to kick them open with his boot. A weird tingling spread through his body and made the hair on his neck rise, but he couldn't figure out what exactly caused it. The hallway looked oddly familiar, but so had the one they found Ann in a few months ago. This didn't mean anything but the feeling in his stomach was different this time.

Nate's body was pulled towards the first door on the left side of the hallway so he carefully stepped towards it and kicked the door open.

On the other side of the door frame was a metal-framed bed, if this was even the appropriate name for it, as it was more of a plank than a bed. A thin beige blanket was crumpled on top of it and Nate could see that it already started to wear away into pieces. The fabric that was left was blotched with dark brown splotches that resembled blood.

In front of the bed he could see the remnants of a wooden chair, fallen apart years ago. He could still see all four legs lying around, with leather shackles on two of them.

He turned his head to the side and saw a metal table on rollers standing right next to the door. It had still different sized knives lying on top of it, the blades rusted.

Nate's heartbeat increased until all he could hear was the galloping of his heart and a loud tinnitus in his ears. His vision blurred and black dots appeared in front of his eyes. Breathing was impossible for him as if his lungs were filled with cement.

The rifle fell to the floor while Nate struggled to stay upright. With every second the darkness came closer and he considered just giving up and diving into it.

But then he heard loud steps echoing through the hallway, straight in his direction. The remnants of his clear mind clawed onto these new sounds and tried to pull him back to reality but only Oliver's large hand on his shoulder was finally able to do it.

"Are you okay, pal?" Oliver asked, but it took Nate several minutes to process his words.

Finally he turned around and looked at his best friend with an expression that looked as if he'd seen a ghost.

# Did you know?

**August 5th, 2022**

"I've been here before, Oliver. Had this gut feeling right from the moment we entered the hide-out, but I wasn't sure. Now I'm sure. This is the hide-out I was held captive in. This is my fucking cell. My fucking cell!" Nate pointed into the holding cell and screamed towards his best friend, his emotions overwhelming his body.

He was hot and cold at the same time, his hands shaking, and he could sweat gathered on his forehead. Oliver on the other hand was unusually quiet. Too quiet for someone who heard this shocking information for the first time.

"Did you hear what I said, pal?"

Instead of answering him, Oliver lowered his head, the eyes locked with the floor underneath them. He was breathing heavily. His reaction was more than strange and suddenly Nate realized what was going on. His lips parted, his eyes wide and the shaking of his hands intensified so that he needed to clench both of them to fists.

"You knew that," Nate hissed.

It wasn't a question. It was an accusation. His voice was low and rough like gravel but with a lot of anger lingering in it.

Oliver was still avoiding his best friend's gaze before he mumbled a defeated "yeah".

"But you didn't tell me?"

"I needed you to be functioning. I needed you for the operation."

"I wasn't even staffed for that operation," Nate screamed back at Oliver.

"You are always my number one choice when it comes to operations, Butch. I just wasn't sure if Lynn would clear you in time."

Oliver finally looked into Nate's eyes, seeing the terror that was swirling inside of them. His best friend had been confronted with his darkest moment. The three months that had almost destroyed his life. That had almost killed him.

"I'm sorry that I didn't tell you," Oliver mumbled, tears brimming around his eyeline.

"You're sorry? Sorry?" Nate leant forward, pointing his index finger towards Oliver.

"A little warning would have been nice. Something like, *hi pal, just FYI this is the hideout you were held captive in.* So that I wouldn't almost suffer a panic attack," Nate was still shouting.

"Listen, Butch. I'm sorry. Really. I thought it would've been the right decision to not tell you but I was clearly wrong."

Oliver looked at him with a pleading look. Pleading to stop the shouting, pleading that this wouldn't break their friendship.

"Is this a test?" Nate had lowered his hand and now looked at Oliver with his eyebrows knitted together.

"What?"

"Is this a test? To see if I'm mentally stable again? Who's idea was this? Yours? Marta's? It was Lynn's, wasn't it?"

"Butch. Stop it. I have no idea what you're talking about. This isn't a test. This isn't about you. Now stop shouting at me and let's get back to the others, we're still on operation."

It was now Oliver's turn to scream back at his friend. He was in command and Nate's mind was spiraling down so deep and so fast that Oliver knew it was the only way to avoid Nate freaking out in front of the others as well. He was able to handle this, he deserved his best friend's anger, but he didn't want Nate to look unstable in front of the SEALs and Peter.

Nate looked at him with his jaw on the floor but no words came out of his mouth. Instead he shook his head in disbelief, let out a loud huff, and turned around to head out of the hide-out and back to the vehicles.

Oliver looked after him, his urge to say something almost eating him alive, but he knew it wasn't the right time. He turned to look into the cell once more, letting his gaze wander over the metallic bed, the broken wooden chair and the greasy toilet.

Although it had been over ten years since he'd found his best friend lying in this cell, almost dead, it felt like yesterday.

Oliver would never forget the moment he opened the door and looked around the cell. Full of hope, full of relief that they'd found Nate and that they'd made it in time. When he saw the huge puddles of blood on the concrete floor and an unconscious man right behind them, his hope was devastated.

He thought Nate was dead.

His body was frozen, like someone had poured liquid ice in his veins. He didn't want to go and check for a pulse. He didn't want to have the final evidence that his best friend was dead. That he was too late.

Oliver felt like he was stuck in a tunnel. He didn't hear his SEAL colleague storm into the room to check for Nate's vitals. He was still glued in the doorframe, only seeing the lifeless body of his best friend in front of his eyes until his eyesight was blocked by his colleague who shouted something at him.

"… to the hospital," were the only fragments Oliver was able to understand when he crashed back to reality.

"What?"

"He's alive, but we need to get him to a hospital asap."

"Oh my god. You sure?" He couldn't believe the words his comrade was saying, so he finally rushed to Nate and looked at him for the first time. Properly looked at him.

His skin was pale, the beard long and wild and his hair messy and curly. It had been really short when they left for Pakistan. Blood was all over his body and the tattered clothes that he was wearing. He was in black boxers and a dark gray shirt that was torn apart around Nate's middle. He did look dead but thankfully he wasn't.

Now that Oliver was standing in that exact same door frame he could see the scene in front of his eyes again. Saw Nate lying on the floor on his back, himself kneeling next to him while their colleague tried to find the nearest hospital, mumbling into his comm about which obvious injuries Nate was suffering from.

Tears started to fall down his face, blurring his vision. After a few blinks, the scene was gone. His mind was back in 2022 and, although it was the same place, the entire situation was all different. Nate was better, right?

With a last shake of his head, Oliver started to get out of the building so that they were able to go home. He also needed to contact Marta to let her know that Atef was able to flee and that they'd found plans for attacks in New York City and Washington. He couldn't even imagine what rumble would go through the heads of the CIA, the military, and the government when they told them that there might be an attack soon.

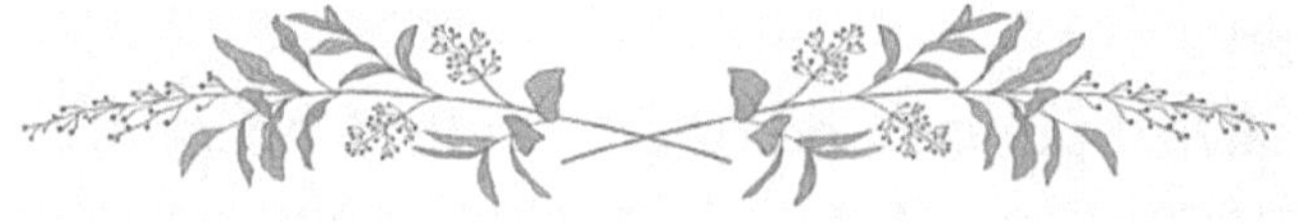

**August 6th, 2022**

The flight back home was the most uncomfortable flight in Oliver's life. Nate gave his report to Hyena and talked to Peter about the operation but avoided speaking to Oliver as much as possible. While talking about what they had found in the hide-out he added stuff to Oliver's verbal report, but neither of them mentioned their fight.

"Are you okay?" Peter asked Nate as he took a place next to him.

"Yeah. How about you?"

"I'm fine. Happy to be home soon." Peter smiled, but Nate didn't return it.

Oliver's seat was on the other side of the plane, easy to avoid another confrontation and make them look unprofessional. His mind spiraled between the scenes from 2011, his fight with Nate, and the fear that he had driven a wedge into their friendship. He grabbed his phone and texted Marta.

Oliver
On our way back home.
Atef was warned so he could flee before we arrived.
We found plans about potential attacks in NYC and
Washington, the SEALs are currently preparing the report.
You should have it soon.

Marta
Oh shit. Sounds like a lot of work...

Oliver
Had a fight with Butch

Marta
What? Why?

Oliver
He found out about the hide-out and freaked out.

Marta
Is he okay?
Should I let Lynn know?

Oliver
No, please don't tell Lynn.
He's fine, he's just super pissed.
Don't know if I ruined our friendship with this.

<u>Marta</u>
It will be okay. Your friendship survived worse.
Let's talk about this when you're back home.
Te quiero.

<u>Oliver</u><br>
Te quiero también.

While Oliver was texting Marta, one of the SEALs, Gorilla, approached Nate and Peter and took a seat on the other side of the aisle. He gave the two Agents a smile before he said,

"Agent Sheppard, I just wanted to tell you that you have my full respect. Returning to the place you've been tortured is more than brave. I don't know if I'd be able to do that. Good to see you back in the field."

Nate just looked at him with a blank stare until he realized that the man was waiting for an answer. He cleared his throat and tried to ignore the uncomfortable silence in the plane. He was sure the other men around them had heard Gorilla's words as well.

"Thank you." He nodded and Gorilla gave him another smile before he turned his attention to the phone in his hand.

Peter gave Nate a side-eye but wasn't brave enough to say anything.

Nate wasn't in the mood to talk about this topic right now. There was a thunderstorm passing through his heart and mind right now. It was dark, it was depressing, and all his thoughts were swirling around. He couldn't finish a single one, while his mind drifted off towards the holding cell and all the memories he connected with it.

BBeing lost in his mind meant he didn't even realize when the plane landed and they had returned to Washington.

"Butch, are you coming?" he heard Peter say and turned his head in confusion.

The young Agent was standing next to him, his backpack hanging off one shoulder and his eyebrows raised towards his colleague.

"Yeah, sure." Nate quickly jumped to his feet, grabbed his own backpack, and sprinted after Peter to leave the plane.

Standing on the runway next to the plane they said goodbye to the three SEALs before another soldier led them out of the base and towards the car that was already waiting for them.

The car ride towards headquarters was quiet. Peter tried to engage in some conversation but both Oliver and Nate only gave him single word answers leading to every conversation falling dead after only a few seconds. After the fourth try Peter just huffed and stared out of the window, watching the trees pass while they drove closer and closer to Langley.

They passed the gate and Oliver parked the car almost right in front of the main entrance. All three Agents left the car and grabbed their backpacks out of the trunk before they entered the foyer. They passed the memorial wall and the front desk, crossed the first building and the small green on their way to the main building, and entered an elevator to head to the third floor and directly into Marta's office. She had sent a message to all of them as soon as they had arrived back in Washington. They needed to talk about the operation.

That was what they did. Well, mostly Oliver did. He gave Marta the best possible verbal report to add to the report from the SEALs that she'd already received a few hours ago.

Peter made a few additions to Oliver's report and Nate remained silent.

"Thank you, Oliver, Peter. Butch, do you have anything to add?" Marta asked and looked at him demandingly.

Nate was still completely lost in his own mind, he hadn't even listened to Oliver and Peter so even if he had something to add, he wouldn't know what had already been reported so he quickly shook his head and continued to look at his combat boots.

"Okay. I gave the SEALs report, the pictures, and the other scanned material to Liam. He's trying to get as much information as possible. Unfortunately the SEALs refused to give him the found laptop or the burner phones. They want to do their own research first, but I hope we get our hands on them soon," Marta explained.

"Let us know as soon as Liam finds something," Oliver said and Marta gave him a smile.

"Sure. You three go and get some sleep now and we can have a meeting with Liam tomorrow. I'm pretty sure he will have something for us by then."

Oliver smiled back at his girlfriend, Peter nodded, but Nate remained in the same position as before.

"See you tomorrow then," Peter said and left the office first.

Marta shot Oliver a concerned side-eye before she looked at Nate. The brunet man was still staring at his shoes and it seemed like he didn't even notice the world around him.

"He's been like that since I saw him again on the plane." Oliver mouthed to Marta in the lowest possible voice.

Nate seemed to be stuck in his own mind but they weren't sure.

"Butch?" Marta asked with a commanding voice.

The Agent raised his head and looked at them with empty eyes. Oliver's heart ached when he saw the extent of his friend's mental breakdown. The weight of making the wrong decision by not telling him about the hide-out was almost crushing his shoulders.

"We're done here. You can go." Marta smiled at Nate, who raised to his feet and left the room without saying another word.

Nate shambled along the hallway, entered the elevator, and left it again on the second floor. A moment after he passed the med-bay the automatic door opened and Lynn exited her working area. When she turned left to head to her room she saw a familiar man walking along the hallway. Her heart skipped a beat when she realized it was her boyfriend. But why didn't he text her?

"Honey?" she asked loudly but Nate didn't turn around.

"Nate?" she repeated, thinking that he might not have heard her the first time but he still didn't react and continued his walk towards his room. His shoulders were hanging low, as if the weight of the backpack was pulling them down, but she knew that he only had a few clothes in it as the operation had not been planned as a longer stay. Lynn turned her head around to see if she could see Oliver but she couldn't see anybody else at all. The doctor furrowed her brows and deep lines appeared on her forehead. Nate's behavior was weird.

She decided to follow him and ask about the operation. Whilst she had been looking for Oliver Nate had already entered his room and closed his door. Lynn stood in front of it and connected her knuckles with the cold wood.

One knock. No answer.

Another one. Still no answer.

"Nate? Are you okay? It's me. Can you let me in?" she asked through the closed door, hoping that Nate was only in the bathroom and hadn't heard the knock on the door.

She knocked one more time. Still no answer.

Something in her gut started to feel off. Maybe there was a logical explanation for Nate's behavior but with every second the panic within her body started to grow. Tiny hot stones moved in her gut while she tried to figure out what was going on. This wasn't one of her usual panic attacks, this felt different. Something really was off right now but she didn't understand what.

"Nate. Please open the door," she demanded. Pleaded. She needed to see him. Needed to know that he was alright.

She needed to feel his strong hands on her waist, calming down the panic inside of her. Last time she had seen him like that was in May, right after he had found out that Lynn was working with Az-Zawahiri in order to save her sister's life.

That time he had hurt himself by hurting his freshly operated knee. Lynn didn't understand why he had done that back then but she knew that he was always in danger of falling back into the rabbit hole of his mind. Listening to the demons again that she was able to silence over the past few months with their therapy sessions.

"Nate. Please," she partly screamed, partly sobbed.

She hadn't even realized that she was crying, only when her tears started to drop off her chin and soak her scrubs.

Suddenly she heard a female voice say her name. She turned her head towards the sound and saw Marta and Oliver standing only a few feet away from her.

When did they arrive? She hadn't heard them.

Marta's face was furrowed and she looked at her friend with worry behind her honey-colored eyes. Oliver's gaze was fixed to the floor and Lynn couldn't interpret his expression.

"Lynn," Marta repeated, reaching out one hand in order to touch her but Lynn flinched back.

"What did he say?" Marta asked. Lynn needed a moment to regain the ability to speak.

"He... He didn't say a word. I called his name a few times, knocked on his door, but there was no reaction. Is he okay?" Lynn felt her heart rate increase, her mind drifting off to possible injuries that could have been the reason that he didn't respond.

"He's fine. No injuries. They didn't get Atef but the operation went without any other complications." Marta tried to calm Lynn's nerves.

"Okay but why is he like that?"

Lynn let her eyes wander to Oliver, who was still looking at the floor. Marta followed her gaze, looking at her boyfriend before sighing. It was his story to tell but he had been in that devastating state since they arrived at her office. She had only gotten him down here so he could have something to eat before they went to her room to have a long conversation about what happened.

"The hide-out they were going to... it was the hide-out where Butch was held captive," Marta said with a low voice.

"What?!" Lynn exclaimed, her mouth open and her eyes wide.

Marta stepped towards the doctor, grabbed her arm and carefully guided her towards the communal kitchen so they didn't have to talk in the middle of the hallway. Lynn turned her head around the entire way to the kitchen in a desperate hope Nate would open the door and tell her that everything was okay. Marta placed Lynn on the couch and took a seat next to her.

"That's not all," she started, carefully watching her boyfriend taking his own seat on the other couch.

He was still silent, avoiding Marta's and Lynn's eyes with a lot of effort.  Lynn just stared at Marta with pure shock on her face. She needed a moment to process the words, but Marta didn't give her a chance to drift off.

"We knew that it was this hide-out. We'd known it for weeks. But as we weren't sure if you would clear him for this operation, we didn't tell him about it and when he was cleared we kept on with the same strategy and didn't tell him. We weren't sure if it would trigger him and risk the mission. He'd only been in a few rooms in the entire hide-out so the risks of him realizing that he'd been there before were very low."

"But he found out..." Lynn's eyes filled with tears while she imagined how shocked Nate must have been.

"Yes. He and Oliver had a huge fight about it."

Both women looked at Oliver and saw that tears were streaming down his face. Marta immediately rose to her feet and crashed down next to her boyfriend, wrapping her arms around his shoulders and pulling him close. Oliver continued to cry silently while Lynn didn't know what to say or do. All she wanted was to take her ID card, enter Nate's room and pull him into her arms the same way Marta was doing  with Oliver.

"I didn't know it would send him down a rabbit hole again. I expected him to be angry, but not this. I'm so sorry," Oliver sobbed.

"What do you mean?" Lynn asked and finally Oliver raised his gaze to look at her.

"He didn't say a word to me the entire time. Not in the plane, not in the car. At first I thought he was pissed and he has every right to be but when he looked me in the eyes, I saw that his mind had drifted off and he was listening to his demons again. It's always easy to tell by his eyes. They were completely empty."

Oliver was hard to understand as he was mumbling in between sobs. Lynn had never seen him so emotional before. She should feel sorry for him but she was so overwhelmed by Nate's weird behavior, the information she was still processing, and Oliver breaking down in front of her, that she only panicked. Panic about her boyfriend's mental health, him hurting himself as result of his devastating state, and that he might never let her come near him again.

"Oliver..." Lynn started but needed another moment to figure out her feelings and thoughts, "...I'll check on him again. To make sure he's okay. Physically."

Oliver looked at her, his eyes swollen and with so much sadness in them. Lynn wanted to be angry at him. Angry about the tremendous amount of stupidity that led to him not telling Nate about the hide-out. She knew how hard Nate struggled to trust people and how insecure he still was. He had improved so much, but he was still like a little seedling that needed love and comfort to grow into a big plant. He was still so fragile. Lynn had worked so hard over the past few months to make him feel better, to make him forgive her about the betrayal, but this whole situation had thrown him back. The demons of his past had caught up with him and thrown him to the mat like an MMA fighter.

"I don't like that you kept that secret from him but right now we should focus on making sure he isn't spiraling down even further," she added and rose to her feet.

She would deal with Oliver and his stupidity later. Marta was there to comfort him and make sure he was okay.

Lynn's focus was on Nate now.

# How to save a life

**August 10th, 2022**

The past few days have been more than challenging for everybody. Lynn had tried to talk to Nate several times after his arrival but he ignored her. He wasn't answering when she called him, he wasn't opening the door when she knocked on it. The only reaction she got was when she threatened to open the door with her ID card and check on him.

"I'm okay. I need some time alone," he had said through the closed door.

His voice had been more than rough, gravelly, and trembling with a huge amount of anger. Lynn wasn't sure if Nate was able to assess his condition by himself but she didn't want to upset him even further.

"I love you, Nate. You're not alone. I'm here. If you want to talk, you know where to find me. I understand that you're angry and hurt. You don't have to go through those emotions alone, okay?" she answered, but Nate didn't respond.

The next day Lynn was standing in front of his door again, asking him if he was okay. He gave her a short "I'm good", but Lynn grew more and more impatient, hurt, angry, and confused. There were so many emotions inside her body.

She was so overwhelmed that tears started to fall the moment she turned around to head to the med-bay and do her job.

Marta saw her coming in her direction and was immediately concerned when she saw Lynn crying.

"What's going on?" she asked, before opening her arms and engulfing the doctor in a hug.

Lynn sobbed into her shoulder, letting all the emotions out that had gathered in her body over the past few days.

"He's not talking to me but I didn't do anything wrong. It's not my fault."

"I know, sweetie. He's being a dick. I was on my way to tell him exactly that."

"What?!" Lynn stepped away from her and looked at her with shock on her face.

"Just kidding but I am indeed on my way to him. He hasn't been to work for a few days. That's unacceptable. He needs to work or I need to admonish him officially and I really don't want to do that. I don't want to draw any attention to him or Director Burns could get suspicious about his mental state," Marta explained with a concerned frown on his face.

"Oh."

Lynn wasn't able to say anything else as her mind was going crazy about Nate getting confronted with his mental state in an official internal investigation or something. That would throw him so deep down his rabbit hole she was scared that nobody would ever be able to help him out of it again.

"I'll do anything I can to avoid that but he needs to work."

"Go tell him that. Maybe he'll listen to you if he's not listening to Oliver or me," Lynn sighed, the tears again on the brink of falling down.

"It'll be alright." Marta smiled at her, gave her another hug and left towards Nate's room.

She knocked on his door loudly.

"Butch, if you don't start to work again today, there'll be legal consequences for you. I know it was a more than shitty idea to not tell you about the hide-out but keep it together and do your fucking job. Understood?"

To her surprise the door opened and a miserable-looking brunet man appeared in the doorframe.

"Understood. Where do you need me?"

"Oliver expects you down in the team's office. Can you do that?"

"Yes, Ma'am," Nate answered and closed the door in Marta's face.

She hadn't seen him that bad in a while. His hair was a mess on top of his head, his beard long and untrimmed, and the black bags under his eyes more than visible. With a loud sigh she turned around and saw that Lynn was still standing in the hallway, curiously listening to Marta's conversation with her boyfriend. Marta was glad that from Lynn's position it was impossible for her to see Nate because his appearance would have triggered her urge to help the Agent again.

"He's going to work with Oliver. Don't overdo it, okay? Let him have his space," Marta said when she arrived back in front of the doctor.

"But…"

"No buts. Give him a day to get settled again. Then you can talk to him. Trust me. It's for the best." Marta shot her another smile, before heading back to the elevator.

Lynn sighed loudly but continued her work in the med-bay as well.

Nate waited for the voices in the hallway to subside before he stepped out of his room and quickly jogged towards the elevators to get to the room where Oliver was waiting. He looked with sad eyes towards the automatic door of the med-bay but decided to go past it and head to Oliver. He wasn't ready to face Lynn yet. Of course he knew that she had nothing to do with the whole situation, but the demons in his mind were loud at the moment. Telling him that nobody was trustworthy. Especially not Lynn, who had betrayed him once. She was anything but trustworthy.

With his demons screaming at him as if they were having a rock concert inside his mind, he entered the team's office. Oliver sat on one of the desks, scrolling through something that Nate couldn't see from his position. Peter and Eliana were nowhere to be seen which was weird because it was a Wednesday, which was usually a regular working day for them.

"Where's the rest of the team?" he asked, leaning on the doorframe with a neutral face expression.

"Butch..." Oliver started but saw in the face of his friend that now was not the time to talk about the happenings in Iraq. So he swallowed the lump in his throat.

"They're on their way to the WPD headquarters, organizing how to make sure none of the attacks will happen. Marta will be with them on a call. I'm still here going through the translated communication logs of Atef's phones. The SEALs sent them over yesterday."

"What about Liam? Why isn't he working on that instead. Sounds like one of his specialities?"

"Liam got Atef's laptop yesterday. The SEALs are done with that, too. Haven't found a single clue where and when the attacks will happen but Liam is optimistic that he'll find something."

"Sure he is. What can I do?" Nate asked, pushing himself off the door frame and walking to the desk next to Oliver's.

"Butch, I…"

"What can I do, Oliver?"

The blond Agent sighed in defeat. There was no way he would be able to talk to his best friend today. The silence between them was more than uncomfortable, something that had never happened ever since he'd known Nate.

"I'm not even halfway through the communication log. I started at the beginning. You can start at the end and we'll meet somewhere in the middle."

"Understood."

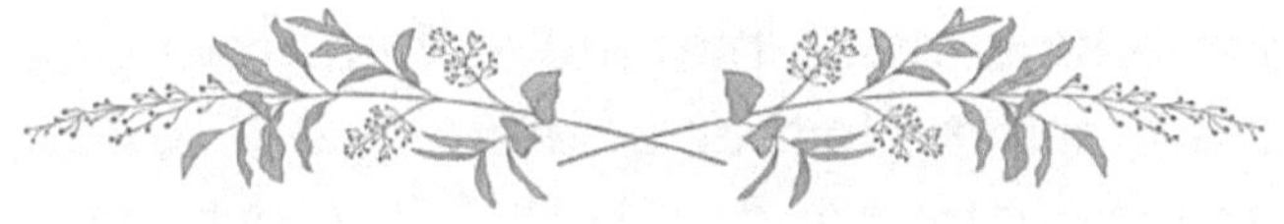

**August 12th, 2022**

Of course Nate hadn't talked to Lynn and she didn't try to talk to him again. She was too scared to get rejected again. Her fragile little heart wouldn't be able to take it again. Sleep had been a rare occurrence for her over the past few days so she tried to kickstart her body back to life with an unhealthy amount of coffee and energy drinks. Of course she knew that this wasn't exactly how she should treat her body but there was no other way. The second pillow on her bed still smelled like Nate and she wasn't even able to kick it out of her bed. No, she grabbed it in her arms and cried herself to sleep every night only to wake up an hour later because she smelled Nate and hoped he had returned to her. The cognition that it was only the pillow and not Nate made her cry herself to sleep again. And again. And again.

That morning she scuffled into the communal kitchen to get some breakfast and a big coffee into her system before she started her shift in the med-bay. Her eyes weren't even fully open so she didn't see the man already in the kitchen. Only when he turned around and looked at her with ocean-blue eyes, Lynn realized that it was Nate.

Her lips parted, her eyes suddenly as wide as they could be, but no sound left her mouth.

His gaze fixed with hers and he could see the tears in her eyes. The demons were screaming at him to look away, to ignore her, to go back to his room or down into the office where he was still working on the communication log.

But something inside him pulled him towards Lynn as if she was a magnet. Neither of them said a word but when Nate reached out his hand and carefully touched Lynn's small fingers with his own, a warmth flooded his body like the sun on a summer day. The cracks in his heart started to heal the longer he held her fingers and for the first time in days he felt like himself again.

Nate Sheppard.

Both remained silent, too afraid to scare the other one off and lose them completely.

For an uncertain period of time they stood there, a female hand in a male one, looking in each other's eyes, communicating without words.

"Have dinner with me tonight," Lynn mouthed barely above a whisper.

"Okay." His voice was rough, as if he hadn't used it a lot in the last few days.

"I love you." Her words were emphasized by tears streaming out of her eyes and a single sob.

"I love you, too." His voice broke as if he didn't believe his own words.

Lynn's heart was heavy, confused, hurt. When he let go of her hand and stepped out of the communal kitchen without even taking his sandwich with him, she looked after him. Her mind was like a swirling storm, unsure what to think, what to feel but this had been a step in the right direction. She hoped.

Later that day, when her stomach was growling so loud that she couldn't lay in her bed again and read, she stepped out into the hallway and towards Nate's room. Her heart was full of hope. She was excited, she was happy. A normal dinner with the man she loved. Her boyfriend. Everything would be okay. She felt it in the pit of her stomach.

With three loud knocks she signaled to Nate that she was ready for dinner. A few seconds passed, but Nate didn't open the door or shout that he was about to come.

"Nate? Are you in there? I'm hungry and ready for dinner," she said through the closed door.

"I can't. I'm sorry." His voice could be heard through the door. It sounded still rough, as if he were crying.

"What do you mean? Should I come back later?"

"No. I'm not hungry."

"Will you at least spend some time with me, while I eat?"

"No. I'm sorry. I can't. This was a bad idea. Please leave me alone."

"But Nate."

"No. Please. Leave me alone."

He was clearly crying. She heard his sobs between the words. Lynn was crying too. Mourning the evening she had been excited about for the entire day. Mourning her relationship that was about to burst into pieces. Mourning the love and happiness that this man had brought her. Until a week ago. Now all emotions when she thought about him were madness, sadness, and despair.

"I love you, okay?" She now sobbed herself but instead of an answer she could hear his loud cries through the door.

Her heart finally couldn't stand the pressure anymore and burst into a billion pieces. She crashed down on her knees, the palms of her hands pressed into her face while she cried more than she had  since her sister died.

Suddenly she felt big hands on her shoulders and hope inflamed in her body. Was Nate caring for her?

But when she looked up and expected the brunet man with the ocean-blue eyes, she got hurt all over again, when her eyes looked at Oliver kneeling next to her.

"What's wrong, Lynn?" he asked, concerned.

His eyebrows were furrowed and she could see the shock shining in his eyes.

Instead of answering him she started to cry once more, collapsing into Oliver's arms when the emotions took control over her body. Oliver turned his head around and looked helplessly for his girlfriend. They were meeting in the kitchen to cook but she wanted to get her notebook from her office first. The elevator doors opened and Marta stepped into the hallway. When she saw Oliver looking at her with a slight panic on his face she rushed to his side as quickly as possible. Together they pulled the still-crying Lynn to her feet and managed to get her onto one of the couches in the communal kitchen.

Marta engulfed her in a strong hug, letting the doctor cry on her shoulder until exhaustion hit her like a train and she fell asleep in Marta's arms. Carefully Marta laid Lynn down on the couch, grabbed a blanket and placed it on top of her.

"What the hell was that?" Oliver asked after making sure Lynn was fast asleep.

"I have no idea. But I'm pretty sure she'll tell us as soon as she's awake. I've never seen her like this."

Marta's heart felt heavy and she forced herself to take a deep breath as she was shocked about Lynn's breakdown. She stepped towards Oliver who already waited with open arms. He pulled her close, giving her the comfort and security of a tight hug to calm her nervous mind.

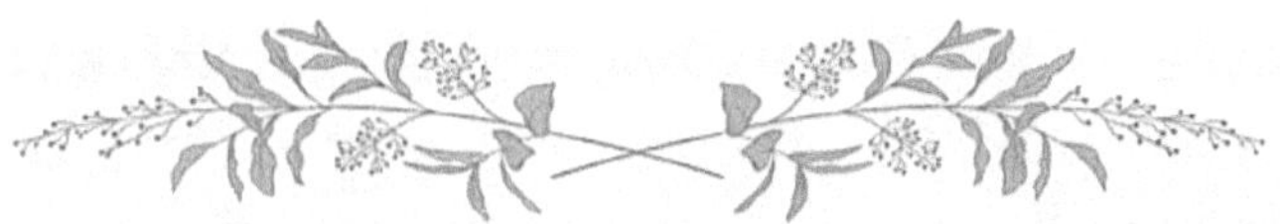

**August 13th, 2022**

Lynn slept through the night and almost the entire morning. Marta had checked with Tia and Birdie that they could postpone the planned appointments with Agents to the afternoon. Oliver had watched over her like a mother hen, making sure everyone who entered the kitchen was quiet so that nobody woke her. He had his laptop with him, checking on the communication logs until he found something that could have been a hint on an attack. So he ran to the elevator to head to Liam Thomas and look at the log with him.

It was noon when Marta quickly ran into the communal kitchen and knelt in front of the still-sleeping Lynn. She took a deep breath and carefully shook Lynn's shoulders.

"Lynn, sweetie. You have to wake up. We need you to treat a gunshot wound," Marta said while still shaking Lynn's shoulders.

The doctor's eyes fluttered open and the moment the words "gunshot wound" reached her brain she was in work mode. Her eyes clear, she quickly rose into a sitting position and looked at Marta. The stains of her dried tears were still evident on her face but other than that she was fully functioning.

"What happened?" She asked.

"It's a long story, I'ill tell you on our way to the interrogation cell."

Marta rose to her feet and stepped aside so that Lynn could stand as well. The two women practically ran out of the kitchen and into the med-bay where Lynn grabbed her emergency pack before they sprinted to the elevators.

"Is it one of us?" Lynn asked during the way-too-long elevator ride.

Her heart was beating fast, anxiety rising in her body together with bile as she imagined treating one of her friends.

"No. We caught one of Atef's men but he got shot in the shoulder while Oliver's team secured him."

"What?" Lynn looked at her with furrowed eyebrows. They had reached the level of the interrogation cells and were walking along a long and clean hallway.

"Oliver found something in Atef's communication log this morning and Liam was able to locate one of his men in an apartment in Washington. Looks like they were planning an attack here soon," Marta explained after they came to a halt in front of one of the interrogation cells.

"Okay, wow. When did that all happen?" Lynn looked at her watch and realized it was later than she had thought.

"Woaaaaah," she added, looking at Marta in shock and slowly remembered what had happened yesterday.

"You needed a good sleep. Let's talk about this later, okay. Abdul is already in there. Oliver, Butch, and I are waiting in the observation room. Turn around and look in the mirror if you need our help. Understood?"

"Yes, Marta. Thank you."

Marta nodded at her and stepped towards the door next to the one Lynn was standing in front of. The doctor took a deep breath and saw her friend enter the observation room. Then she placed her ID card on the lock of the room, saw the light turn green and entered the interrogation cell.

The terrorist was sitting on a metal chair, his hands cuffed with a long chain to a ring in the middle of the table. This gave him a little range of movement without being able to attack any Agents that were interrogating him. His face was slightly furrowed in pain and Lynn saw immediately that the wound was bleeding more than she liked to see. How long had he been sitting there? Bleeding and in pain? He was still human after all.

"Hello. My name is Doctor Summers and I'm going to treat your wound."

The man remained silent, only nodding slightly at the doctor. She placed the emergency pack on the floor next to him, pulled rubber gloves over her hands, and grabbed the stuff she needed. Then she stepped towards him.

"I need to cut the sleeve of your shirt to access the wound," she explained to him and waited for his nod before she went to work on his wound. There was an exit wound on the back of his shoulder, which was good, but she still needed to stitch it together or he wouldn't stop bleeding.

After explaining this to him, Lynn took her time and stitched the wounds on the front and the back of his shoulder. After she was done she placed dressings on top of both of the wounds.

"So, it's all done. You'll need to wear a sling for the next few days to prevent the wounds from opening up again. I don't have one with me but I'll bring you one. Okay?" She smiled at him.

The man placed his arm in a recovery position in front of his stomach, resting the hand right above the pocket of his pants.

Instead of smiling at Lynn he looked past her and right into the mirror. A smile appeared on his face and something shimmered behind his eyes.

Nate, who watched the interrogation cell intensely, suddenly had a very bad gut feeling.

# One more smile

**August 13th, 2022**

The scene in front of Nate happened in slow motion. One second he watched as Lynn stitched the wound on the man's shoulder and the next the terrorist leaned forward and stabbed Lynn's body several times. The man had grabbed a knife out of the pocket of his pants, although they had checked him for any weapons. Nate had no idea how the hell he was able to hide it.

He was forced to watch the love of his life stumble back a little before her hands touched her stomach to check for injuries. She was obviously in shock, and so were Nate, Oliver and Marta.

A loud tinnitus filled his ears, pushing away every other sound. The moment Lynn raised her hands from her stomach to reveal them stained in blood, Nate could only feel one emotion: fear.

"Oh God." Marta was the first one to react.

"Call an ambulance," Oliver whispered in a shockingly low voice before he started to run out of the observation room and into the interrogation cell.

Nate wasn't able to move.

Nate wasn't able to speak.

All he could do was watch Lynn's eyes widen in shock while she turned her face around and directly into the mirror. Although she didn't know where Nate was exactly standing, her eyes met his in an instant and he could see the confusion in them, paired with pure fear.

It was like the world around them was frozen while their gazes were locked and they communicated without even saying a word.

"Butch."

Marta's voice sounded like she was standing miles away. She needed to shake his shoulder for him to break his gaze from Lynn's.

Nate was dizzy, his body heavy like it was made of solid rock and he would never be able to move his legs again. His heart dropped so much that he expected it to fall out of his chest and onto the floor beneath him. At the same time his chest was burning. The pain was almost unbearable until he realized that it was his body screaming for oxygen. He hadn't even noticed that he was holding his breath. He allowed his lungs to fill with fresh air again and the pain in his breast subsided almost immediately.

While taking another breath he saw Oliver storm into the room and point his gun towards the terrorist, who was smiling widely while still sitting on the metal chair.

"Butch," Marta repeated and slowly Nate turned his head to look at the woman standing next to him.

His lips were parted but no sound escaped his mouth. He just looked at her while his veins were filled with ice.

"She needs you now. Keep it together."

Marta placed one of her palms on Nate's shaking shoulder. He was oblivious to the fact that his whole body was trembling.

Marta stood next to him with her phone in her hand. The call was still active and an emergency operator was giving some instructions but Nate didn't listen to the man on the phone. All he had heard were Marta's words.

*She needs you now.*

They kicked his senses back to life again and he managed to take a deep breath and move his legs. Out of the room, around the corner and into the interrogation cell. A second later he found himself next to Lynn, carefully placing his palm on her upper arm.

She turned her head to look at him and he could see her eyes still wide, her eyebrows slightly furrowed in shock and confusion, and her mouth parted. She held her blood-stained hands palms up in his direction, as if she wanted to show them to him.

Wanted to show him that something wasn't as it supposed to be, but she didn't understand what exactly it was.

"Nate," she whispered.

Tears gathered in her eyes, making the chestnut color shine stronger than ever before.

"I know, darling. I'm here," he answered and carefully placed his other hand on her hip.

Nate could feel her starting to shake when shock flooded her body and he strengthened his grip.

The color on her face changed almost in an instant from slightly tanned to almost ash-gray and Nate knew that she was about to collapse in his arms.

"Darling, you need to lay down, okay?" he carefully said, guiding her body towards the floor.

"But I'm fine," Lynn responded.

She was sitting now, Nate kneeling by her side and never removing his hands from her body.

Their eyes locked with each other, glimmering, and full of love.

He tried to push her upper body down so that she was lying completely flat, but she protested.

"I'm fine."

"Darling. You were stabbed," he carefully whispered and could see her open her mouth but without saying anything she closed it again, broke the gaze with Nate and let her eyes wander down her body.

With shaking hands she touched her stomach once more and inhaled sharply. Then she raised her gaze again and with tears now streaming down her face she looked at Nate.

"I was stabbed."

"Yes, darling, but it's going to be okay. The ambulance is on its way and Tia and Birdie are as well. It's all going to be okay."

He tried to assure her but also himself. He really needed to tell himself that everything was going to be okay because if not he knew he would die.

"I was stabbed," Lynn repeated over and over again, obviously still in shock.

Nate managed to finally push her upper body down into a lying position while she continued her mumbling.

"Lynn."

She was looking everywhere and nowhere, her gaze wandering around the room while she still mumbled the word "stabbed" over and over again.

"Lynn," he now said with a louder voice, making her quickly turn her head to look at him.

Her irises contracted a little when she tried to focus on him.

"There you are. I need to put pressure on the wound. This will hurt, okay?"

Lynn nodded in response while her eyes were still pointed towards him but Nate needed to break their gaze. He knew that he needed to hurt her while trying to save her life and he couldn't look into her face. He couldn't see her face the moment he hurt her. He just couldn't.

Lynn's t-shirt was completely soaked with her blood by now and he couldn't see where the stab wounds were. He grabbed the hem of her shirt and pulled it towards her breasts.

There was so much blood.

He couldn't see where it was all coming from, so with a swift movement of his hand he tried to wipe the blood away.

Lynn hissed in response.

It was the first time after being stabbed that she actually seemed to feel the pain, that her body was able to react properly. Nate was relieved as with her solely being in shock it was hard to see if her condition was changing, although he didn't like that she would feel the pain full force now.

He looked at her stomach and a chill ran down his spine. He could see three stab wounds on her right side. All of them bloody and deep.

The first one was right underneath her rib cage, the second one slightly underneath the first one and the third much lower. Right above her pelvis. They were too far apart for him to be able to put pressure on them simultaneously with one hand, so he placed the palm of his left hand on the two wounds on top and the right palm on the one above her pelvic bone.

"Ahhh, that hurts," Lynn cried out and hearing her high-pitched voice followed by a loud sob broke Nate's heart.

"I know, darling. I have to apply pressure to stop the bleeding," Nate responded with his gaze fixed on his hands.

He couldn't look at her.

"Honey, you hurt me. Please stop. Don't hurt me. Please," Lynn whimpered, but Nate tried to focus on the only thing he needed to do now; applying pressure to her wounds, trying to save her life until the EMTs arrived. He leaned in even more when he saw blood still seeping through his fingers.

Lynn let out something between a cry and a scream and Nate's heart crumbled again. He felt Lynn stiffen underneath his hands, but that didn't stop him from pressing down.

"Stop. Please. It hurts," she groaned.

Her voice broke and he knew that she was crying but he still couldn't look at her. His own tears made his vision blurry. He could see them dripping from his chin onto Lynn's stomach, where they split into tinier drops that spread in different directions.

For moments it was only Lynn's pleas of him to stop, her whimpers of pain, and the constant sound of his tears dripping onto her stomach while his hands never left her wounds. Where were Tia and Birdie? He really needed professional support here.

Suddenly they heard noises from outside of the room, growing louder with every passing moment.

It was the first time that Nate had raised his head and looked around him. All that time he'd been solely focused on Lynn and hadn't even noticed what was happening around them.

The terrorist was gone, so were the others. He turned his head in confusion but couldn't see Oliver or Marta inside the interrogation cell.

"Almost there!" Nate swore it was Oliver's voice, but his still-shocked brain wouldn't allow him to understand what was going on.

Only when Oliver and Marta wheeled a gurney into the interrogation cell did Nate allow himself to breath and feel relief.

The ambulance had arrived and finally someone was really capable of helping the love of his life.

But something felt off.

There were no EMTs following Marta and Oliver.

"Get her on the gurney, Butch!" Oliver practically screamed at his best friend.

"The ambulance?" Nate asked, confused but Marta shook her head.

"No time for explanations. We need to get her into the OR as soon as possible," Marta responded and Nate nodded.

For a second he pulled back his hands and grabbed Lynn's shoulders instead. Oliver sprinted to her feet and grabbed her ankles.

In a swift movement they lifted Lynn's small body and placed it on the gurney next to them. She left a huge puddle of blood on the floor and Nate almost slipped on it, while he rounded the gurney to apply pressure again.

"Where are we going?" Lynn was semi-conscious by now. The blood loss had taken a toll on her and she wasn't able to understand what was going on around her.

"To the med-bay, sweetie. You gotta get patched up." Marta smiled at the woman lying on the moving gurney.

Lynn weakly smiled back at her, her eyes half closed and her mind fuzzy.

"Stop!" Nate suddenly exclaimed and Oliver stopped the gurney immediately.

"What's going on, Butch?" Marta asked, confused.

"I can't put enough pressure on it while we're moving. Give me a second," the man with the ocean-blue eyes responded before hopping on the gurney.

Oliver raised his eyebrow at his best friend. Nate placed himself on Lynn's lap and leaned forward to apply pressure again. It was much easier when he was on the gurney as well and with the amount of blood Lynn had already lost, he needed to prevent her losing more.

Oliver continued to push the gurney and they soon found themselves in the elevator. Thankfully it was only a short ride from the first to the second floor.

During their elevator ride Lynn slipped in and out of consciousness and Marta slapped her cheek a few times.

Lynn needed to stay awake to help her blood pressure remain elevated. It was also easier to examine her breathing when she was still awake, something Marta needed to know as she knew she would panic if she saw one of her close friends stop breathing right in front of her.

Was it selfish? Sure, but they all tried their best to keep Lynn alive until she was in the OR and in professional hands.

With a loud "ding" the door opened again and Oliver pushed the gurney towards the med-bay. Nate pressed his upper body down while they were walking through the door, his hands never leaving Lynn's wounds.

Tia was already waiting for their arrival. The nurse was standing next to the counter and screamed,

"Get her into OR1!"

Oliver didn't know where that was but he pushed the gurney into the hallway that led towards the ORs.

"On the right!" He heard Tia scream behind him and he maneuvered the gurney into the room on their right.

It was a small, square room with a gurney in the middle and a lot of medical equipment surrounding them. On the wall opposite the entrance was a huge sliding door. Through a small window Oliver could see two people rushing around in the OR, preparing everything for Lynn's arrival.

Nate, who was still on top of Lynn, let his gaze wander around until he saw Tia storm into the room. He was confused.

Confused why the hell they weren't on the way to the hospital.

Confused who was supposed to operate on Lynn.

"Agent Sheppard, you need to get off the gurney. I need to prepare Lynn for the surgery," Tia said, friendly but demanding.

"But I have to apply pressure," Nate responded.

He fixed his gaze with Tia. He had a fearful frown on his face and tears never stopped running down his cheeks.

"I know but now it's more important that I prepare her for surgery and we get her into the OR," Tia argued, sounding more desperate than before.

"Butch, come on," Oliver said, trying to help Tia get Nate off the gurney.

"Thirty seconds. Can I have thirty more seconds?" Nate sobbed.

"Agent Sheppard..."

"Please. Only thirty seconds."

Tia saw the desperation in his face, the trembling lower lip and the little waterfalls of tears.

"Okay. Thirty seconds," Tia sighed while shooing Oliver and Marta out of the room.

Then she went to a cabinet on the side of the room and prepared a few syringes. Nate jumped off the gurney and walked towards Lynn's head.

"Lynn. Darling," Nate started.

He raised one of his blood-stained hands to her cheek. Her eyes fluttered open a little and she looked at him the best she could. Nate started to draw small circles with his thumb and felt her leaning her head into his touch.

He didn't even know if she was able to process what he was about to tell her, but he needed to do it anyway. In case she wouldn't make it...

"I love you, okay? Everything's gonna be okay. You'll push through this and then I'll bring you breakfast to bed every damn day. I promise. I just need you to know that I need to see your smile again. I need to see just one more smile of yours, okay? Please stay with me. Don't leave me alone. I can't do this alone. I need you. I love you. Ever since we shared that first orange juice. I love you and nothing in this world can change that."

Nate struggled to keep his emotions at bay. Just a few more seconds then he would allow himself to fall apart.

"I. Love. You."

He placed a kiss on her forehead with every word and a last one on her nose.

"I love you too, Nate," Lynn whispered barely audible but it was all Nate needed to hear at that moment. No matter what happened over the next few hours she loved him and she knew that he loved her, too.

"Agent Sheppard, I really need to prepare her now," Tia said harshly and Nate looked at her before he nodded.

"I'll be by your side when you wake up, darling," he whispered towards Lynn before stepping out of the room.

Tia closed the door behind him.

Nate stared at the closed door in front of him when he suddenly felt a large hand on his shoulder.

"She's gonna be okay. She's a fighter," Oliver's voice sounded behind him.

In that moment Nate allowed himself to be vulnerable for the first time, allowed himself to realize that there was the chance that Lynn wouldn't make it and that he'd said "I love you" to her for the last time.

Nate's stomach turned and his legs gave up. He crumpled to the floor and let out a loud and desperate whine while pressing his hands onto his face.

They were still full of blood. Lynn's blood.

Oliver was shocked to see his best friend collapse right in front of his eyes, so he quickly went down on his knees and placed his hand on Nate's back.

"I can't lose her. Oh God, I can't lose her." Nate sobbed, his body shaking heavily with every wave of panic, fear and sadness.

"You won't, Butch."

"I just need to see her smile again. I need her smile to survive. It's the fuel for my heart."

# Stay with me

**August 13th, 2022**

Oliver's slight snore was heard in the waiting area of the med-bay. It had been more than three hours since Lynn had been taken into surgery and they hadn't heard anything from the OR yet.

After Nate's breakdown Oliver had led him to the bathroom to clean the blood off his face and hands and then here, where Marta was already waiting.

The Deputy Director had explained that the emergency operator on the phone suggested they call their on-call doctor Toby, so that he could perform surgery on-site. With the severity of Lynn' injuries and all the blood she had lost, it was uncertain if she would have survived the drive to the hospital. So Marta called Toby who arrived within fifteen minutes and started to prepare the OR together with Tia and Birdie. The female doctor was lying on an operating table in the OR ten minutes later and Toby immediately started to open up her abdomen to stop the internal bleeding.

It was Lynn's only chance of survival.

None of them dared to say it out loud but they all knew.

Now, three hours after Toby took his scalpel in hand, Marta, Nate and Oliver were sitting, waiting for any news out of the OR, hoping that it would be good. Well, not all of them, as Oliver had managed to fall asleep in the most uncomfortable-looking position with his head on Marta's lap. She carefully caressed her finger through Oliver's blond hair while she watched Nate sitting on the other side of the room. His head was in his hands, elbows resting on his thighs while he watched the floor in front of him, as if it were the most interesting thing in the world.

It was a rare sight from over the last three hours. Most of the time he'd been pacing around the room, mumbling to himself and the others in a desperate attempt not to fall apart again. He probably looked insane and maybe he was.

Watching the love of his life bleed out right in front of him had catapulted Nate into a mental state that he'd never been in before.

The moment he visualized Lynn's pale face again, his tears started to fall, dripping through the gap in his thighs and onto the linoleum underneath his feet.

"Butch," Marta said quietly, but concern lay heavy in her voice when she saw him crying again.

The brunet man raised his head to lock his red and puffy eyes with Marta's honey-colored ones.

Marta had never seen him so broken, nor had Oliver and he was the one who'd found him after az-Zawahiri had tortured him for three months. Yes, back then he had been mentally and physically destroyed, being in a medically induced coma for two weeks.

But this was different.

This was a different kind of broken.

"She's going to be okay. I know it," Marta added when she saw the empty look in Nate's eyes. as if his body was only a shell and his soul had left to be with Lynn.

"Why are they not done yet? They should be done, shouldn't they?" His jaw trembled while he mumbled into his hands and Marta needed to concentrate to understand his words.

"I don't know, Butch. I'm not a doctor but maybe that's a good sign. The longer they need to help her, the better she will be after the surgery."

"You and I both know that's utter bullshit," he sighed in response, pressing his palms to his thighs and rising to his feet.

He couldn't sit still anymore. His mind was driving him crazy, the demons telling him about all the worst-case scenarios that could happen. It became harder and harder for him to ignore them and believe in Toby, believe that Toby was able to save Lynn so that he would see her smile again. Would hold her in his arms again. Smell the peach of her perfume and feel her hot skin under his lips.

"I wish I could switch positions with her," he said to himself, but of course Marta had heard him.

"What do you mean?" she asked confused while watching Nate pacing up and down the waiting area again.

"I wish I was the one lying on the operating table right now. She doesn't deserve this. All that pain. It's not fair."

Nate punched his clenched fist against the wall with so much power that he left a small dent in the white surface. It hurt like hell so he grabbed the injured left fist with his other hand and rubbed his fingertips over the skin that had made contact with the wall.

He hissed in pain before another sigh left his mouth.

"Are you okay?" Oliver asked with furrowed brows.

He had almost fallen off Marta's lap the moment Nate punched the wall. It was an old habit from their time serving together. He had always been a light sleeper but after joining the SEALs they were trained to always be ready to fight. Nate used to be that way too.

Until the kidnapping and torture that left him with nightmares.

Nightmares that appeared way too realistic and kept him in the dream no matter what happened around him.

"Ye- Yeah. It only hurts like a bitch. It's probably nothing," Nate responded with his eyebrows still furrowed in pain.

Oliver quickly looked at Marta who simply shrugged her shoulders before he responded.

"Maybe you should let Toby check your hand if it still hurts later."

"You don't think Toby has more important things to do right now, like saving Lynn's life?" Nate hissed at his best friend.

His eyebrows were knit together, his lips in a thin line, and his injured hand clenched into a fist again. He didn't even feel the pain anymore while his skin was burning.

"Come on, pal. That's not what I was trying to say. I was just worried you'd broken your hand or something."

Nate's face dropped and from one second to the next his anger was gone. Oliver was right. His reaction was exaggerated and it wasn't fair. His best friend and Marta had been by his side since the moment he was shoved out of the OR. Since the moment he had his breakdown.

"I'm sorry," Nate mumbled, his gaze wandered down to the floor again.

He let himself collapse onto the chair, covering his face with his palms. The tears had started to fall again and his shoulders were shaking with every sob.

Oliver quickly sat next to his friend and wrapped his arm around his upper body. Marta watched the two best friends with tears glistering in her own eyes.

This whole situation was just so fucked up.

"I'm so scared," Nate mumbled into his shaking hands.

Oliver tried to assure him while rubbing his hand over the top of his back, but it didn't work.

"Everything's going to be okay. She's strong, she's in a good physical state and she's a fighter," the blond Agent said.

Marta had risen from her feet as well and knelt in front of Nate. She placed her hands on his thighs.

"Butch, look at me."

The brunet man with the ocean-blue eyes did as he was told.

"It's Lynn we're talking about. The woman that didn't stop trying to help you with your nightmares even after you hurt her. The woman that lost her sister and still managed to find her happiness again. Because of you. She was so happy the past few months. Only because of you. She would never leave you right now."

It was the first time that someone other than Lynn was able to calm the demons in Nate's mind. The first time he didn't fall into the devastating and destructive chaos that mostly ended with a panic attack.

Maybe Marta was right. Lynn wouldn't leave him now. Not when he was finally willing to give their relationship a real chance.

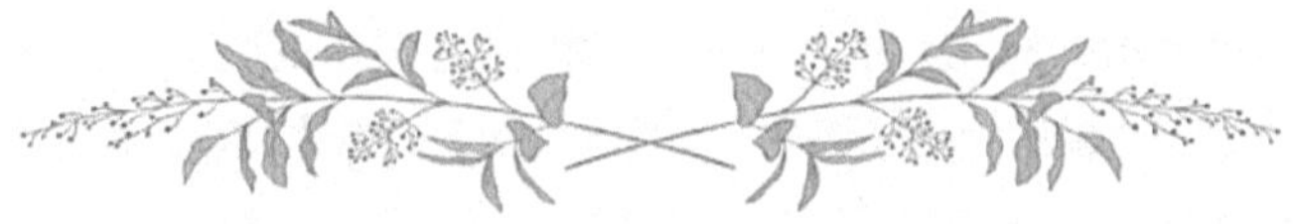

"Why the hell won't it stop bleeding," Toby shouted through the operating theater.

He had already closed the stab wound on Lynn's lower abdomen. Thankfully it had missed the large intestine so he was able to stitch it back together pretty easily. It would limit Lynn's movements a lot because it was a nasty position but at least it was nothing severe.

The two stab wounds on the upper right side were way more serious. They had both punctured her liver and Toby was currently trying to stop the bleeding.

Lynn had already lost so much blood and they were trying to get as much of it back into her as they could via an IV but it was still a fight against the clock. It was imperative that Toby stop the bleeding in her abdomen soon.

With forceps in his hand he carefully lifted the liver to check for other wounds beneath it. He had closed one of the holes with stitches but out of the other one blood seeped like lava from a volcano.

"Shit. Tia, can you suction off some of the blood? I can't see anything," he mumbled and Tia immediately held the suction inside Lynn's abdomen.

The heart rate monitor next to the operating table started to change its beeping, indicating that something wasn't the way it was supposed to be. Toby raised his gaze from the liver in front of him to the monitor and observed it for a few seconds.

"Toby," Birdie said with a tremble in her voice.

"Give her some adrenaline. That should stabilize her," Toby responded, focusing again on checking for other wounds than the obvious ones in her liver.

He cursed under his breath while Tia tried to give him a clear view with the suction tube.

Birdie grabbed a syringe and a bottle with liquid adrenaline in it. She filled the syringe and injected the medicine through the IV on top of Lynn's hand. Her eyes watched the heart rate monitor but instead of stabilizing, her heartbeat became slower and slower.

"It's not working," she said with a slight panic in her voice.

The edge of the monitor started to blink with bright red lights and Toby was forced to stop again.

"It's the blood loss. She is losing more than we can pump back into her. She's hypovolemic."

Toby's hands were trembling a little while he tried to think of a strategy to save Lynn's life. The doctor closed his eyes and steadied his breathing, ignoring the beeping and blinking of the heart rate monitor as well as Tia's and Birdie's words full of fear and panic.

They were all professionals but it was always different if you had someone on your table that you knew.

One final deep breath and Toby opened his eyes again.

"I'm just going to stitch the wound back together and then we close her. I'm not 100% sure if there are other veins or arteries damaged but she doesn't have any more time. It doesn't look like there are other casualties though," he said as calmly as possible before locking his gaze with Tia.

She nodded in response before grabbing the surgical needle and sutures to give to Toby. He quickly closed the second wound on Lynn's liver but before he was able to start closing her skin completely the heart rate monitor showed a code blue.

Lynn's heart wasn't beating anymore.

"Shit," Toby hissed, placing the needle and suture on a metal table next to him before placing his hands on Lynn's bare chest to start compressions.

"Preparing another shot of adrenaline, increasing the blood flow on the blood bag into the IV," Birdie said while Toby was still compressing Lynn's chest.

Up and down.

Up and down.

"Twenty-eight, twenty-nine, thirty." Toby panted.

CPR was physically really exhausting, like a full body workout.

Tia was standing next to Lynn's head with an Ambu bag in her hand.

Toby detached Lynn's ventilator and attached the Ambu bag instead so that Tia was able to press a larger volume of oxygen into Lynn's lungs in between his chest compressions.

One.

Two.

Tia nodded at Toby who continued pressing on Lynn's chest. It wasn't ideal that she had a big open wound on the right side of her chest and Toby had to be very careful while compressing. He didn't want the freshly closed wounds to open again.

"Give her some Amiodaron and prepare the defibrillator," he shouted towards Birdie.

Sweat was covering his forehead when he finished the second round of chest compressions. Tia squoze the Ambu bag twice again and Birdie wheeled a defibrillator on a small table next to Toby.

He quickly grabbed the external pads of the machine and placed them on Lynn's upper body. The left pad on Lynn's right shoulder and the right one under her left rib cage.

"Clear!" Toby shouted and Tia and Birdie raised their hands in front of their bodies before Toby pushed the button on the machine and shot an electroshock through Lynn's fragile body.

They saw her jolt upward, before all three of them fixed their gazes on the heart rate monitor.

"Stay with me, Lynn," Toby whispered.

Thankfully her heart started to beat again.

"Get more fluids in her system, prepare another bag of blood and give her some sodium bicarbonate. I'll check the stitches real quick and then close her abdomen. We gotta get her in an ICU bed and let her body rest as much as possible," Toby instructed.

That was too close.

He didn't have time to think about the "what if's" right now as he needed to finish the surgery.

Lynn was still not out of danger.

The two wounds looked good and hadn't opened again so Toby could finally check for other wounds around the liver, while Tia cleared the remaining blood from around it. Thankfully no new blood could be seen but Toby double-checked the area before he was 100% sure that Lynn didn't have another wound. Finally he decided to close her completely. With steady movements of his hands he moved the needle through her skin and closed the wound with 15 stitches.

Afterwards Tia placed a huge dressing on top of it before she and Toby moved to Lynn's head and inserted a central venous catheter in the side of her neck. This was for all the medicine her body would need to heal after this traumatic event.

Birdie had already left the operation room while Toby was still sewing to prepare a heart rate monitor, a saturation monitor including a ventilator, and multiple syringe drivers. She practically turned a regular patient room into an ICU.

"I think we've prepared her as best as we can. Now it's her job to heal," Toby said to Tia, before carefully brushing his thumb over Lynn's cheek.

He had never seen his friend in such a miserable state and his stomach was about to turn. He quickly ran to the trash can and emptied his stomach inside it.

Tia watched him concerned but when Toby gave her a thumbs up she continued to prepare the gurney where Lynn was lying to wheel it out of the OR and into her room.

It was the first time in five hours that Toby's body and mind fully realized what had just happened. That he'd had one of his best friends on the operating table and that she'd flatlined during the surgery. That he'd needed to quickly finish the surgery without being completely sure he didn't miss anything, because Lynn's body wasn't able to take it any longer.

It was the first moment Toby realized that Lynn almost died under his watch. That it was still not certain that she would survive.

And that he had to tell Nate.

# Despair

**August 13th, 2022**

Oliver and Nate were still sitting next to each other in the waiting area, a thick tension lingering between them. Neither had said a word in over half an hour because there wasn't much to say. Nate had made it very clear that he didn't want the whole "she's going to be fine" speech and Marta's assuring words had only lasted for a couple minutes. Long enough to prevent him going completely insane, but not long enough for him to not be scared and concerned the entire time.

Marta was sitting on a chair on the wall in front of them, playing Candy Crush on her phone. It was already over five hours since they had last seen or heard from Lynn. Since the moment the door closed in front of Nate.

Five hours of fear and despair but also hope and praying.

Five hours since the moment nobody knew if Lynn would survive or not.

When the door to the hallway with the operating theaters opened, all three Agents jumped to their feet and looked at the man who entered with expectation written all over their faces.

"She's alive," Toby immediately said and could see the tension fall from their shoulders.

A single tear slid down Nate's face and he let out the breath that he was holding.

"But..." the doctor started to continue before stopping again.

He needed to take a deep breath. It wasn't easy for him either. Lynn was one of his best friends.

He'd known her way longer than the others although he had to admit that Nate was probably suffering the most out of all of them.

"She's still not out of danger. She lost a lot of blood and she flatlined during the surgery."

"What?" Nate croaked.

His skin turned pale and his legs started to tremble. Oliver saw it and, before Nate collapsed, he guided his best friend back to the chair so that he could sit down. Both of Nate's hands were shaking like branches in a storm and Oliver alternated his gaze from Nate to Toby with furrowed brows.

The doctor cleared his throat and stepped towards the two Agents. Nate's eyes were half closed and he had trouble staying conscious. This was all too much for his body.

Toby grabbed his wrist and quickly checked Nate's pulse with a concerned frown on his face. The moment he touched the bruise on the outside of Nate's hand, the Agent hissed in pain. Toby turned the hand around and looked at the swollen and bruised skin.

"What the hell happened to your hand?" he asked, shocked.

"Punched a wall," Nate mumbled, his eyes now fully closed while he tried to focus on his breathing.

He was struggling to stay conscious and prevent the upcoming panic attack.

"We should take an x-ray. Maybe it's broken," Toby suggested and Oliver nodded at him. He had suspected that hours ago.

"Toby," Nate hissed while opening his eyes and staring into Toby's brown ones.

Anger was shining behind the ocean-blue eyes of the Agent and the doctor let go of his hand immediately.

"Stop talking about stuff that's not important and let us know about Lynn," Nate added.

"Ye- Yeah. I'm sorry. She flatlined during the surgery but we were able to get her back. Her body was so weak that I had to finish the surgery early. I've closed all three wounds. Two of them punctured her liver but thankfully missed the lung. I wasn't sure of that because of the location of the wounds. I didn't have time to check whether she had additional injuries. We need to give her body time to rest and monitor her closely."

"Can I see her?" Tears brimmed in his eyes and Toby could see relief wash over Nate's face the moment he nodded.

"Tia and Birdie are getting her to her room now. As soon as she's settled, you can see her."

"Thank you so much, Doc. I don't know what would have happened if you weren't here so fast," Marta said and Toby turned around to look at her with a shy smile on his face.

The door behind them opened again and an exhausted looking Tia entered the area.

"She's all settled," she almost whispered.

Her eyes looked heavy and she was paler than usual. Toby smiled at her, before stepping in front of her and placing his palms on both of her upper arms.

"You and Birdie get some rest. You did an amazing job in there. I'll look after her," he said in a calming voice.

Tia was only able to nod before the door opened again and Birdie entered the room.

She looked as devastated as Tia.

"I'll try to get 2-3 hours of sleep in and then I'll be back so you can rest, too," Tia responded with a smile on her lips as well.

Toby nodded at her before Tia grabbed Birdie's arm and led her out of the med-bay.

"Ready to see your girl?" Toby said towards Nate, who was impatiently stepping from one leg onto the other.

As caring as the little talk between the doctor and the nurse had been, he was desperate to see Lynn. See that she was indeed still alive and hadn't left him.

"Yes, more than ready," Nate croaked.

It was hard for him to swallow, as if he had cotton balls stuck in his throat.

Before they could head towards Lynn's room, Toby turned around to Marta and Oliver.

"She needs a lot of rest now. That's why it's better for her if only one person visits her at a time. As Butch is her boyfriend, he has the priority card here but you can see her tomorrow."

"Understood. Say Hi to her from us," Marta said towards Nate with a little smile on her face that Nate didn't return.

Finally, after five hours of waiting, he was about to see his girlfriend again. The love of his life.

They entered the hallway to the patients rooms and came to a halt in front of one of them. The door was closed and it didn't have a window in it..

"Butch," Toby said while standing in front of the door, blocking Nate's way.

"I really need to see her, Toby." He almost pleaded.

"I know. Just listen to me real quick."

"Okay." Nate let out the loudest possible sigh.

"It will probably look very scary to you. Lynn is hooked up to different machines that are monitoring her vitals. I also needed to intubate her. She has a central venous catheter on her neck that we need to get all the drugs in her system," Toby explained in a calm voice.

"She's in a coma?" Nate's face fell and there was sadness glimmering behind his puffy eyes.

He really wanted to hear her voice. He needed it.

"Yes. Her body needs to focus on healing. She lost so much blood and the damage to her liver was severe. We need to give her time."

Nate turned his head to stare at the wall next to him. A few tears escaped his eyes and slid down his cheeks, although he had tried so hard to not cry again.

He wanted to be strong for Lynn.

He wanted to be her rock while trying to do everything he could so that she could recover as fast and best as possible but this situation was all too familiar. Almost twelve years ago he was the one laying in a coma. He was the one lying in the hospital bed, his best friend by his side, hoping and praying he would wake up.

Now Nate was standing here, in the same miserable situation as Oliver had been back then and hell, he had never been more useless than at this moment.

"Okay," was the only thing he managed to say.

"Are you ready?" Toby asked while placing his hand on Nate's upper arm.

The Agent flinched a little, then turned his head and nodded at Toby.

The moment Toby opened the door and revealed Lynn lying in the hospital bed, surrounded by machines and monitors, Nate's heart shattered into million pieces. This was a moment that would haunt him for the rest of his life.

Tia and Birdie had placed a chair next to the bed that looked so large in comparison to the small body of the brunette woman inside it. Nate halted in his movement and observed his girlfriend for a moment longer. Shock rose inside his chest and his heart weighed a tonne. He had trouble breathing, as if someone had wrapped a rope around his chest way too tight. The voices inside of his mind became louder.

This must be another nightmare.

This can't be reality.

Maybe, if he tried really hard, he would just wake up and find Lynn peacefully sleeping next to him. He would grab her face and place hundreds of kisses over it, and he would tell her how much he loved her and that he never wanted to spend a single day without her.

It took Nate tremendous effort to get his body moving but the entered the room and walked straight towards the chair. His eyes never left Lynn's pale face. He frowned when he noticed the tube coming out of her throat. He had known that it would be there but seeing it in reality hit differently.

Lynn didn't look like a living human being. With tubes coming out of her throat, the catheter attached to her neck and another IV on her hand as well as dozens of cables that observed her vitals like heartbeat and oxygen saturation. If Nate hadn't heard the steady beeping of the monitor next to Lynn's head, he would have thought she was dead.

Maybe she was.

Only the machines kept her alive at the moment.

He stared at said machines around him before collapsing on the chair he was currently standing in front of. He hadn't even noticed the tears that were streaming down his face. With trembling hands he reached out to grab Lynn's small and fragile hand but he stopped before his fingertips touched the back of it. He turned his head to look at Toby, waiting for a silent permission that he was allowed to touch her.

That he wouldn't break her.

Toby gave him a sad smile and a nod and Nate extended his hand again and finally touched Lynn's.

Normally, when he touched her hand, the warmth of it crawled through his arm and directly to his heart. It had been like that since the first time she'd ever touched him and it hadn't changed ever. Nate even felt addicted to the warmth that Lynn radiated and that was the main thing that calmed the demons in his mind.

Now her hand was cold. Too cold.

He gently brushed his thumb across her pale skin while he stared at her beautiful face. He would give anything to see her chestnut eyes again. To see her smile and reassure him that everything was going to be okay. He didn't like it when Oliver and Marta said that to him earlier but he would do anything to hear those exact words out of Lynn's mouth right now.

"Her vitals look good but I'm monitoring her very closely." Toby's voice was heard in the room, bringing Nate back to reality.

He didn't want to, but Nate raised his head to fix his gaze on a still-smiling Toby.

"How long?" Nate asked.

"I can't tell you. It depends how fast her body recovers. We're trying to give her as much blood as possible to replace the pints that she lost but she still needs time. Maybe a day or two, maybe longer," Toby sighed.

He didn't like that either. He knew that every day in a coma meant a longer recovery. Muscle wastage was especially a risk.

"Toby?" Nate's voice was barely louder than a whisper, the tone serious with a little tent of fear vibrating with it.

"Yes?"

"What is the likelihood that she survives and makes a full recovery?"

Toby needed to swallow. He'd expected that question, actually he'd expected it the moment he'd told Nate that Lynn still wasn't out of danger.

"Butch..." he started, trying to avoid answering the question directly.

"What is the likelihood?" Nate repeated with a sterner voice this time.

His gaze bored into Toby while his hand still heldLynn's.

"I can't tell you," Toby sighed.

"You can't or you don't want to?"

"I... both. The damage on the liver was severe but we were able to stop the bleeding just in time."

"But?" Nate asked.

Toby didn't answer right away so Nate repeated his question.

"Literally anything can happen right now. All we can do is monitor her as best as we can so that we can intervene if her condition worsens again."

"I just want her to be fine again," Nate sobbed and Toby noticed that he had started to cry again.

Properly this time. Not only tears streaming down his face. His body was shaken by waves of sadness while he pulled Lynn's hand towards his face to place kisses on it. He was constantly sobbing between the kisses, his tears covering Lynn's small hand.

Nate was falling apart and Toby's eyes brimmed with tears as well. There was nothing they could do at that moment. All they could do was wait. And it drove them both nuts.

"I know, Butch. Me, too," Toby said sadly.

After a few moments of silence and Toby checking the monitors as well as the syringe drivers, he excused himself and left the room.

Nate had realized it, although his eyes were closed and he held Lynn's hand still in front of his face. From time to time he placed another gentle kiss on it, while he prayed for her to be fine again soon.

He took another deep breath and opened his eyes again. His legs were still weak from all the emotions that were overwhelming his body but he managed to stand and gently caress the back of his hand over Lynn's cheek, careful not to nudge the tube coming out of her mouth.

"Hi darling," he said with so much love in his tone.

His face relaxed and he forced himself to smile. He didn't feel like smiling, especially because her cheeks felt cold too. They weren't supposed to feel cold.

Nate had heard that people lying in a coma were possibly able to hear what he was saying and feel his presence. He hadn't eleven years ago, but that didn't mean that Lynn couldn't.

Maybe she felt that he was there and for that he forced himself to smile at her. Comfort her. Make her feel better.

"You look awful," he chuckled.

It was so out of place and he didn't understand why he'd done it, but he chuckled.

"I'm just messing with you. You look beautiful as always," he said before leaning over the bed and placing a tender but shy kiss on Lynn's forehead.

He was so scared that he would break her even more.

She looked like a porcelain doll, ready to break at the smallest impact. He didn't want to be the reason for that. He stilled in his movement, his face only inches apart from Lynn's. He waited for the familiar peachy scent to reach his nostrils, but it never came.

All he smelled was disinfectant and that was worse than anything else before.

A tear slipped down his cheek and onto Lynn's forehead. He quickly grabbed his thumb and swiped it away, careful to not disturb her peaceful sleep.

But was it a peaceful sleep?

Inside her body every cell fought a brutal war to keep her body alive. If he could listen closely enough, he'd be able to hear her organs scream at each other in frustration and despair. Her body was in shock from the traumatizing experience and had to do all the work to bring Lynn back to life. Yes, the coma might help to shut down every other function so that her body had enough power to fight against the injuries, but it was still a very tough time.

Nate took his place on the chair again and grabbed Lynn's hand with both of his own.

"You need to fight for me, darling. This is the only thing you need to promise me. Fight," he whispered towards her fingers before carefully placing a kiss on each one of them.

"These past five hours have been the worst in my entire life. I'd prefer another three months as az-Zawahiri's hostage, including all the torture, but I never want to experience this again. Sitting and waiting. Helpless. I've never felt so helpless, darling," he sobbed before he remembered he wanted to be her rock.

Well, he failed miserably at that.

For a moment he didn't say a word and watched the line on the heart rate monitor, the only proof that Lynn was still alive. Seeing the constant up and down of the line in combination with the subtle beeping, let Nate slip into a trance.

He didn't know how long he was zoned out, but with a few blinks he came back to reality just to realize that nothing had changed. He was still in this horrible place with the love of his life lying in front of him in a hospital bed.

"I'm scared," he confessed, leaning back in his chair after placing Lynn's hand back on the soft mattress.

"I'm scared to lose you because I can't. I just can't. You're the light in my darkness, the reason I wake up every morning with a smile. I know I've been behaving like a dick over the past days and wasn't exactly the best boyfriend but I promise you that this will change. All you have to do is wake up. Please, Lynn. You need to wake up."

Nate brushed his own hand through his messy and slightly curly brown hair while watching Lynn's face.

For a short moment he expected her to wake up. Like in every romance book or movie. Where the person sitting on the bedside confesses their love and the one in the coma suddenly awakens and tells them that they love them too. That's how he wished it would have been now.

But Lynn didn't wake up.

Actually even if she wanted, she wouldn't have been able to. Toby had given her strong sedatives so it was physically impossible for her to wake up now, no matter how heartbreaking Nate's words were.

He laughed when he realized how ridiculous it was to hope for her miracle awakening.

"I'm sorry, I got carried away. What I wanted to say is that I love you, Lynn Summers. I really do. And I hope you heard that I said this to you right before you went under because I want to be sure that in whatever state and place you are right now, you know that I love you."

There were no tears anymore. Nate was convinced he had used them all. All the tears that were stored in his body, used within the last five and a half hours. He raised from his chair, leaned over Lynn again and placed a few tender kisses along her face to underline his previously said words.

"I'll be back later, I promise. Need to let Toby check my hand. To be honest it hurts pretty badly and I think it might be broken. Of course I'd never tell Oliver that he was right, but I know you'd want me to get it checked, so I will. Because I want to be strong for you. I wish you could see me now. Getting medical treatment on my own free will. There's a first for everything."

He ended his monologue with a little chuckle. Obviously a mechanism to cope up with the lingering fear inside of his heart.

The heart that still felt like it was made out of concrete, because the only person that filled it with warmth and love wasn't able to do that at the moment.

"I love you. Don't forget that," he whispered before placing a last kiss on her pale nose.

Nate made his way to the door, turned around once more, smiled a little, and left the room. On his way out of the med-bay he came across the doctor's office.

Lynn's office.

He knocked on the door with his good hand and heard a muffled voice from inside so he opened the door and found

Toby sitting on Lynn's desk, reading a patient's file in front of him.

The doctor looked up and raised both of his eyebrows in confusion when he saw Nate standing in the doorframe.

"Butch. Is everything okay?" he asked.

"Yes, considering the circumstances."

"Good. What can I do for you then?"

"I... Maybe we should do an x-ray of my hand. It hurts more than I like to admit," he mumbled with an insecure frown on his face.

Nate didn't like anything that came with the med-bay, but at least an x-ray wasn't a needle and he knew that even if the hand was broken, he would be okay with getting a cast. After months of working on his fears with Lynn, he was okay with smaller stuff.

"I'm glad you came. Let's get it over as quickly as possible. Follow me," Toby said, rising from his position and walking past Nate.

He turned to his left and headed straight towards the radiology part of the med-bay that contained an x-ray machine as well as an MRI.

Ten minutes later Nate sat on the table in one of the examination rooms while Toby was zooming in and out on the iPad in his hands.

"And?" Nate asked with a mixture of concern, impatience and curiosity in his voice.

Toby sighed and turned on his swivel chair to face Nate.

"Congratulations, you broke your hand. It's not a big fracture actually, only a small crack, but I still need to immobilize the hand with a cast so that it can heal properly."

"Oh shit. Thankfully it's the left hand, as I'm right-handed."

"Yeah. At least that's something..." Toby chuckled.

While Toby prepared the black cast on Nate's left arm, he asked,

"Why did you punch the wall?"

Nate sighed heavily, his lips in a thin line and the jaw clenched. After some moments of silence, he mouthed,

"Despair."

# Soulmates

**August 14th, 2022**

Nate hadn't slept the entire night.

He'd tried. He really had.

He knew that he needed to be fit, strong and rested for Lynn. It'd been 18 hours since she'd come out of surgery. Toby told him that he didn't know how long Lynn needed to be in a coma but there was this slight hope that she could wake up today. This hope was like a flame inside of Nate's dark heart, growing with every minute that passed and giving him a reason to get ready as soon as possible and storm towards the med-bay.

When the automatic door opened in front of him he almost crashed into Marta, who was about to leave the room.

"Wooooah. Butch. Hi. You look terrible by the way," she commented after stepping back a little and pointing on the large black bags underneath Nate's eyes.

"Good morning. Yeah, you too," the brunet man answered.

Marta chuckled a little in response before her face fell into a serious frown again.

"I just visited her," she almost whispered, not able to look into Nate's eyes, but watching the floor underneath their feet instead.

"How is she?"

"Toby said her vitals are still good. No sign that her situation worsened over the night. Which is good."

"But?" Nate asked with a raised eyebrow. He'd known Marta for years and by the way her voice sounded he knew that a "but" was about to come.

"But he won't wake her today. He thinks she's still too unstable. Maybe tomorrow," Marta sighed.

"Maybe tomorrow," Nate repeated with sadness very present in his voice.

"Listen, Butch…" Marta started, but he interrupted her immediately as he raised his hand in front of his chest.

"Save it," he said and was about to walk past Marta and into the med-bay but the Deputy Director placed her palm on Nate's chest and pressed him back into the hallway.

Nate huffed and saw the angry expression on Marta's face.

"No. You listen to me now. Lynn is my friend, too. You're not the only one here who's suffering and going nuts because she's lying in a coma. I was the one to comfort her over the last few days, when you were too much of an idiot and ran away from her again instead of fucking talking to her. I was there. I held her in my arms when she cried for hours because you called off the dinner she was so excited for. Because something in your stupid brain can't accept that being happy with her is a fucking good idea. That you should finally fucking forget that she worked with az-Zawahiri to save her sister. She did it because she didn't see another way to save Ann. Don't you think she feels guilty enough, that we weren't able to be there in time to save Ann? Don't you think she's destroyed enough?"

Marta needed to take a deep breath and Nate used the small break in between her rant, to respond.

"I know that. I've been in therapy sessions with her."

"Then why the fuck are you still behaving like a twelve-year-old?!"

"I am not behaving like a child," Nate said, his voice louder than before and trembling with anger.

His eyebrows knit together while the flame of hope inside his heart was replaced by a raging typhoon of anger.

"Oh yes, you do. If she hadn't been stabbed yesterday, you'd still be acting like a teenager in puberty. One day smiling and kissing her and the next avoiding and ignoring her. That's not how adults solve problems, Butch. That's not how relationships work."

"Listen, I'm trying. I really am!" He screamed at Marta.

"Yeah? I can't see it. Why is it always Lynn who has to suffer so that your stupid brain can finally move on? It needed her to get hurt during your nightmare so that you finally really tried to improve your PTSD, it needed her to suffer after the funeral so that you were finally able to give her a chance and take her on a date. Lynn came and held happiness right in front of your nose and you were too stupid to just accept it."

"You don't understand," Nate responded.

"What do I not understand?"

"It's all because of my trauma and I..."

"Nate Sheppard. You won't use your fucking trauma as an excuse to behave like an asshole. I've been through horrible things in my life and it took me years of hard mental work and patience to get out of my darkness and heal my heart. You can't even imagine how guilt can crush you into pieces.

How it feels when it's your fucking fault that your husband and unborn child died and you weren't able to protect them. Even though the only thing I was supposed to do was keep the fetus in my body alive. That was my only job but I failed and it destroyed me. But do you see me use this as an excuse to behave like a bitch? No. Because one day I decided that I needed to find closure and that I needed to focus on the future. That even with everything that happened to me, I deserved to be happy. Do you even want to be happy or do you simply need drama in your life?"

"Don't you dare say another word," Nate hissed at her with contempt in his voice.

His right index finger pressed in Marta's chest, his face only inches away from hers. He was about to snap and Marta couldn't wait for it to happen.

She was angry at him, and had been for weeks. Not enough sleep and a friend in a coma was enough for her to be right on the edge of her own aggression all the time. This confrontation wasn't supposed to happen but now, as it did, they were both willing to fight with bare hands.

"ENOUGH." Oliver's voice could be heard behind Marta's back.

"Enough. Both of you. Are you fucking serious? Lynn's fighting for her life and you two are trying to rip each other's heads off?"

Nate stepped away from Marta, who turned around to look at her boyfriend.

"Why are you already out? I thought Toby said that you had thirty minutes?" She asked, confused.

Oliver averted his gaze from her but his face showed all that Marta and Nate needed to know.

"What happened?" Nate asked and the bile rose up in his throat.

"Toby said her blood count doesn't look good. I don't know what exactly he meant, but..."

Oliver didn't have a chance to finish his words when Nate stormed past him and towards Lynn's room. Toby was standing in front of it while looking at the file in his hands that showed Lynn's blood count. A phone was laying on the table in front of him. It must be on speaker, as Toby was talking towards it while checking the numbers on the paper over and over again.

"She's in a coma that's why we haven't seen the discoloration of her eyes before. Her skin still looks normal. Well as normal as a coma patient looks like. She's pretty pale, so I thought I'd have seen it right away, but nothing."

Nate stood in front of Toby, his heart beating so loud that for a moment he wasn't able to hear anything else. He pinched the bridge of his nose and tried to focus on the doctor in front of him, listening to what he was talking about to the person on the other end of the line.

*"What about blood pressure and respiration?"* Toby's colleague from the MedStar Washington hospital center asked through the phone.

"She has very low blood pressure, that's why I checked her blood again. As we already have her intubated there's no change in the respiration. Oxygen saturation is also still good."

It was the first time Toby raised his gaze from the paper in front of him and jumped in shock when he saw Nate standing only a few feet away. The Agent's lips were parted, his brows furrowed in concern.

*"Okay. I'd suggest giving her liquid glucose to stabilize the blood pressure. Other than that you can only wait. Prevent opening her up again as long as it's not hundred percent necessary. It's just additional stress for her body."*

Toby nodded a few times in response before he said,

"Thank you, Gary. You've helped me a lot."

*"Call me again if the situation changes. I'll be on-call if you need me for surgery."*

"Thank you again. I really appreciate it."

With that the call ended and Toby let out a loud sigh before he shifted his attention fully on Nate.

"Toby…" he started with a trembling voice.

"Butch, I know that sounded frightening and I'm not gonna lie to you. The situation has worsened. Her liver isn't working the way it should be. But there's still no need to worry or panic."

He reached out his hand to place it on Nate's upper arm, his lips curled upwards into a small smile.

Nate couldn't answer, all his anger gone, that had built inside of his body a few minutes ago. Again it was like he was drowning without even being in the water. His breaths became more and more shallow when his mind dove into the different "what if" scenarios that came the moment he overheard the two doctors talking about Lynn's vitals.

"How's your hand doing?" Toby suddenly asked.

He'd noticed that Nate was about to get a panic attack and he knew he had to distract him.

"Good. I think."

"Can I check the cast real quick?"

"Yeah, sure. But why?" Nate asked, confused.

"Well your hand was pretty swollen yesterday. Sometimes the cast can be too loose when the swelling reduces overnight." Toby answered and grabbed Nate's left arm to observe the black cast.

He took some time to turn the arm around and wiggle Nate's fingers. He didn't need that time to access the cast, he had seen within a few seconds that it still looked good but he tried to distract Nate for a few more minutes before both of them had to steer the conversation back to Lynn and her liver failure.

"It all looks pretty good. Just let me know if the pain increases or something feels odd."

"I will. Thanks, Doc."

A silence lingered between them after the short conversation.

"What's going to happen now?"

"Like my colleague said, we need to give her some more time. I'ill administer some liquid glucose and check her blood every hour. I want to make sure we catch any changes as soon as possible."

"Okay. Can I do anything to help you?" Nate asked.

"Yes. Stay with her. Maybe that will help reduce her stress levels."

That was all Nate needed to hear before he opened the door to Lynn's room, put some disinfectant on his hands, and marched towards the love of his life who was still lying unconscious in the hospital bed.

"Hey darling. Told you I'd come and visit you today."

He smiled at her before placing a kiss on her forehead. Afterwards he collapsed on the chair. Toby followed him inside and stood next to the syringe drivers. He filled one of the empty spots with a syringe he had prepared outside. It was the liquid glucose he was talking about. He attached the syringe to Lynn's central venous catheter so that it could flow into her system quickly and help raise her blood pressure again.

After pushing some buttons on the other syringe drivers to adjust the dose of the medication, Toby patted on Nate's upper back and left the room.

"Just me and you now, darling," he whispered and grabbed Lynn's hand again.

It was still cold.

All he wanted to do was pull her small body into his arms and hold her really tight but with all the machines attached to her body he knew he wouldn't be able to do that without messing things up so he decided to scoot the chair even closer to the bed so that he was able to lean his head on Lynn's upper arm. It was the closest he could get to cuddling with her right now.

"I love you, darling. I'm so sorry that I've been such an asshole the past few days. You didn't deserve it. You deserve someone who treats you like a princess. That appreciates you the way you are and that is willing to let go of everything that is holding him back. I know I'm not that person at the moment, but I promise I'll try. I'll treat you the way you deserve to be treated. I won't be angry again about the whole betrayal thing. I'll finally let the past be the past, and I'll take more therapy sessions to make sure I'll never fall back into that devastating chaos. I'm so sorry that you cried because of me, that I broke your heart by canceling our dinner, ignoring you and avoiding you. I'm so sorry. I'm an idiot sometimes, but I'm your idiot if you let me be."

He turned his head to press a kiss on her shoulder that was covered by a light blue hospital gown.

"I will always love you," he added, snuggling his head closer to her arm and closing his eyes, remembering all the nice moments they'd had together.

The first time he had held her in his arms. After he successfully managed to realize that he had a nightmare. It was one of the turning points in his recovery and one of the first moments the sparks between him and Lynn were apparent for both of them, although back then they didn't realize it right away.

He remembered their first kiss after he opened up to her and told her about his torture. How soft her lips felt on his when she leaned in and connected them. Oh, he'd give anything for her to kiss him right now.

Somewhere in the middle of his nostalgic memories, Nate drifted off into sleep, his temple still connected with Lynn's upper arm. Being with her brought him enough comfort to allow his body to rest. Even if it were just for a short period of time.

When he opened his eyes again, he was confused to begin with. Hearing only the steady beeping of the heart rate monitor, he needed a moment to realize that this wasn't a flashback to his time in the hospital. That it wasn't him lying in the hospital bed.

He was sitting on the chair next to it. Next to Lynn.

He groaned in pain when he sat up again. His back already hated him for the uncomfortable sleeping position and he stretched his arms over his head with a loud sigh. While he rotated his upper body to crack his back he looked at Lynn.

Suddenly all the oxygen was pushed out of his body and his heart stopped beating. A concerned frown appeared on his face while he jumped on his feet.

Lynn's skin had turned slightly yellow.

It looked like these old articles you found in museums. When paper had started yellowing because the lignin reacted to the oxygen in the air.

He quickly grabbed the panic button and pushed it multiple times while his thumb brushed over Lynn's skin. It was cold but sweaty at the same time. That didn't make sense to him. She was fine before he fell asleep. What had happened?

He couldn't even check how long he was asleep, because at that moment Toby burst through the door.

"What's wrong?" he asked.

"Her skin," Nate only managed to say and Toby lips parted the moment he stepped closer and saw the coloration of Lynn's skin.

The doctor grabbed his phone, clicked the first number on the redial list and pressed the speaker button. Then he threw the phone on the bed next to Lynn's hand and walked around the room to grab a tourniquet, a needle and some blood tubes.

*"Toby, what happened?"* A voice came out of the phone.

"Skin yellowing. Within the hour. She was fine the last time I checked on her. Currently drawing some blood to get it checked."

*"Acute liver failure. Does she have any family members living nearby?"*

"Her sister died last year, her father has COPD, and I don't know how good her mother still is. I bet she wouldn't be fit enough for a donation."

*"Any cousins or anything?"*

"I don't know. She doesn't have time for the regular transplant list, Gary."

*"I know. How severe were the stab wounds again?"*

"They only affected the outer parts of the right lobe so I thought it would be fine. There were enough healthy parts left."

*"Her only chance is a partial liver donation from someone around you. Someone nearby. Maybe call her mum and ask if other family members live nearby. And check the mum, too. Maybe she could be a donor."*

Nate was forced to watch Toby draw blood and talk to his colleagues as if he wasn't even in the room. He didn't understand all of the words but "partial liver donation" was something he did understand and that made a shiver run up his spine and his hackles rise.

*"Call me as soon as you have a donor and I'll help you perform the surgeries."*

"Thank you, Gary. I really appreciate your help."

*"Any time, man. Lynn's one of the good ones. She deserves to live."*

Sadness clouded Nate's mind.

Lynn was one of the good ones. Gary was right.

"Test me," Nate suggested.

Toby had handed the blood tubes to Tia who took them to the lab.

"What do you mean?" Toby raised an eyebrow on Nate.

"You know exactly what I mean. Test me to see if I'm able to donate my liver to her."

"Butch... First of all it's a partial liver donation. Means you don't donate your full liver. You need your liver. Without it your body poisons itself and you would die. Also, it's very unlikely that you're fit to be a donor. The likelihood is much higher when we test family members, and don't even think about saying that we're a family here. This is about biology."

"But you said it yourself. She doesn't have many family members. She never mentioned any cousins to me. If this donation is her only chance, please test me. I'm begging you. Please just give it a try." Nate stood right in front of him now, having his right hand placed on Toby's forearm.

"Okay. But don't get your hopes up" Toby sighed before shaking his head in disbelief.

He pointed to the chair and grabbed the stuff to take blood from Nate.

At that moment Nate realized that Toby would need to inject a needle in his arm to get blood from him. He knew that this was mandatory for Toby to check if he was a potential donor. Panic rose in his chest and his hands started to tremble. Thankfully Toby hadn't seen it and didn't blow off the whole idea of Nate donating. While Nate cleared his throat, he tried to calm down the demons in his mind.

Lynn needed him.

He was stronger than his demons.

He was in charge of his mind.

He could do this.

While Toby placed the tourniquet around his bicep, Nate focused on breathing in through his nose and out through his mouth. He had turned his head a little to look at Lynn's still-yellowish face. He had to push through this. Everything was going to be okay. He aligned his own breathing with the movement of Lynn's chest.

In and out.

In and out.

In and out.

"Alright, next up I need to make an MRI of your abdomen to check that, if you *are* a potential donor, your liver is suitable for donation. I have to check the veins and arteries of your liver as well as the exact anatomy of your gallbladder and bile duct."

Nate turned his head to look at Toby with confusion in his eyes. What was the doctor talking about?

At that moment Nate realized that Toby was already done and pressed a small gauze pad on the inside of his elbow to stop the bleeding.

"Yeah, sure," he simply mumbled, still confused that he totally missed the needle entering his body.

Thirty minutes later the MRI was done and Nate had survived it pretty well. Lying in a tight, loud, beeping machine wasn't his favorite Sunday afternoon activity, but it was better than he had expected. No panic attacks.

"I'll let you know later if you are a potential donor. Now I have to call Lynn's mum," Toby said to him with a smile on his face.

Nate entered Lynn's room again to sit down next to her. Marta had placed a book on her bedside table and Nate grabbed it to start reading to her.

It was a romance book about soulmates. He'd never believed in them as these books always appeared way too unrealistic to him.

He'd never believed in love at first sight and actually Lynn and him hadn't been. Their relationship just slowly shifted from professional to friends to lovers. However that happened. Nate still wondered why this wonderful woman with the brown hair and the chestnut eyes chose to give her heart to him. The broken man with all the demons.

He continued reading to her. Something about everything happening for a reason and believing in miracles will help. About people that are connected to each other without even knowing it and finding their one true love. The soulmates in this book even felt each other's emotions and pain. He raised his gaze from the book and looked at Lynn.

He wished he could share her pain. Only to take some of it away from her, so that she was feeling better, but things like soulmates didn't exist and life wasn't a romance book.

Miracles didn't happen all the time.

The door burst open and a panting Toby stood in the doorway.

"I couldn't believe it, so I tested it three times," he started before placing his hands on his waist and leaning forward a little.

It seemed like he had sprinted from the lab into the room. Nate didn't respond. Scared to be disappointed by the answer, scared that his hope would be shattered.

"You *are* a potential donor," Toby exclaimed, his face lighting up with excitement and a wide smile appearing on his face.

"What?" Nate asked surprised, his jaw on the floor while he rose to his feet.

"Yes. Yes, you are. Gary is on his way so we can start right away. Don't eat anything until I'm back!" he instructed before storming out of the room to inform Tia and Birdie and prepare both operating rooms for the upcoming surgeries.

Nate turned around and grinned towards Lynn.

"Have you heard that, darling? Everything's going to be okay!"

Maybe sometimes life was indeed like a romance book.

# Waiting game

**August 14th, 2022**

"He should wake up soon. The surgery went pretty well and because of his good physical state he should be back on his feet in no time," Toby said to Oliver and Marta.

The three of them were currently standing next to Nate's hospital bed, who was still sleeping because of the sedatives. His head was turned towards Oliver, his lips parted with some drool dripping out of them. Oliver smiled while watching his best friend.

Although the situation looked quite familiar to him, everything was different now. Nate's whole life had changed within a year.

All because of Lynn.

The woman lying in the room next to this one.

"What about Lynn?" Oliver asked.

"Her body reacted better to the surgery than I expected. She was stable the entire time and Gary didn't have a problem attaching the remaining parts of her liver to Nate's donation. Of course there's always the risk that her body rejects the donor liver, but let's hope for the best. We kept her in a coma so that her body has enough time to rest. She's still in a very weak condition." Toby explained while checking the saline solution that was hanging on an IV pole next to Nate's bed.

He adjusted the regulator and checked the IV on top of Nate's hand as well. Everything looked pretty good and he was happy. He would check the surgery site later when Nate was awake.

As if on cue, he started to shift in the bed, furrowing his brow in pain and a loud groan could be heard.

Toby quickly grabbed a bottle with pain medication in it, hung it on the IV pole as well and connected it to the IV on Nate's hand.

"I tried to not drug him up too much, but I'm not gonna lie. This is a very uncomfortable position for such a big wound. He'll be in pain for the next few weeks," Toby explained while placing his palm on Nate's shoulder.

He was shifting more which obviously led to more pain, as he slightly crunched his abdomen. Not the best idea after donating a part of his liver.

"Butch," Oliver said with a loud voice, trying to wake his best friend so that he stopped stirring around.

He got a loud groan in response.

"Is it possible that he's having a nightmare?" Oliver asked, changing the side of the bed to place his hand on Nate's other shoulder.

Together with Toby he tried to hold his upper body down on the mattress to prevent him from hurting himself more or ripping some of his stitches.

"No, I don't think so. It's very unlikely to dream on sedatives. I see this a lot. People stirring around before waking up. Most of the time they need a moment to realize what happened and they're confused, so be prepared for that."

Nate threw his head from one side to the other and didn't stop moving his upper body. If Oliver and Toby hadn't held his shoulders down, he would've sat up in bed.

"Butch. Come on, pal. Wake up," Oliver said with a loud voice.

Finally the brunet man in the bed opened his eyes a little, before closing them again with a loud whine. His brows furrowed and his mouth contorted in a grimace. Oliver raised his gaze from Nate and looked at Toby.

"The painkillers will work in a minute or two," the doctor commented.

Another groan and Nate tried to open his eyes again. It was only a slit, but he managed to see a blurry face with blond hair on top of it.

"How's Lynn?" he asked with a husky voice.

His mind was foggy, he didn't know where he was and who was around him, but the only thing that mattered for him was the love of his life because even in his sedated state all he cared about was Lynn.

"She's okay," Toby answered.

The doctor wasn't sure how clear Nate's mind already was, so he hesitated to tell him the whole story now, just to repeat it several times during his wakening-process.

Nate opened his eyes completely now, letting his gaze wander around the room until he locked it with Toby.

"Can I see her?"

"Butch..." Oliver started but got interrupted by Toby immediately:

"You came out of surgery an hour ago, Nate and it wasn't an easy one. There's a huge wound on the right side of your body so no, you can't see her now. Maybe tomorrow but only if your wound looks good and the pain is bearable."

Nate's face fell, tears glimmering in his eyes. The whole situation was overwhelming him. Oliver gently caressed his thumb over Nate's shoulder and said,

"I'll go and check on her and then come back and tell you everything in detail. Okay, pal?"

But before the man in the bed could answer, Marta cleared her throat and said,

"I'll do that Oli, you stay with him until he's completely clear again. Make sure he doesn't panic. You're his best friend, so you're the best one for that job as long as Lynn is lying in the next room. I'll be back in a few minutes."

Nate turned his head and looked at the Deputy Director before he nodded a silent "thank you" in her direction. Marta gave him a smile, turned around and left the room.

"I'm so proud of you," Oliver whispered after Toby had left the room as well to check on Lynn.

Gary, his colleague, was with her, but he wanted to see her himself.

Nate raised an eyebrow at Oliver.

"Why?"

"Because you decided to have surgery. After everything you've been through, this is something we should celebrate."

"I don't feel like celebrating, to be honest," Nate groaned.

He tried to change his position but gave up, after another strong wave of pain shot through his body. He hoped that the painkillers would start to work soon.

"But you should. Butch, not only did you get your blood tested before the surgery, but also got an IV and went through surgery. Although Lynn wasn't the surgeon, nobody paid attention to your fear of needles and tried to help you with it. But you managed to get that all done. Without a panic attack. That's so awesome, pal!" Oliver was grinning widely and the adoration and pride in his voice was very present.

"I had to. For Lynn," Nate mumbled, his eyes shining like sapphires with the tears in them.

"I know. I'm still proud of you. And she is, too. I know it."

"I just want to see her. I need to see myself that she is okay." A few tears had slipped out of his eyes, but he didn't care and neither did Oliver, who only sighed deeply.

"You can. Tomorrow. It's not helping her if you force yourself out of bed right now and rip some stitches and maybe even get an infection because of the reopened wound. You need to get back on your feet as soon as possible so that you can be there for her. She'll need you and for that you need to listen to Toby right now."

Oliver had always been the voice of reason for him, giving him support when he needed it, but also tough love when he felt Nate needed that as well.

"I know," Nate said but he wasn't able to shut the disappointment out of his voice.

"Get some more rest, sleep a little. Time will fly and you can see her. I'm pretty sure."

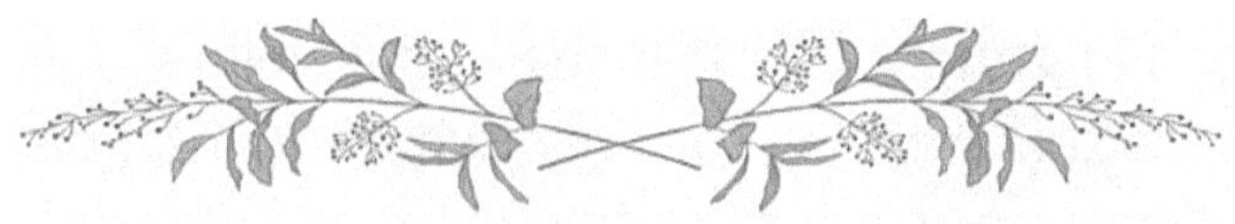

**August 16th, 2022**

Two days later Nate was so insistent seeing Lynn that Toby finally allowed him to get out of bed. Oliver, Tia and Birdie had begged Toby to agree to this because Nate was driving them nuts.

"She's still under sedation so she won't wake up today. You can see her for thirty minutes, then you go back to bed. Sitting isn't good for the wound. Understood?" Toby explained while he and Oliver helped Nate from his laying into a sitting position.

That he still had his left arm in a cast, didn't make it any easier.

The brunet man groaned in pain but quickly shut himself off so that Toby wouldn't change his mind. With clenched teeth and his vision blurry because of the pain, he managed to move his body into the wheelchair. His stitches protested a lot and he was scared that he had ripped them, but Toby checked them over and gave him a thumbs up. Earlier that morning Oliver had helped Nate to change from the hospital gown into t-shirt and sweatpants.

"So that you look respectable for your girlfriend," Oliver had laughed. Nate was very grateful for his support.

He hadn't expected the recovery to be so long and painful and his recovery was nothing in comparison to Lynn's.

"Her blood count looks much better and the discoloration of her skin is gone. I can still see some yellow shine in her eyes but it's still amazing for only two and a half days," Toby explained as he pushed the wheelchair out of Nate's room.

"So her body's accepted the parts of my liver?"

"I can't tell for sure yet. We're still observing her closely but it looks like her liver's started to work properly again."

They halted in front of Lynn's room and Nate took a deep breath. He'd been desperate to see her for the last 48 hours but now, that she was just a few feet away, he was scared.

Every time he had to see her lying in the coma it broke his heart and he wasn't sure if there were enough parts left to keep him alive, if it got broken all over.

"Her condition didn't worsen again. Her blood pressure is stable and we were even able to take her off the ventilator and put her on a nasal cannula instead. It means she's breathing on her own. It's good news, Butch. You should focus on that," Toby said while opening the door.

He had noticed Nate's tense shoulders and his unusually fast breathing.

"Yeah. Yeah, you're right. Focus on the good things," Nate repeated, mumbling.

Toby pushed the wheelchair into Lynn's room and next to her bed.

She still looked so fragile.

It had only been a few days but Nate could already see that she had lost weight. Her jawline was more present than usual and she had big black bags under her eyes although she had been sleeping the past few days. The veins in her hands popped out and Nate was about to lean forward to grab one of her hands with his good right hand, when Toby intervened with a loud noise.

"No leaning forward! That's not good for the wound. Wait, I can give her hand to you."

And that was what he did. Nate clenched his own hand around Lynn's as if he needed to pull her back to the land of living.

Thankfully the fingers of his left hand were outside of the cast so he was able to caress his fingertips along Lynn's hand and arm.

"Hi, darling. Sorry that I haven't been here the last two days. Toby didn't let me out of bed, and you know what? I even listened to him. Can you believe that?" He chuckled a little before pulling her hand towards his mouth so that he could place some tender kisses on it.

"I wish I could kiss you. Now that you've finally gotten rid of the tube coming out of your mouth, Toby said I'm not allowed to stand and lean over. Yet. So I'd better listen to him, or I won't be allowed to be here when you wake up. I'd never forgive myself for that."

Toby smiled at him before he finally left the room while mouthing "thirty minutes" into his direction.

For the next thirty minutes Nate talked to her, telling her about his own surgery, how they found out that he was a perfect donor, and nobody could believe it because the chances of that were so low. But here they were, he was able to donate a huge part of his right lobe. Sections VI and VII to be precise. He didn't understand what that meant but Toby was eager to tell him all the details about the donation before he went under anesthetic.

Nate wasn't interested. He would have given his whole liver if that would have saved Lynn's life.

Even if that meant his own death.

Time flew by and it felt like only a minute before Nate was lying in his bed again, Toby leaning over him and changing the dressing on his wound to check the stitches.

"Everything still looks good. I'll attach you to the painkillers again and you should get some rest. Your body is still recovering from a big surgery."

Nate furrowed his brow while he shifted his body a little to find a more comfortable position. He hated lying on his back but his right side wasn't a good idea with the wound and his left side was also uncomfortable because for some reason the wound hurt then too.

"When do you plan to wake her?" he asked with clenched teeth.

"We're reducing the sedatives this evening. But slowly. If we see that she or her body isn't ready yet, we increase the dose again."

Nate's cheeks pushed upwards while his lips curled into a tiny smile, making the crow's feet next to his eyes appear. It was the happiest Nate looked in the past few days and Toby couldn't help himself to copy the smile.

"I want to be with her when she wakes up," Nate commented.

This wasn't a question. It was a demand.

"Easy, Agent. I still don't want you to sit for too long. You can't even change your lying position without pain. Don't think I don't see that, although I have to admit that you try pretty hard to hide it."

"Shit, you got me." Nate chuckled a little before groaning in pain.

Maybe his little trip to Lynn had been more exhausting than he thought. His stomach was screaming at him, angry about the movement and pulling on the stitches. He totally forgot that it wasn't only the wound on his skin. Toby had removed a big part of his liver. His insides were turned upside down and they were protesting a lot about the disruption of their peace.

"It can take some time until she really wakes up and, most of the time, when patients open their eyes for the first time their mind is still not clear. I had to tell you about your surgery three times."

"You did?" Nate looked at him with furrowed brows.

"Yeah. And every time you only asked about Lynn, which is cute though," Toby snickered before he continued, "Of course I'll let you know as soon as I think she's really awake."

"Thank you. I promised her that I'd be there," Nate whispered, feeling the painkillers rushing through his body while his eyelids became heavier with every second.

"And you won't break that promise. Close your eyes and rest. I'll let you know as soon as you can see her," Toby responded, seeing that Nate struggled more and more to keep awake.

He'd expected that because he'd given him a full shot of painkillers as soon as the IV on his right hand was attached again.

Nate had drifted off by now, his head lolled to the side and he was sleeping peacefully. Toby needed to make sure that he healed as fast and well as possible. He knew Lynn would need every bit of support she could get after a few days in a coma. Regaining strength in her whole body would be hard work and she needed mental and physical support for that. Nate needed to be fit.

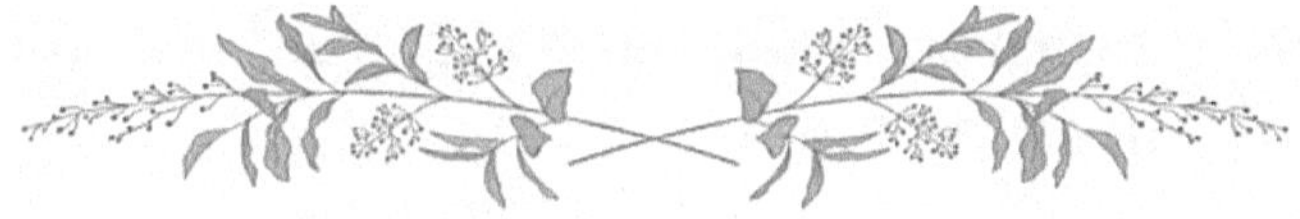

**August 17th, 2022**

"Butch."

"Butch!"

The man lying in the hospital bed opened his eyes in shock and was about to quickly sit-up when an agonizing pain on his right side forced him to fall back into the mattress. He groaned in pain, tears forming in his eyes, because it didn't stop hurting, like someone was stabbing a burning hot knife into his side.

"Oh shit, I'm so sorry. I didn't want to scare you," Toby said and placed his hand on the Agent's shoulder.

"It's okay," Nate hissed between clenched teeth.

"It's almost 7 am and I'm pretty sure she'll wake up very soon. Do you want me to wheel you over?"

Nate opened his eyes immediately, looking at Toby as if he had spoken in a different language. He knew that this moment would come but it still took him by surprise.

Now?

Lynn was going to wake up now?

"Yes. Yes, of course. Please. I really need to see her."

Tears of happiness were seen in his eyes and a smile appeared on his lips. Toby smiled back at him and helped him into the wheelchair.

Nate was still drugged with painkillers and the additional adrenaline of finally hearing Lynn's voice again made it impossible for him to feel any pain right now.

"Toby?" he asked while Toby started to move the wheelchair out of the room.

"Mhm?"

"Promise me that I can kiss her as soon as she's awake."

"You'd do it anyway, even if I said no right now."

"You got me."

# You are my sunshine

**August 17th, 2022**

"She's still asleep."

"I told you that it can take a while until she is finally awake. There's still a lot of sedatives in her body."

"I know. I just can't wait to see these beautiful chestnut eyes again."

Lynn heard a low voice, almost like a whisper next to her ear.

She'd heard this voice before, it was familiar, but her brain wasn't able to connect the dots and it was driving her crazy. Who was this man?

Flutters appeared in her stomach while hearing this voice and her heart was burning. She didn't understand why her body reacted like this while hearing this husky, graveled voice.

Suddenly she felt someone touch her hand. A warm and tender touch. Someone drew circles on top of her hand.

It was the best feeling ever.

She hoped the person would never stop doing it.

It was so careful, so full of love.

Love.

*"I. Love. You."* The male voice had said to her once. Right before everything went black. It's the last thing she could remember and she had told him that she loved him too.

Nate.

He was the love of her life.

Was it Nate sitting next to her?

Lynn slowly opened her eyes because she needed to know if it was him. She needed to see his ocean-blue eyes because it always calmed her. Always made her feel at peace.

Her vision was way too blurry to identify anything of her surroundings. Vision and sound were in asynchrony because she could still hear this voice talking to her but she couldn't see anybody.

With a tremendous effort Lynn managed to move her head a little to her right, finally seeing something other than bright lights.

The blurry outline of a human became clearer with every blink, until she finally saw him: Nate.

His brunet hair was messy on top of his head, as if he hadn't styled it for a few days. His skin was paler than she remembered and he had dark circles under his eyes. Lynn still thought he looked handsome, but also completely exhausted.

She let her gaze wander down his body until her eyes landed on a black cast on his hand.

He was hurt.

Nate was hurt.

Her heart skipped a beat and suddenly there wasn't enough oxygen entering her body.

A loud beeping appeared from the other side of her head, but all she could focus on was the man sitting next to her. With her hand in his. The hand in a cast.

Alarmed by the beeping, Nate raised his head with furrowed brows, shock very obvious on his features.

Chestnut eyes met ocean blue ones.

And the world stopped around them.

No sound could be heard, the surroundings in a blur.

The only thing that mattered were the two of them looking into each other's eyes after days of despair, frustration, sadness and hope.

Nate kept on drawing circles on the back of her hand, when his features softened, one side of his lips curled upwards, and tears streamed out of his eyes.

Lynn didn't understand why he was crying but in that moment the only thing she cared about was the love the two of them shared. The sparks flying between their eyes and the warmth that radiated from Nate's hand into hers and all the way up to her heart.

Neither of them noticed Toby running to Lynn's other side and checking her vitals but, as quick as her heart rate increased, it fell again.

"Your arm," Lynn croaked, her voice hoarse after days of not using it.

She coughed a little after the two words and needed to clear her throat. Toby held a glass with water and a straw towards her mouth and Lynn gratefully took a sip. Her eyes never left Nate's.

"It's okay. It doesn't matter now," Nate answered, his voice soft and loving.

Her heart was full the moment she heard him speaking directly towards her.

She had missed his voice in the darkness.

"But you're hurt," she whispered, ignoring the burning sensation in her throat.

"It's just a broken bone. I'll be fine."

"Lynn?" Toby's voice echoed through the room, making the two lovebirds break their gaze for the first time.

Lynn slowly moved her head to her left, looking into Toby's brown eyes.

"Toby," she said and tried to smile but her body was too exhausted.

Every muscle was so heavy and turning her head had already been draining like running a marathon.

"How are you feeling?" the doctor asked.

"Tired. Heavy. Tired," Lynn answered, her eyelids already closing halfway.

Toby had expected that. He was surprised that she was already able to speak after waking up for the first time.

It seemed as though Nate really did have some healing vibes.

"It's okay. Go back to sleep. We can talk when you wake up again." Toby gently caressed his fingers over Lynn's upper arm.

He was happy that she was finally awake. Not only as her doctor, but mostly as a friend. Having your friends lying in hospital beds in front of you was never easy. Especially not when it was such a dangerous situation.

Lynn gathered all her strength and turned her head to the right again. Nate's gaze was already waiting for her with shimmering eyes.

"Can you lay with me?" she asked, her eyes closed for a few moments, before she forced herself to open them again.

Nate broke his gaze with Lynn and looked at Toby, asking for permission without actually asking. The doctor sighed but nodded. He wouldn't be able to stop them anyways. Both Nate and Lynn were the most stubborn people that he knew. And those two combined? He wouldn't stand a chance, even if he had the better argument.

Toby grabbed Lynn's hospital gown and carefully pulled her towards him so that she was lying on the outer edge of the bed. Lynn giggled in response and hearing her make this sound made Nate's heart scream with love. A warmth spread through his body. A warmth that had been missing over the past few days. But finally he knew everything was going to be okay. For the past few days he had tried to convince himself over and over again. But he never believed himself. He was constantly scared that, in the end, Lynn wouldn't make it and that he would be alone.

Alone, cold, dark and lost.

Now was the first time he actually knew that everything was going to be okay.

With a loud groan he pushed his body into an upright position and slowly sat down on the edge of the bed. Lynn's eyes shot open and she looked at Nate with concern.

"You're hurt," she commented, without actually understanding how true these words were.

She knew that it wasn't only his arm. Yeah, she had been in a coma for days, her mind was still fuzzy because of painkillers and sedatives and whatever else Toby was pumping into her body but she was still a doctor, one of the best.

Nate was hurt and not only on his arm.

"It's okay. It was worth it because I have you back," he said between clenched teeth.

His stitches were protesting a lot and he had black spots in his vision. This was probably way too much movement for his recovering body, but he didn't care.

Finally he was lying next to her again.

Both of them on their back, heads turned towards each other, and their hands connected. At least as much as possible, because it was his broken hand in the cast, but she had laid her fingers into his and felt him squeezing them. It was the best they could do with their broken bodies, but it was enough for the moment.

Lynn had closed her eyes again, exhaustion flooding her body.

"I love you, Lynn," Nate whispered with a shy smile dancing around his lips and his eyes shimmering with unshed tears.

His words made her open her own eyes once again. It took her a lot of strength because every cell of her body screamed at her to finally sleep but she needed to look him in the eyes.

"I love you too, Nate," she whispered.

Neither of them had enough strength or were in the best physical condition to lean over and connect their lips, so they just lay there, looking at each other before both of them closed their eyes and fell asleep.

Next to each other, their bodies connected through their intertwined fingers. Hearts beating in the same rhythm.

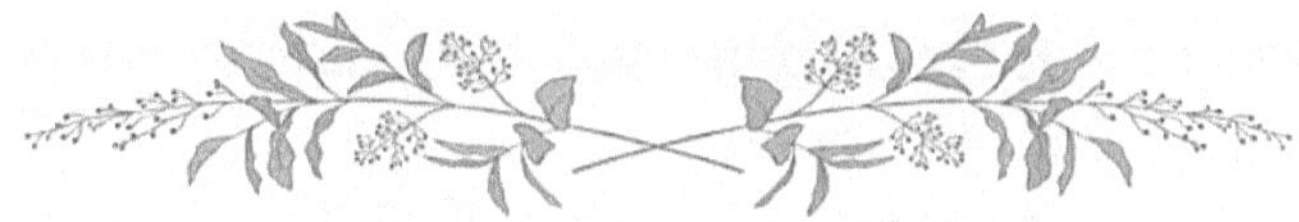

When Lynn opened her eyes again she could see the love of her life sleeping peacefully next to her. She was still very tired and exhausted but her brain was clearer this time, so she took her time and watched him from head to toe.

The obvious injury was the cast on his arm and she really wondered what happened for him to break his hand. The last time she saw him, he definitely hadn't. He was fine.

Her eyes wandered along his body and she could see his abs popping out from underneath his t-shirt. It had slid up a little, revealing his stomach and the six pack she loved to let her tongue caress along.

Distracted by his sculpted body, Lynn hadn't noticed the outlines of a white dressing peeking out of his t-shirt but now she saw it and was confused. She tried to lift her arm and grab the shirt to pull it away even more. She was curious but her weak body failed her, so her hand landed with a thud on Nate's abs.

His eyes fluttered open and he whined a little "ow".

"Lynn. You're awake, darling." He smiled at her, covering the fact that he was in pain.

"What happened to you?" she asked with her eyebrows knit together in concern.

Tears shimmered in the corner of her eyes.

"It doesn't matter. The only thing that matters is that you're fine again," he responded and managed to turn his whole body onto his left side with a loud groan.

He was obviously in pain and that didn't reassure Lynn. She was even more concerned.

"But it matters to *me*," she whispered to his face that was now only inches apart from hers.

Instead of answering her, Nate leaned forward. He tried really hard to hide the amount of pain he was in, but of course Lynn noticed it. The moment his lips were lingering on top of hers she whispered,

"I can't remember the last time I brushed my teeth."

They both giggled a little before groaning in pain in unison. Stupid stubborn idiots.

"Shut up and kiss me."

She could feel his breath on her lips and moved her head to finally close the gap between them.

It wasn't the epic romance book reunion-kiss Nate had expected but the moment her rough lips touched his he swore he could hear a choir singing in the background along with fanfares. Fireworks exploded in both of their stomachs and they were both sure that this was the best kiss they ever shared.

After a few seconds they broke apart, their bodies still too sore and weak for longer interactions.

A wide grin could be seen on Nate's face. He had imagined this moment non-stop for the last few days and now that it had finally happened, he was on an adrenaline rush.

"Can you now tell me why you are hurt?" Lynn asked carefully.

"We'd better let Toby explain it to you when he comes to check on you later," Nate responded, leaning forward and resting his forehead against hers.

His right side was still screaming but the adrenaline of having his girlfriend back was able to block out the pain.

"Okay. Let me call him." Lynn was looking around for the call button that was laying next to her head.

She still felt weak but managed to raise her arm next to her head and grab the device.

"Wait, what are you doing?" Nate asked, confused. He had watched her movement.

"Calling Toby."

"This is a panic button, darling. Not a service bell. Don't you think Toby will freak out when you use this just to call him?"

Lynn rolled her eyes and sighed loudly, the device still in her hands.

"I've been sleeping for the last few days, so some action should do him good. Don't want him to be bored," she chuckled a little but stopped as soon as she saw Nate's straight face.

Something was shining behind the blue of his eyes. Was it anger?

"The last few days weren't exactly a picnic," he whispered and averted his gaze from her.

Tears glistered in the corner of his eyes and he blinked a few times to prevent them from falling.

"I'm sorry," she whispered.

They didn't have a chance to continue their conversation because the door opened and a smiling Toby entered the room with his iPad in his hand.

"Oh you're awake," he commented, his smile getting even bigger when he saw Lynn turn her head towards him.

Her eyes looked clear, the color of her skin slowly but steady returning back to normal. She still had the nasal cannula in but that didn't stop her from smiling. Nate turned back onto his back with a loud whine and Toby could see his t-shirt slip up and reveal some small dots of blood on the white dressing.

"Toby, can you please tell me why my boyfriend is hurt?" she asked, the smile fading from her face and she sounded a little annoyed.

"You haven't told her?" Toby asked Nate with a raised eyebrow.

"Thought you could explain it better, Doc," Nate responded through clenched teeth.

Toby sighed, tilted his head a little and looked Lynn directly in her chestnut eyes.

"He donated part of his liver to you."

"He did what?" Lynn exclaimed louder than anybody in the room had expected.

So Toby explained everything to Lynn in detail. What damage the stab wounds had done, how he treated them until the liver failure made it necessary for them to find a donor. How nobody expected it, but Nate turned out to be a donor and that they performed surgery on him an hour later. It was a lot to process for Lynn, although she had expected something like that.

At least the part with the coma. She knew she had lost a lot of blood, but the liver failure still surprised her.

"Your blood count looks much better, your liver is working again, and it seems like you're finally coming back to life. Although you know recovery will take some time. Especially until you have your strength back, but one step at a time. Do you have any questions?" Toby smiled at her again.

"No. Not right now. It's a lot to process." She smiled back at him weakly  before turning her head to watch Nate.

He had his gaze fixed on Toby, who was rounding the bed to stand right next to him.

"Can I?" the doctor asked and Nate nodded.

Toby grabbed the hem of his shirt and lifted it to reveal the dressing underneath.

"There's some blood on the gauze. I'll change it to check if you ripped some stitches."

"Sure," Nate answered.

He'd expected something like that as the pain was killing him. It hadn't hurt like that over the last two days but kissing and cuddling with Lynn was worth it.

Toby pulled the dressing off and Nate flinched because of the pain. He had his eyes closed and was oblivious that Lynn was watching him with furrowed brows. She was concerned.

"One of the stitches opened a little, but it's okay. Let's keep an eye on it, but you should be fine," Toby explained before placing a new dressing on top of the wound.

"Amazing," Nate said with his eyes still closed.

When he opened them, he saw Lynn's chestnut ones glistering with tears.

"Hey, darling. What's up?" He asked, raising his right hand to place it on her cheek.

He had to twist his upper body a little, but the pain was acceptable.

"You're hurt because of me," she mumbled, a single tear slipping out of her eye.

"I'd do it again. It was totally worth it," Nate whispered, leaving featherlight brushes with his thumb on her cheek.

"But why?" More tears slipped out of her eyes as she wasn't able to keep her emotions at bay.

"Because you're my sunshine. I can't live without you. You make me smile, you make me laugh. Your warmth is addicting and it's made me a better person. Just the thought of losing you... I've never been so lost and in so much darkness than I have the past few days. So of course I wanted to do everything possible to save your life. Even when that meant getting surgery."

"Oh, Nate." Lynn couldn't say anything else while tears streamed out of her eyes again.

"I mean every word of it," he added and tried to change onto his left side again so that he was able to kiss her but halfway into the movement his right side protested so loud that he needed to let himself fall back on his back. Another wave of pain shot through his body making him see stars so that he needed to close his eyes for a moment. Lynn gathered her strength and moved her arm on his thigh. Carefully she caressed her fingertips over his fabric covered leg.

"After everything that happened over the last few weeks, I wasn't sure if you still loved me," she whispered.

Her words made Nate open his eyes in an instant. They were shining with guilt.

"I will always love you. Every moment until I die. My heart belongs to you and nobody else. There is no one I'd rather spend my life with than you."

"I... I'm sorry. I know I messed up with az-Zawahiri and..." she started but Nate placed his right hand on top of hers, that was still caressing his thigh.

"No. Well, yes, you messed up, but you only did it to save your sister. I already told you this while you were still in the coma, but it's all my fault that I was too stupid to finally let go of the past. I don't know why I wasn't able to just move on and focus on the happiness you bring to my life. I hate that it needed something like this for me to finally understand but I promise you, the betrayal will never be a reason for me to avoid you or ignore you or make you believe that I don't love you anymore."

"I don't deserve you." Lynn turned her hand around to entangle her fingers with his as much as she could.

"No, I don't deserve you. Someone so patient, so brilliant, so caring and so loving. You are my sun and my moon. My everything. Wait, I gotta save some of those words for another occasion," he chuckled and Lynn giggled as well.

"I love you, Nate."

"I love you too, Lynn. My little sunshine," he responded before raising his left arm to boop his index finger on her nose.

She started to laugh before hissing in pain.

They were both physically and mentally broken, but they were willing to fix each other.

They were finally willing and able to move on in their life.

Together.

# Recovery Process

**August 23rd, 2022**

The week after Lynn finally woke from the coma had been an emotional rollercoaster for all of them. Although it had only been a few days, her body was emaciated, and she was shocked how weak she actually was. Toby had checked her vitals frequently, but it wasn't her general constitution that she was struggling with.

It was the weakness and soreness of her muscles, making it almost impossible for her to stand without support. Of course she was a doctor too, but as she had always been in charge of the ER, she never really saw the recovery process of the patients.

She felt like a burden to everyone as eating was the only thing she was able to do on her own. She couldn't go to the bathroom alone, couldn't move from her back on her side or the other way around without hurting the surgery site.

She was groaning and huffing and cursing the entire time and Toby tried his best to lighten her mood. Very unsuccessfully.

Of course there was only one person that could make her smile in this miserable situation and that person was Nate.

Although Toby hadn't been very happy with it, Nate was starting to be able to walk after his surgery, allowing him the freedom to sneak out of his room as much as possible. It would help prevent him getting a blood clot, but Toby hated it when his patients overdid it. Nate didn't care because spending time with Lynn, reading books to her, watching TV shows and movies while cuddling in bed as best as they could was all he cared about. Of course he was monitored as well, making sure that his wound looked good and no infection could be seen. Even with moving way more than Nate should have, his healing process was exactly how it should have been so, after laying in the med-bay for a little over a week, Nate was finally allowed to move back to his room.

But because Lynn was still lying there, he was around almost 24/7, only getting shooed out of the room when Tia and Birdie needed to wash Lynn and help her change her clothes.

Eight days after the liver-donation Lynn took her chance and bombarded Birdie with a request as soon as she entered the patient room.

"I really need to shower," Lynn pleaded while making the best puppy dog eyes she was able to do. She even tried the trembling lip, but to be honest it looked more like she was having a seizure than a cute face to convince Birdie.

"You know Toby will kill me if I allow you to shower," Birdie responded, while stepping next to Lynn's bed and noting down the vitals that were showing on the monitors.

"But I finally got rid of the catheter yesterday and I even improved with the PT and strengthened my muscles a little. The PT and Toby were very happy about it this morning," Lynn whined.

"I'll have to check with Toby again, but he's in surgery right now. Agent Richards broke her leg and he needed to fix it."

Birdie was currently checking the different medicine bags that were hanging on the IV pole. Yes, Lynn got rid of the syringe pumps, but she still needed to get some medicine through the IV on her hand.

"Wait. Agent Richards? Eliana Richards?" Lynn asked, her eyebrows raised so high, they were almost lost in her hairline.

"Yeah. She got hurt on a mission."

"Oh shit. Hope Peter's doing okay. I know the two have been out on a simple mission."

"Agent Davis seems to be okay other than a few bruises and scratches."

"Thank God. Birdie pleeeeeaaaassseeee. See, I can even sit on my own. With a chair in the shower it won't be any problem. Really. Trust me, I'm a doctor, too." Lynn quickly went back to the original request, scared that the change of topics would destroy her chance of a much needed shower.

"But you're not in charge right now, and I don't know if you can assess your condition correctly." Birdie sighed.

"I don't feel like a human anymore. Look at my hair. It's so greasy. And my muscles are so sore and full of knots. I don't even understand how that happened because I haven't done anything other than lie around for the last two weeks, but it feels horrible. I could really use some warm water to soothe my muscles. That's good for my recovery process, too." Lynn had started with a pleading voice but changed into her doctor-voice at the end, making Birdie laugh, but the nurse didn't respond as she was focusing on changing the medicine bag and attaching it to the IV again.

"Darling, you can really be a pain in the ass sometimes," a male voice could be heard from the other side of the room.

Lynn and Birdie turned around simultaneously to see a brunet man with ocean blue eyes and a wide smile standing in the doorframe. He had a bouquet of flowers in his hand that was shining with different colors. Bright blue forget-me-nots, purple sweet peas, purple snake's-head fritillary, as well as some branches of cherry blossom. The beautiful flowers were combined with different branches and grasses, giving the bouquet a good contrast to the colorful highlights.

"You brought me flowers." Lynn's lips curled upwards into a wide smile.

"Of course. Now that your room isn't an ICU anymore, I'm finally allowed to bring some. But to be honest, Oliver got them for me at the farmers market he and Marta went to this morning. I didn't feel well enough for a trip into the city," Nate answered while closing the door behind him and stepping next to Lynn's bed.

"I'll bring you a vase," Birdie said and was about to leave the room when Lynn screamed after her,

"And bring some waterproof dressing as well."

Birdie only chuckled and then closed the door behind her.

"Waterproof dressing?" Nate asked, confused, as he took a seat on the chair next to Lynn's bed.

The moment he leaned back, he whined a little. His wound was still bothering him as soon as he put pressure on it, which automatically happened as soon as he leaned back. As Lynn already had a wound from stitching her back together after the stabbing, Toby had just reopened that one for the transplant. It was on the front of her body, right under her breast.

But for Nate's surgery, Toby had decided to open his back to have access to his liver. The front of Nate's chest was full of scars from the torture and the surgeries to save his life afterwards.

Toby didn't want to cut through these scars so he decided to choose a scar-free area on Nate's back and side. This was very thoughtful of Toby, but it caused Nate to struggle a lot with sitting and lying down after the surgery.

"Yeah, I really need to take a shower. I feel awful!" Lynn whined with her head turned towards Nate.

"But you look beautiful as always, darling." Nate tried to reassure her, but only got a huff back.

"You don't have to lie just because you're my boyfriend," the brunette woman complained.

"I'm not lying. You're the most beautiful woman I've ever dated," Nate responded before leaning forward to press his lips on hers.

Birdie re-entered the room with a "that's disgusting" on her lips, making both Nate and Lynn laugh out loud before breaking apart.

She held one hand up in the air and wiggled a package, making Lynn's eyes shine in excitement.

"I'll let you shower, but only under one condition," Birdie said with a serious frown on her face.

"Anything!" Lynn exclaimed happily.

"Loverboy here has to shower with you. As he's already released from the med-bay and I know he can stand and all that stuff, he can wash your hair and make sure you don't collapse or fall off the shower chair."

"Roger that," Nate answered and saluted sloppily, before all three of them burst into laughter.

"Also, Agent Sheppard. You stink as well. You need a shower," Birdie commented with a giggle.

"Hey!" Nate responded, a pout very present on his face.

"I'm sorry, I'm just being honest." Birdie was still giggling.

Nate raised his arm and sniffed underneath his armpit before making a grimace of disgust.

"Maybe Birdie's right," he mumbled, shrugging his shoulders and looking innocently at his girlfriend.

Lynn didn't know if she should burst into laughter or grab Nate's hand, pull him close and place kisses all over his face, because he looked so damn cute with that pout on his face.

"I love you even when you stink," she mouthed in his direction, getting a smile back.

"And I love you even with greasy hair," he responded.

"Hey, you said I look beautiful! Liar!" Lynn grumbled with a theatrical exaggerated pout on her own face.

"Stop flirting, I need to change your dressing for the shower," Birdie said with a commanding voice.

"Yes Ma'am!" Lynn and Nate responded simultaneously, struggling hard to hold back their laughter.

Birdie rounded the bed and motioned for Nate to lean forward. Then she grabbed the hem of his shirt and pulled the white gauze off the wound on his back. Afterwards she placed the transparent waterproof dressing on top of it and clapped Nate's shoulder to signal him that she was done. She repeated the same procedure with Lynn's wound.

"What about my cast?" Nate asked while raising his left hand in the air that was still surrounded by the black cast.

"Hold on a minute," Birdie responded and grabbed the iPad that was laying on the small bedside table.

She scrolled through it to check for Nate's patient file and the comments and instructions Toby had made. She mumbled a few things to herself before passing the iPad over to Lynn. The brunette woman grabbed it, confused, and looked at Birdie with a raised eyebrow.

"If he was your patient, would you allow him to take the cast off for a quick shower?"

Lynn studied the x-ray of Nate's hand as well as Toby's report and notes. She had stuck out her tongue again and Nate couldn't help himself but smile when he saw. He really missed her being back in her element.

"Well, the crack is pretty small and it's surrounded by intact bones, so no risk of displacement in that short period of time. It's been nine days since the break, so I'd do a check-up x-ray and if that still looked good, I'd allow it if he was my patient," Lynn commented while placing the iPad back on the bedside table.

The nurse raised her head and looked at Nate.

"You heard her. Let's do an x-ray and see if your hand looks better."

Nate just nodded in response and rose from his chair to follow her out of the room. Meanwhile, Lynn grabbed the iPad again and opened the surgery reports for her first and second surgery. She was so lost in the report that she almost jumped out of bed when the iPad made a loud "bing" to indicate Nate's incoming x-rays. Lynn quickly opened the pictures and zoomed in to examine the crack in the bone.

"Wow, it looks pretty good already although it's only been nine days. We can cut the cast off and change him to a wrist brace instead. That makes stuff easier for him and he can take a shower from time to time," Lynn said to Birdie when she and Nate re-entered the room.

"Thank God!!" Nate exclaimed and added, "I really hate that thing. It's smelly and annoying."

Lynn smiled at him, and Birdie pointed to the chair before grabbing a cast saw and some scissors to free the man from the black monstrosity.

"Don't move your finger and hand around too much while we're in the shower. It's still broken!" Lynn warned her boyfriend with her no-nonsense doctor-voice.

"Of course, Doctor Summers," he teased in response.

Lynn reached out her arm and slapped him on his thigh as hard as she was able to with her weakened muscles. He barely felt it but hissed a loud "ow!" to make her feel better. Nate knew how frustrated Lynn was with her weak body.

A minute later Nate's arm was finally free again and he was about to help Lynn out of the bed and into a wheelchair when Birdie quickly stepped between him and Lynn. She had a serious, almost angry frown on her face when she huffed loudly towards Nate.

"You're not supposed to grab anything heavy with that hand. Go to the bathroom but keep your clothes on until I'm gone!" Birdie instructed and Nate quickly marched into the attached bathroom.

Birdie followed with Lynn in a wheelchair and placed some of Lynn's clothes on the side of the wash basin.

"She's not allowed to stand for more than a minute and you're not allowed to lift her up with that hand. I know that makes things complicated but I know you can do it. The shower chair is already prepared and you should have enough space to put the wheelchair right in front of it. I brought her favorite shampoo and some shower gel as well. It's already in the shower. If you need me or any help in general, there's a call button next to the door but also a red rope inside of the shower. If you pull that, I'll see the alarm. That's only for emergencies though. Remember to only pull it in an emergency because I don't want to see you naked unless I have to," Birdie chuckled while trying to light the mood a little.

There had been a weird silence between Nate and Lynn while Birdie was explaining everything to them.

She left the room a minute later and Nate carefully helped Lynn out of her clothes until she was sitting naked in the wheelchair.

He took his time to look up and down her body. Part of him was shocked at how thin she had become with her ribs popping out from her skin and her thighs way thinner than he was used to. The little belly he loved to kiss in the mornings was gone.

Another part of him couldn't help himself as he was automatically pulled towards her. Longing for her. It had been a while since they'd been intimate because of him avoiding her and the stabbing incident afterwards. He could feel his cock twitch while he leaned forward to place a loving kiss on Lynn's lips.

To avoid the situation running out of hands while he observed his naked girlfriend longer, he stripped out of his clothes as quickly as possible, revealing his half-hard cock. He tried to turn around, so that Lynn wouldn't see it, but of course she already had.

"I think Toby would kill us, if we have our normal shower ritual today," she whispered with a little giggle, pointing to Nate's manhood. Of course thinking about their usual shower ritual, which was a codeword for shower sex, made him even harder and he needed to laugh as well.

"See what you do to me. It's not fair." He whined, while giving himself a few strokes.

"I wish I could take care of that, but I don't think I have the strength for this already." Lynn responded with her gaze locked on the floor. Her happy face fell and showed a sad expression, while she felt guilty.

Nate grabbed her chin with the good right hand and tilted it upwards, forcing her to look him in the eyes.

"We have the rest of our life to take care of each other. It's fine. I haven't even thought about sex for the last two weeks. But seeing you naked in front of me... I couldn't control it. I'm sorry," he mouthed before leaning down and kissing her once again.

To think about something else than shower sex with his girlfriend, he placed the wheelchair only inches away from the shower chair. Lynn pushed herself off the wheelchair and managed to maneuver her body onto the chair without additional help from Nate. Her face was furrowed a little and he knelt in front of her, placing his arms left and right of her body to catch her in case she would collapse.

"You're good?"

"Perfect," she answered and smiled at him.

"Okay. Great. Let me know as soon as you get dizzy or feel any bad pain. Then we get you out of the shower as quickly as possible," Nate said with a slight tremble in his voice.

"It'll be alright."

Nate stepped behind her, started the shower, and turned the water as warm as possible without burning their skins. He knew that Lynn loved to shower hot, and he bet it would help her tensed muscles to relax.

Slowly he grabbed the peachy shampoo and placed some of it in Lynn's hair. He wanted to massage it into her hair and scalp, when he remembered that he wasn't allowed to do much with his still-broken hand so he carefully started to give her a massage with only his good right hand. It wasn't the same and he struggled a lot to work against the knots in her hair, but he tried as best as he could.

Lynn closed her eyes and enjoyed the intimacy between her and Nate as well as the little head massage he was giving her but when some curse words left his lips, she opened them again and asked,

"What's wrong, honey?"

"The damn hand. I wanted you to relax after everything you've been through, but I didn't manage to give you a proper head massage with one hand," he whined and she could hear him sigh deeply.

"Hey," she said while turning her head and upper body a little but the moment she felt a sharp pain in her side, she moved her upper body back in the old position.

"It's okay. You have the rest of our lives to give me a head massage," she added and could feel her heart skip a beat.

"That sounds good," Nate responded before grabbing the shower head from the mount on the wall.

He carefully tilted her head back and started to get the shampoo out of her hair. When he was done, he gave her the body wash and placed some of it on her back to rub the parts she couldn't reach herself. They worked in unison, rubbing everything off their bodies until they both smelled like they fell into peach juice. Nate didn't care. He was going to love smelling the familiar scent when he was sleeping in his bed all alone tonight.

When they were done with the shower, Nate turned off the water and reached out for the towels. He wanted Lynn to be dry before changing into the wheelchair. He was scared she could slip and fall down while changing from the shower chair back into the wheelchair.

Ten minutes later they were both dressed and left the bathroom to move back to Lynn's bed.

"Wait, I'll get Birdie to help you back in bed," Nate said, but Lynn stopped him.

"No need to disturb her. I can do this alone."

"Lynn," Nate grumbled loudly into the room, letting the doctor flinch a little in the wheelchair.

"You wait for Birdie. I don't want you to get hurt again. I know you're annoyed that you can't do anything on your own but this time for your own good. We all suffered a lot while you were in the coma and I never want to see you so lifeless again so please, do me a favor and have a little more patience. With your body and yourself. I know it sucks." He stepped next to the wheelchair and placed the hurt left hand on her shoulder.

She grabbed it and placed a kiss on it. Nate held back a small hiss, as she grabbed his hand a little too roughly.

"Okay. I'm sorry that you suffered so much over the past few days. I remember feeling helpless too when I heard your story and saw you getting hurt. I can't imagine how it must be for you seeing me lying here."

Nate was surprised how understanding she was, as Lynn had a tendency to be stubborn when it came to her recovery process.

He called for Birdie and the nurse entered the room a minute later with a bigger package in her hand that she gave to Nate. He looked at it and saw that it contained the wrist brace he needed to wear for the next few weeks.

"Wait a second. I'll take care of your girlfriend first before I show you how to get in and out of the brace without hurting your hand even more," Birdie said before stepping in front of Lynn with a big smile.

"Feeling better?" she asked the doctor.

"Much. Thank you for allowing it," Lynn smiled back at her.

"Anything, if it helps your recovery, but now you need to do me a favor and make big progress in physical therapy so I can let you shower alone soon." The nurse smiled after Lynn was lying in the bed again.

Birdie connected the IV with the medicine again before asking,

"Do you need anything else, sweetie?"

"Lunch would be great. I'm starving," Lynn chuckled.

"I'll bring you something as soon as I have loverboy's hand secured again," the nurse winked at her.

Birdie showed Nate how to put the wrist brace around his hand and take it off again. She also instructed him again that he was still not allowed to lift heavy things and should be careful to not break the bone again.

All in all it had been a pretty successful day in Lynn's recovery.

# Cuddling is the best medicine

**September 2nd, 2022**

The Star Wars main theme was heard in Lynn's bedroom, disturbing her peaceful sleep in a brutal way. She loved the music, getting chills every single time she watched one of the nine movies, but she hated Nate for having it as his alarm tone ever since they watched the first movie together.

What she hated even more was the fact that it never actually woke him. He told her that he used to be a light sleeper before the nightmares started but, to be honest, she never saw that version of him. Even without having nightmares he slept like a rock, Lynn always needed to wake him in addition to the alarm clock. It was the same every morning.

She scooted closer to Nate, who had tossed his own blanket almost completely off his body. Because of him still having nightmares from time to time they'd decided to sleep with two separate blankets. Lynn could continue sleeping while Nate tossed around and pulled on the blanket frantically.

Her boyfriend was lying on his back, his lips parted while slightly snoring, all of his four limbs stretched in different directions. It looked adorable. His right arm was outstretched towards Lynn and she remembered he had caressed her back until she fell asleep last night. She grabbed his arm, slid it over her shoulders, and laid right next to him. Lynn turned onto her left side and carefully placed her hand on Nate's stomach. She leaned forward and kissed along his shoulder, collarbone, neck and jaw until she reached his lips.

He was wide awake already but kept his eyes closed. Only the little twitch in his lips, while he was trying to hide his smile, gave him away. While nibbling on Nate's lower lip she drew small circles around his belly button, carefully not to tickle him, but her touches were so light that he struggled to not burst into laughter. His abs engaged and the sixpack popped out of his skin. Immediately Lynn stopped her movements and laid her palm on his abs instead.

"Good morning, sunshine," Nate whispered against her soft lips before moving his head just a little to give Lynn a proper kiss.

"Good morning, honey. Did you sleep well?"

Nate opened his eyes and looked at her with a sleepy gaze. She looked beautiful this morning, and he almost got lost in the depth of Lynn's eyes. Something was different this morning because she was glowing. She looked at him with a wide smile on her face, her cheeks having a wonderful pink tint. He couldn't tell what exactly it was and why but she looked like an angel today.

"I slept amazing. What about you?"

"Me too. It's the first night that I actually didn't wake up because I moved on my right side and hurt. Don't know if I just didn't turn on the right side, or if the pain is gone. Don't want to try though," Lynn whispered.

Her eyes were still shining and he could practically see how happy she was.

"That's amazing, darling." Nate smiled before pressing a few kisses along her face.

The last one landed on her nose, like always.

"Hungry?" she asked, the smile on her face never fading.

"Oh yeah, I could use some breakfast. Let's get ready and head to the communal kitchen!"

Nate was about to sit when he heard Lynn whine a little. His head shot around to look if she had hurt her wound but he only looked into puppy dog eyes.

"What is it?" he asked with a raised eyebrow.

"Let me make breakfast and bring it to you," she pleaded.

Nate let out a loud sigh and changed into a sitting position to lean back on the headboard. Lynn slowly raised as well until she was sitting cross-legged in front of him, still waiting for an answer.

"Do you think you're strong enough for that already?" he asked carefully.

"Yes!" she exclaimed immediately and then added, "I made great progress with Becks the entire week and she even let me do some squats. Squats, Nate! That's kind of working out."

Nate couldn't help himself and chuckled a little. He'd seen Lynn's last session with Becks and the 'squats' she was referring to. It was nothing compared to a real squat. It was more like standing up and sitting back down on a box.

Nate had worked with Becks after his knee surgery as well. As the whole situation around Lynn wasn't clear at that time, Toby had decided to call a friend to help. Toby and Becks had worked together a few years ago until Becks decided to open her own practice instead of working in hospitals around the region. Nate really respected her because Becks wasn't only following strict plans. She was the most flexible physical therapist he had ever worked with in his life. Constantly observing his recovery and changing the plan so that he would get the best possible outcome. It was thanks to Becks that he was back in the field so early after his surgery and he knew that she was the best person to help Lynn get back on her feet.

"You've only been discharged from the med-bay for a week, darling. And yes, you're doing some work with Becks, but you're still weak. Especially because you're doing so much PT. Your muscles need time and rest," he argued but knew that it was useless with his girlfriend.

She wanted to prepare breakfast, so she would do that.

"Don't treat me like I'm broken, Nate," she scolded him.

They had talked about this several times over the past few days, always with the same outcome: Lynn convincing him that she was okay by doing activities she wasn't actually cleared for yet. Like carrying stuff around and walking on the treadmill without supervision. It was super hard for Nate to find the fine line between supporting Lynn in her recovery and stopping her from doing too much. It had been a constant fight and struggle the last few days.

"I'm not treating you like you're broken. I'm just trying to protect you from hurting yourself, Lynn," he sighed.

He was looking at her with his brows slightly furrowed, making three lines appear on his forehead.

"I won't hurt myself by doing fucking breakfast." She rolled her eyes and was about to get out of bed and prove to him that she was indeed capable of making breakfast and carrying it to his room.

"Let's make a deal," Nate suggested the moment Lynn slowly rose to her feet.

Her strength had improved over the last week but she was still slightly dizzy every time she stood. She tried to hide it as best as possible when turning around to Nate but he saw her cheeks turning pale. Thankfully he kept his mouth shut about it.

"What kind of deal?"

After a few seconds, Lynn steadied herself a little but she still stood next to the bed like a baby deer right after it was born.

"You do the breakfast and you carry it to the dinner table, but I'll be there just in case your legs give out on you."

Lynn rolled her eyes. This was exactly what she had expected him to suggest but at least he let her do stuff on her own now. The first few days he hovered behind her with his left and right arm outstretched next to her waist in case she collapsed. What would he have done anyways? His left hand was still in the brace, he wasn't allowed to catch her. She hated every single second of her recovery process. All she wanted to do was go back to work and continue living her life but her muscles were weak from lying around for weeks and she really underestimated how sore she became. How long it would take to regain the strength in her legs, her mobility, and moving around without pain.

"Okay," she sighed, watching Nate swing his legs over the edge of the bed and practically jump to his feet.

He grabbed black sweatpants and a navy-blue shirt with the SEALs logo in golden letters on the front. He quickly changed into the clothes before grabbing Lynn's pair of sweatpants from the chair of his desk. Lynn had stepped towards it as well. She tried to appear strong in front of him, but her first steps every morning were still a little wobbly, until her legs were cooperating and accepted that lying in a bed wasn't their new life now.

Nate threw the sweatpants towards Lynn who quickly raised her left arm and caught them in the air. The Agent watched her curiously, seeing that she didn't lose balance while catching the pants but he also realized that she had caught it with her left hand although she normally preferred her right one. Raising her right arm was still painful for Lynn, as the surgery wound was on that side. He felt the same although his wound was already looking pretty good. Toby had been surprised by how fast he was recovering and said that "it must be because he was in such a good physical state". Nate wasn't so sure about that as he had always recovered fast, even as a child.

Lynn held on to the desk for some stability before slipping into the sweatpants.

"Don't test me, honey," she groaned, well-aware of the intention of the pants-throw.

"Sorry," he mumbled before adding: "Just for the record, you passed the test with flying colors."

Lynn started to laugh while Nate stepped in front of her, grabbed her face in his large hands, and placed a tender kiss on her forehead, her nose and on her lips last.

"I love you," he mumbled.

"I love you more."

Hand in hand they left his room and headed towards the communal kitchen. Marta and Oliver were already sitting at the dining table, chatting about something Lynn couldn't hear.

"Good morning," she shouted in the room, making both of her colleagues turn their heads around.

"Good morning, Lynn." Oliver smiled.

"Good morning! Look who's walking to get breakfast all on her own, huh?" Marta mocked.

"Don't get too excited, Marta. It's only walking," Lynn huffed.

She walked in front of Nate now, making her way straight towards the fridge to grab some ingredients for breakfast. With a little grimace she observed the contents of the fridge, silently considering what she wanted to eat.

Nate had halted in his movements for a moment, awkwardly standing on the other side of the island. He looked at Lynn for another second before stepping towards the table and taking a seat next to Oliver.

"Hey, pal. How are you feeling?" the blond asked.

"Good actually. Barely feel the wound anymore. It's just a matter of time until I'm cleared to work again." He directed the last part towards Marta who nodded with a smile.

Lynn had grabbed some eggs, an avocado, bagels, butter, and sriracha sauce out of the fridge and was currently cracking some eggs into a pan to make scrambled eggs.

"You okay with her doing this all alone?" Marta asked in a low voice, careful that Lynn wasn't able to hear it.

"Tried to talk her out of it, unsuccessfully as you can see," Nate commented, his eyes locked on Lynn.

Carefully observing every step she took, every movement with her upper body. He was alert, ready to jump off his chair and run to her side in case she gave any small signal that it was too much, but he let her do it alone.

"Seems like you finally found someone to match your stubbornness," Marta chuckled.

Nate only huffed in response but couldn't hide the smirk that danced around his lips. Lynn had almost finished preparing the avocado bagels and was finishing them off by putting some sea salt and black sesame on top. Then she shoved the scrambled eggs from the pan onto the two plates and placed both plates on a tray she had already got out of one of the cabinets.

So far she was still smiling, no sign of her injury. She turned around to another cabinet and was about to get two glasses out of it but because they were placed very high, Lynn needed to stretch her arm in the air to reach them and that movement pulled her stitches a little. She whined a small "ow" but scolded herself immediately for it. Screeching noises could be heard as Nate rose from his chair.

"Don't you dare!" Lynn exclaimed.

"You're good?" Nate asked, still standing next to his chair.

"Yes. Just pulled the stitches a little, but I'm fine. Sit down."

"Yes Ma'am."

Lynn placed the glasses on the tray and grabbed the orange juice out of the fridge to place it beside them. Then she grabbed the whole tray and carefully carried it towards the table. Nate, who was sitting again, watched her, concern written all over his face. He didn't like it. It was still too early in his opinion but he knew it would only end in another fight if he helped her right now.

It took her a little longer than usual but in the end the breakfast and orange juice ended on the table and Lynn was smiling from ear to ear. She quickly wiped away the sweat on her forehead and took her place in front of Nate.

"Told you." She winked at him.

"I'm proud of you." Nate smiled.

"Wow, I'm impressed. Seems like Becks is really making improvements with you," Marta commented.

"Yes. She's an angel. Challenging me a lot every day. I'll have my next session with her at 11."

"Then you can tell her about this morning," Oliver added.

"Absolutely. I'll tell her that I improved a lot thanks to Nate," She giggled before loading her fork full of scrambled eggs.

"Thanks to me?" the brunet man asked, confused.

"Yeah. Cuddling is the best medicine!" she laughed. Nate reached out his hand to Lynn's face and booped his finger on her nose.

"Only if you listen to the one that gives you the cuddles," he commented, making all four of them laugh again.

They enjoyed the breakfast afterwards, both couples shooting loving gazes between them while eating in silence.

Nate was sure that it was only his imagination but that morning the avocado toast tasted even better than usual.

# Thank you

**September 16<sup>th</sup>, 2022**

"Come on, Lynn. You can do 3 mph, right?" Becks mocked her patient walking on the treadmill.

"I'll try, " the doctor sighed, already sweating and panting like she was running a marathon.

They had increased the intensity of her PT a lot over the last two weeks, preparing her for finally getting back to work. Toby had pulled out her stitches a week ago, making her able to work on mobility for her upper body. That was what they did in the afternoons: mobility, stretching, flexibility, and balance. Everything to get her body back to 100%. Every morning she and Becks worked on her endurance and strength.

Warming up was walking on the treadmill or riding the indoor bike and then they strengthened her muscles. Focus was on her legs as they had been the sorest from her time in the med-bay.

From time to time Nate joined their morning sessions, doing his own workout to slowly but steadily get back into field-shape as well. He was able to do way more exercises early in his recovery but the upper body stuff had to wait until he was freed from the stitches. His entire right side had been covered in bruises for a while, making him not even thinking about training his core, but the bruises were fading and under the supervision of Becks he was able to get back into his normal workout routine.

Today was one of the mornings he joined them training, curious as to how much Lynn had already improved. In her everyday life you could barely see the injury anymore. She moved around effortlessly, only wincing once in a while when she turned her upper body too fast or stabbed her elbow right in the fresh scar of the surgery wound. She wasn't up to full strength yet but nobody expected that anyways.

Except for Lynn.

The doctor was more and more impatient, itching to get back into the med-bay. As a doctor, not a patient. She was thankful that Toby had been there to treat the Agents in the time she wasn't allowed to but she missed her job. Nate tried to fill her days with spending time together, doing the PT exercises, cooking together, they even started to do a puzzle together. Just to stop it ten minutes later when they were about to scream at each other because they were both way too impatient for a puzzle.

"Do you want to get back to work, or not?" Becks asked with a mischievous grin on her face.

After a few weeks of working with Lynn the PT knew exactly how to motivate her.

"Of course," Lynn answered, turning the speed of the treadmill on 3 mph to prove to Becks that she was more than capable of going back to work.

Nate had started with some foam rolling as he had trained his legs the previous day and his muscles were really sore. He stepped on the treadmill right next to Lynn and started to walk. He didn't feel like jogging today but keeping Lynn company during her warm-up was always something he liked.

Lynn looked over to his treadmill and saw that his speed was 3.5 mph. She rolled her eyes and shot Nate a challenging glance before increasing her own speed to 3.5mph as well.

Becks tilted her head a little, alternating her eyes between the two lovebirds and smiled again. Every time Nate joined them in PT Lynn was extra motivated, trying to show him how much she had improved and that she wasn't broken. Becks liked that, it made her job easier, because she didn't need to motivate Lynn to test her limits.

"This isn't a battle, darling," Nate's voice trembled with a warning when he increased the speed of his treadmill to start jogging.

He knew Lynn wasn't able to do that yet and he didn't want her to over-exert herself just because she saw a battle in absolutely anything.

Instead of accepting it Lynn shot him a fiery look, increasing the speed of her treadmill as well until she wasn't able to do normal steps and needed to run instead.

"Lynn," Becks warned.

"It's okay. I can do it," the doctor panted between shallow breaths.

"Lynn," Nate said as well, his voice was less warning, more demanding now. Demanding her to stop the bullshit she was doing right now.

"You don't need to prove anything to us," he added and Becks supported his statement with a nod.

Lynn didn't listen, just kept on focusing on placing one foot in front of the other as well as her breathing. It worked much better than she expected and that made her happy and motivated her even more. She felt the burning glares of Nate and Becks on her skin but she kept on jogging. After almost five minutes she reduced the speed back to 2.5mph and returned to walking. Sweat was trickling down from her forehead onto her nose before it dropped down on her crimson-colored shirt. A smile formed on her lips when she looked at Becks. Then she turned her head towards Nate.

"Told you," she said before sticking her tongue out.

Nate couldn't help himself and started to laugh. A loud and rumbling laugh echoed through the room while he tried to maintain his balance on the treadmill.

"I love you, my little stubborn sunshine."

"Stop it before I need to vomit. Lynn, wipe off that sweat and follow me to the dumbbells. We're doing upper body today, Nate, if you want to join us, feel free." Becks' voice brought them back to reality.

Lynn giggled and stepped off the treadmill to follow the PT to the dumbbells. She pursed her lips to blow Nate a kiss who grinned at her in response.

An hour later they were done with their workout session, both sweaty as Becks had challenged them a lot. Upper body was still uncomfortable, stretching the sore muscles after their surgeries and strengthening them at the same time. Nate was still struggling with pullovers and chest flies so of course Becks let him focus on those. Thankfully he'd gotten rid of the wrist brace a few days ago and was now able to do those exercises again, even if it was with baby weights.

Lynn opened the door to her own room, Nate following right behind her. He closed the door behind him, placed his palms on each side of Lynn's waist, and left wet kisses along her exposed neck.

"Hey, I'm all sweaty," she whined.

"I don't care," Nate mouthed between kisses.

"We really need a shower," Lynn whispered, with no intention of moving as she really enjoyed his lips on her hot skin.

"I know."

With a swift movement Nate spun Lynn around and grabbed her butt to lift her up in the air. She gasped in surprise but wrapped her legs around his middle and her arms around his neck to steady herself. She could hear him stifle a groan when a sharp pain radiated in his side. His lips crashed into hers when he started moving them into the attached bathroom. He placed Lynn on the wash basin in front of him and continued to fiercely kiss her. His hands roamed over her body, starting to get rid of the clothes that were sticking to her sweaty body.

"Nate. Nate. Naaaaatteee," Lynn whined in between the kisses.

She managed to successfully hide a moan from him when he pressed his hips into hers and she could feel his manhood right next to her core. He stopped his kisses, framed her face with his large hands, and looked her deep in the eyes.

"Yes, darling?"

"I... I think I'm too exhausted for that right now. Every muscle in my upper body hurts and my right side even more.

I'm sorry," she turned her head to the side, avoiding his gaze while the guilt was mirrored in her eyes.

"Hey. Look at me," Nate demanded in a loving voice.

She followed his command.

"Totally fine, darling. It's me that should be sorry. My lust got the better of me. You're right. It was a hard workout. My side hurts as well. Let's have a relaxing shower and then get some food."

"You're really the best boyfriend ever." Lynn smiled before giving him a last kiss.

Nate stepped away from her, quickly stripped out of his clothes, and started the shower. Lynn's eyes were fixed on his beautiful butt and she sighed a silent "what a shame".

In the shower Nate took his time to give Lynn a proper head massage with her favorite peachy shampoo. She leaned into him, her eyes closed, and she was humming 'Mockingbird' by Eminem. Multiple praises left her mouth while she enjoyed Nate taking care of her. She didn't need to do a single thing on her own as Nate also soaped her entire body with the shower gel. The smile on her lips never faded until Nate turned off the shower. She opened her eyes and looked at him with a pout on her lips.

"Don't be disappointed. I'll take care of you tonight as well." He winked and threw the fluffy towel towards her.

She wasn't fast enough to react so it crashed into her and covered her entire head. Nate's laughter could be heard around the whole headquarters and when Lynn grabbed the towel from her head she saw him kneeling on the floor in laughter, steading his shaking body.

She stepped next to him and placed a loving kiss on the top of his head, not caring that it was all still wet.

"Love you, idiot," she said while drying her body.

Nate couldn't answer as he was still laughing.

"I'm so sorry, but that looked so hilarious and adorable at the same time," he managed to say after a few deep breaths. He was standing now, wrapped his arms around Lynn from behind, and rested his chin on her shoulder.

"I love you more," he added.

"Speaking of tonight..." Lynn started and saw Nate raise an eyebrow on her in the mirror in front of them. She wiggled out of his wrap and turned around to him.

"I have a surprise for you tonight."

"A surprise? Should I be scared?" He mocked.

"No, idiot. I'll pick you up at 7. Don't eat too much today!" Lynn responded while slapping her palm on his upper arm.

"Wait. You're picking me up? That means we're not spending the day together?" Now it was Nate's time to throw a pout at her.

"No, honey. Not today. I'm busy with the surprise. You can ask Oliver if he wants to do a puzzle with you."

Nate rolled his eyes and shook his head in response.

"Sorry for trying something neeeewwwww, but it's noted. Never try something new with Lynn Summers or she'll remind you all over again that it was a big fail."

"Awwwwww, don't feel offended. You tried and we both agreed it was a failure," Lynn answered with another wink. Nothing could ruin her good mood today. Not even the memories of the puzzle disaster.

"Okay. 7pm sharp. I'll be waiting for you!" he retorted with a smirk.

"You'd better."

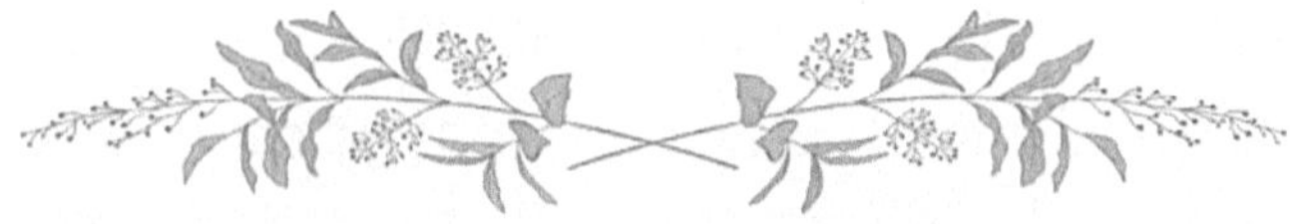

It was 7:05 pm and Nate was pacing up and down his room while mumbling stuff to himself. Did she forget him? Did something happen to her? Did she still love him?

Then he shook his head intensely to get the intrusive thoughts out of his head. She was only five minutes late. Five minutes. That didn't mean anything. At exactly that moment he heard a loud knock from his door. He sprinted towards it and opened it with a quick pull.

Standing in front of him in an emerald-green loose fit skirt and a white t-shirt, was the love of his life. His eyes widened when he checked her out before his features softened and he shot her a loving look.

"You look amazing, darling."

Nate was wearing his favorite black jeans combined with a white shirt as well. It was casual but he was comfortable in it. Lynn stepped aside so that he could join her in the hallway.

"Thank you. You don't look too bad yourself. I like the way your butt looks in those jeans. They're my favorite," she said and quickly pinched into one of his butt cheeks, making Nate jump in the air.

They both chuckled while Lynn slipped her hand into his and intertwined her fingers.

"So where are we going?" Nate asked.

"Actually it's not a long walk, but I wanted to pick you up anyways."

After a few steps they stood in front of the doorframe to the communal kitchen and Lynn stepped inside, practically pulling Nate after her. The Agent froze in his movement when his eyes were illuminated by hundreds of candles all around the big room. The dinner table was already set with two plates, glasses, a bottle of wine, and candles in different sizes and colors. It looked like Lynn had gathered all the candles in the building and lit them tonight.

"Wow, darling. This is beautiful," he mumbled with his mouth still open in awe.

"I know it's not a lot but because of my house arrest I'm not able to take you out to a fancy restaurant," she whispered and he could hear a slight sadness shining through the words.

"I love this even more than a fancy restaurant," he answered before placing a kiss on her cheek.

He felt make-up on his lips and was surprised. Lynn normally never cared for make-up. But today she had.

Their hands were still connected and she gently pulled him into the room and towards the dinner table. On one of the plates Nate could see a letter with his name in calligraphy on it:

*Nate Sheppard*

"Oh wow, did you write that?" he asked in awe.

"Yeah. Don't ask how many attempts it took until it looked like I wanted it to look," she sighed.

"How many?"

"Let's say... if you look into the bin in my room there might be around 30-40 screwed up envelopes." She let out a stifled laugh.

"Oh wow. You really wanted it to be perfect then." He smiled at her.

"Yes. Because it's for you."

"You're super adorable, you know that?" Nate turned around to give her a kiss on the nose.

Lynn closed her eyes and smiled into the kiss. She loved it when he did that. She couldn't remember when he started it but it was their signature. Something she had never done before with a boyfriend. It was adorable and unique.

"Open it while I finish the appetizers," Lynn softly commanded before letting go of his hand and rushing into the kitchen.

She fumbled with the oven and after a few seconds Nate lowered his gaze and looked at the envelope on the plate. He carefully grabbed it, opened it, and pulled the letter out. He immediately recognized Lynn's normal handwriting although it looked like she tried to write as neatly as possible. Especially because she hated the cliché that doctors always had bad handwriting.

Nate ♡
I know one dinner is not enough to express how grateful I am for your support during this hard time. You've been by my side in

all the moments I needed you the most. After the stabbing, while I was in the coma, and you even donated a part of your liver so that I could survive. A simple dinner really isn't enough to thank you.
I will show you every moment for the rest of my life how much your support means to me.
But that's not all I want to thank you for (although it's a huge  thing). Thank you for giving me another chance after I fucked up. Thank you for being patient and for suggesting therapy sessions. Thank you for all the wonderful dates.  Every minute I share with you is wonderful. Sorry for the puzzle disaster but patience is really something we're not  good at.
Thank you for trying all over again.
But mostly:
Thank you for ignoring the demons in your mind.
I know they were pretty loud in the beginning, making you doubt everything between us. I'm so fucking proud of you that you got out of that rabbit hole alone. You've improved so much since I first met you. You are so strong, Nate. And I'm so fucking proud of you. It still feels like a dream to call you my boyfriend and I just hope I never wake up again.
I love you forever, Nate Sheppard.
Thank you for staying with me. Thank you for fighting for us over the past few months. Thank you for being the light in my life.
Lynn ♡

Tears were falling down his cheeks when Nate looked up from the letter in his shaking hands. He turned his head to look for Lynn whose chestnut eyes were already waiting for him. She had been anxious about how he would react to the letter. Tears had gathered in her own eyes and the moment she saw him crying because of her letter, they slid down her face as well.

"Darling," he mouthed so low that she hadn't heard him but she didn't need to. She knew exactly what he wanted to say.

Lynn gave another look into the oven, threw the gloves on the counter next to it, and slowly stepped in Nate's direction. He saw her coming, placed the letter on the plate again, and took one step to meet her. He didn't need to say anything, Lynn automatically crashed into his embrace, wrapped her arms around his middle, and snuggled her nose into his chest. Nate held her close, placing kiss over kiss on top of her head while the tears were still falling.

"I love you so much," he whispered in her hair.

"I love you more."

She wanted to step out of his embrace but Nate still had his arms around her shoulders, pressing her even closer towards him. Lynn giggled a little, lovingly caressing the fingertips of one of her hands over his spine.

"I've never got such a beautiful letter. This means a lot to me. Thank you."

"No, thank you. For everything. It was the least I could do," she mumbled in his chest, her voice muffled through the fabric of his white shirt.

With a little more strength this time she was able to get herself free of his arms. She stood on her tiptoes to place a kiss on his lips, before rushing back to the oven.

"Sit down, food is ready."

"Yes Ma'am," Nate responded with a laugh.

Lynn slipped her hands into the gloves and grabbed the casserole out of the oven. It had a weird shape and Nate was sure that he hadn't seen this one before. He saw Lynn getting different muffin shaped things out of the casserole and was curious. He had smelled this dish before but it had been a long time ago and he wasn't really sure what exactly it was. Lynn placed two muffins on each of the small plates and carried them towards the table.

"We have Cornbread as a starter, one flavored with different herbs, the other with cheese," she explained and placed the smaller plates onto the big plates that were already standing on the table. Nate saw that they had each of the flavored cornbread muffins on their plates.

"Oh wow. I love that. Haven't eaten those since I was a teenager," Nate exclaimed with sparks in his eyes.

He took his time to observe both of the muffins before raising his head to look at his girlfriend that had taken her place in front of him.

"I know. Your mom told me it was your favorite while you were still living at home." She smiled.

Nate's eyes widened and his lips parted.

"What did you just say?"

"I said your mom..."

"Did you... did you talk to my mom?" Nate was completely and utterly shocked.

"Yes. It took me a lot of research and Oliver's help to find the rehab home she is in."

"But she is not responsive. She doesn't even recognize me anymore. That's why I haven't visited in a while. The nurses always told me it freaks her out when I call and she's forced to talk to a stranger." Nate's face contorted while thinking about all the painful memories he had when he tried to call his mom. On her birthday or Christmas. It was always the same panicked answer, so eventually he stopped doing it.

"I know. It took me around six calls to get her at least to talk to me. The nurses and I figured out that in good moments she still has memories of you as a child. So I told her I was your primary school teacher and we wanted to prepare a surprise lunch for your birthday. And I asked her what you liked to eat."

"Lynn you..." Nate started but wasn't able to finish his sentence. He swallowed the lump in his throat.

"I know. I wanted to. You've been through so much since you joined the SEALs. I thought re-creating a happy memory from your childhood would be nice."

The woman smiled at him, her own tears falling down as she wasn't able to hold her emotions at bay. His reaction was priceless, better than she had expected. All she wanted was to make him happy.

"Thank you," he mouthed, extending his hand over the table to give hers a squeeze.

They both tried the different flavored corn cheese muffins and agreed that the cheese one was a 10/10 and the herbs one an 8/10.

"When your mom told me your favorite main dish, I started to laugh. I didn't know what to expect, but Mac and Cheese? That is the most American thing ever, Nate." She laughed while bringing the smaller plates back to the kitchen.

She placed them in the sink before carefully portioning the main dish into plates that were more like a bowl than a plate.

She carried them to the table and placed them on the large plates in front of them.

"I love Mac and Cheese. It just tastes like home for me. Mom struggled a lot to pay all the bills after dad's death, so this was easy to make and cheap. I mostly did it myself when mom was at her day-job," Nate explained with a slight frown on his face.

"Day-job?" Lynn asked before she stood from her chair again and ran back to the kitchen to grab a small bowl she already prepared.

"Yeah. I told you she had two jobs. She worked as a cashier in her day-job and cleaned office buildings in a night-job. It was the only way we could afford to live. That's why I cooked on my own a lot. Well, mostly I got myself take-away or stayed at my friends' houses for lunch. They all knew about mom's struggles and helped as best as they could."

"Wow, that's very supportive." Lynn sat down in front of him again, placing the bowl between them.

"Yeah. Wait. What is this?" Nate asked confused, eying the bowl with suspicion.

"Caramelized onions. That's a Summers' family tradition. We always eat them on Mac and Cheese," Lynn explained.

"Oh wow. Never heard about that. Where did you get that from?"

"My great-grandmother is German. Over there you eat something similar to Mac and Cheese and they always have caramelized onions on top of it."

"I didn't know you were German. Can you speak the language?" Nate asked before taking the first mouthful of food.

"Nope. She fled right before WWII and was scared that people would recognize her as German. So she never taught my grandfather to speak it and he never passed it to my mom. Give it a try. I promise it tastes amazing."

Nate looked at her with a small grimace on his face, unsure if he should follow her suggestion to not upset her or politely decline. He sighed, placed a single slice of caramelized onion on his loaded fork, and maneuvered it into his mouth. Lynn watched him curiously and when his eyes lit up she started to laugh.

"That's better than I expected!" Nate exclaimed, placing some more of the onions on his plate.

"Told you." Lynn winked at him.

"So this is now a Sheppard-Summers dinner tradition. Mac and Cheese with caramelized onions. I like that." The brunet man smiled widely at her before eating more of his dinner.

"It's the first of many traditions to come," Lynn added.

# Dinner Date

**March 26<sup>th</sup>, 2023**

Time flew by faster than Lynn and Nate wanted it to. As soon as she was back in the med-bay every day felt like a blur.

Waking up next to each other, cuddling, working, working out, having dinner together, falling asleep in each other's arms.

And then all over again the next day.

They were lost in the tracks of daily business, trying to maintain the love and care for each other every single day but it wasn't easy. Some nights they were so tired that Lynn fell asleep even before Nate came back from his workout with Oliver. Yes, they still spend their time together as much as possible but as they were still limited to stay at headquarters, they were not able to break out of the comfortable daily bubble they created.

Lynn only had less than hundred hours left of her sentence, meaning she would be free to leave headquarters soon. Nate couldn't wait to take her out again, to do stuff outside of headquarters. Movies, theaters, restaurants, fairs. He would do it all with her.

As long as they were still trapped inside the CIA headquarters, they had started a new tradition: memorial dinner. This was different to their regular dinner, as they tried to only cook dishes that were connected to some memories of one of them. Some weeks they even included Marta and Oliver, cooking recipes from their pasts as well.

Today was such a special dinner with all four of them and they decided to grill some steak, potatoes, and green asparagus. It was the exact thing Nate and Oliver loved to grill when they were back home between operations, like on the day of the photo in Nate's bedroom. Lynn had looked at it again a few days ago and asked Nate if he remembered what they had cooked that day.

Ever since Lynn suggested to re-cook this memory, Oliver and Nate couldn't stop talking about this summer.

"My parents were so overwhelmed when I told them that I was bringing a friend home. I remember dad saying to mom 'what is this? High School? He's a grown man. He can't just bring friends over'. It was hilarious." Oliver's laugh echoed from the hallway.

Lynn and Marta were already in the kitchen, preparing the potatoes and vegetables. They had decided to change the recipe a little, so Marta prepared some rosemary potatoes in the oven and Lynn sautéed the asparagus in a pan. As they didn't have a big barbecue grill at headquarters, they weren't able to make it all outside. It was still the CIA headquarters at the end of the day, not a summer house with an outdoor kitchen and lounge chairs.

To be able to grill at least the steaks Oliver had organized a small portable grill from Jakob that they had placed in front of the main building. It was a Sunday so the best day without disturbing too many people. Most of the central function employees had their classic 9 to 5 job but the Agents were around however long they needed to be when they had an urgent case. But this weekend was pretty quiet, making it the perfect opportunity to grill some steaks outside.

"But in the end they loved me," Nate said the moment they entered the communal kitchen with a huge plate full of steaks.

"Of course they did. You were prince charming," Oliver laughed.

"Prince charming?" Lynn raised an eyebrow at her boyfriend.

"Believe it or not, darling, but there was a time where I was so carefree that people actually liked my company," Nate said, rounding the kitchen and giving Lynn a peck on her nose.

"We still enjoy your company, Butch," Marta intervened. She had her face in front of the oven window, inspecting to see if the potatoes were already good or not.

"Just because this wonderful woman made me a tolerable person over the last few months. Before I wasn't actually the best company and you don't have to say that it's not true. It *is* true. We all know it."

Marta only huffed in response. She stepped away from the oven and towards her own boyfriend, wrapping her arms around him and resting them on his butt cheeks. Oliver had placed the plate on the counter and now inhaled his girlfriend's scent.

"Good that you were tolerable from the day I met you. And that never changed," she whispered and gave him a kiss.

"Well, I hope I'm more than just *tolerable* by now," Oliver answered between kisses.

"Get a room. It's disgusting," Nate whined loudly, making all four of them laugh.

Although both couples were like love drunk teenagers, they had the habit of mocking each other with it. Lynn poured them all a glass of wine before they changed location and went to the couches. The veggies still needed a few more minutes to be done and the steaks needed ten more minutes in the oven to be medium.

"So how's the med-bay doing? Haven't heard from you in a while about it," Marta asked.

She had her palm placed on Oliver's thigh and leaned into him. His arm was around her shoulders, giving her better access to his chest.

"It's doing good. The past few months were pretty basic business. A lot of check-ups and a few minor injuries. Nothing severe. But there hadn't been any big operations for the teams. The drug trafficking task force does have an op at the beginning of April, so I already contacted Toby to be ready if I need him."

"Oh that's great to hear. How is he doing?" Oliver asked because Marta had taken a large sip from her wine.

"He misses the CIA. He liked working here. Said, and that's a quote, it's so much cooler than the lame ass hospital he's normally in," Lynn chuckled.

"I don't know about you, but I'm happy that we don't have drama every day. That's exhausting," Nate commented with a loud sigh.

"That's true, pal. We were all a mess when you were hurt, Lynn," Oliver added.

"I know. I don't need drama every day. Working in the ER was very stressful. Of course we had people coming for bullshit injuries as well, but most of them were actual emergencies like accidents. We also had a lot of people that came too late for stuff that should have been treated weeks ago. Just because they weren't able to afford a doctor. It was really like Pandora's box some days."

"It's a fucked-up system," Marta sighed while jumping on her feet to get the potatoes out of the oven.

"Cheers to that," Nate said and clinked his glass with Oliver's. Lynn rose to her feet as well to help Marta in the kitchen while Oliver and Nate continued the conversation and talked about the advantages they had because of working for the government. Eventually they stood from the couches to help their girlfriends in the kitchen but were shooed away to the dinner table.

"I wouldn't have been able to afford the long rehab and three therapists if the military hadn't paid for it," Nate commented while collapsing on one of the chairs.

"And in the end, you got a therapist for free who helped you," Lynn shouted from the kitchen, shooting Nate a warm smile.

"In the end I got way more than only a therapist, darling."

"Glad you see me as more than your therapist." Lynn winked at him.

"From what I hear through the walls, he sees you as a god, too. At least he's moaning that a lot," Oliver commented casually without making a grimace.

"Oliver!" Marta, Nate and Lynn exclaimed in unison, but Oliver simply took a sip from his wine and shrugged his shoulders.

They finished the preparations of the veggies and placed the different plates and bowls on the dinner table.

Without hesitation Oliver and Nate both loaded their plates, happy about all the memories this dish brought with it.

"One day we should all meet up at your parent's house and do one of those pool parties again," Nate suggested with a chuckle in his voice.

"Oh yes. That would be fun. Maybe we can do that when they're cruising around the world. I need to go down to Georgia anyways once a month to check if everything's alright."

"Cruising around the world?" Lynn asked, surprised.

"Yes, his parents decided to do a one-year cruise around the entire world. Starting in the Caribbean and then going all over South America," Marta answered instead of Oliver.

"Yeah. They told me they'd waited long enough to care for grandchildren but as neither my brother nor I have kids now, they decided to do something they'd always dreamed of. Traveling around the world." Oliver added as an explanation.

"I didn't know you have a brother, Oliver." Lynn was surprised again.

She had been at the CIA for a little over a year now but never heard of Oliver having a brother. To be honest they never really talked about their life outside of the CIA. She knew Marta didn't do it because she didn't want to be reminded about her husband and unborn child being killed because of her job. But she didn't understand why Oliver never talked about it.

"They're not really close. Simon had always been jealous because their parents were so proud of Oliver joining the SEALs. He works in a sales department of a bigger computer company and never got the same praises and attention as Oliver. It's a tense topic within the McGreen family," Nate leaned into her and whispered in her ear.

"Oh," Lynn only responded, feeling herself reminded of her own complicated family constellation. She had been on good terms with her parents and they even visited her a few times after she was stabbed but the missing puzzle piece of the family, Ann, was always hovering like a shadow over the family.

"I didn't talk about this with you because I didn't want you to be reminded of your own family. It's just not fair to share all the funny family moments while you're still mourning your sister," Oliver sighed before loading another plate full of food.

"That's very kind of you. But you don't have to stop talking about normal stuff just because I lost my sister. Nate's been through way more and we still talk about terrorists and Iraq," she argued, shooting small smiles to the others.

"True. Not talking about it can lead to ten years of not talking to anyone. Can't recommend that," Nate chuckled, lighting up everyone's mood a little.

Lynn nudged her shoulder into his boyfriend's while giggling slightly.

"No, not gonna do that," Oliver agreed.

"I wanna have that too one day. A big house with a pool. Living outside of the compound." Nate suddenly changed the topic, making the other three turn their heads towards him.

"You do?" Lynn asked him in a low voice.

"Yeah. I'm thinking a lot about changing from a field-job to a desk-job, too. I could work with Liam and be the operator when the team is out on operations. Doesn't matter if it is national or overseas," he responded casually as if it wasn't the first time that Lynn, Marta, and Oliver heard about this.

"Where has that come from, Butch?" Marta raised an eyebrow at him while Oliver stopped eating and just looked at his best friend with a shocked expression.

"I don't know. Been thinking about it from time to time. I wanna have a family someday. Don't want to be a ticking time bomb for Lynn and the kids just in case I get triggered on a mission. I mean let's be honest. It's not unrealistic that we'll find people that worked with az-Zawahiri in the future as well. And regarding how much I was triggered when we went to find Atef... I just thought that I was done with the risky business. I'm okay with settling down now."

He had side-eyed Lynn the entire time, watching the shine in her eyes when she heard his words. They weren't completely new to her. She knew he wanted to have kids and she had hoped he could imagine that with her. But hearing him say this out loud in front of their friends was a special moment for her. Especially as Nate had never been on the emotional side. She placed her hand on his thigh and drew small circles with her thumb. Her head was turned in his direction and her lips curled upwards in a smile.

"You don't have to decide now, honey. But it sounds like you thought about this well," she said with a soft tone.

"I did. I'm ready to settle down. With you." He smiled back at her.

"You know, pal. That actually sounds like a good idea. Preventing yourself from getting triggered will help you heal even more. I don't like being alone on operations, but I like that idea for you. This could do you good," Oliver said after thinking about Nate's words for a while.

"You're not alone. You still have Peter and Eliana."

"Yeah, well. Those two still have a long way to go until they're on your level of professionalism. When they're not busy battling each other, they try to rip each other's heads off. I really need to watch that, because I don't know how long I can take it anymore. We need to be able to trust each other 100% when we're out on an operation." He sighed.

"I thought they'd improved?" Nate asked.

"They get along better, but on operations it's still a little tense..."

Marta furrowed her eyebrows and looked at her boyfriend.

"We'll talk about that later, Oli. But Butch? If you ever want to change to a desk-job then let me know. I promise you, we'll find a solution."

"Thank you, Marta. That means a lot to me." Nate gave her a wide smile and relief flooded his body. This topic had been a weight on his shoulders for a while and he never found the right timing to talk about it. Not even with Lynn although he shared everything with her. Nate hoped that she wasn't hurt that he hadn't told her about his plans before but it really became clear in his mind today. When they were wallowing in memories of their summers at Oliver's parents, a switch was turned in Nate's mind because he realized that this was exactly the life he was always looking for.

"But only if I'll be the godmother of your children!" Marta laughed, earning herself a slight slap from Oliver for it.

"Hey," she mouthed in his direction but couldn't stop laughing because Nate and Lynn looked at her with shocked faces.

"Sorry, didn't want to make it uncomfortable for you," she added and saw both of them relax.

"No, yeah, well. We haven't talked about the whole family thing in detail. So don't get high hopes of being a godmother sooner," Lynn said with a wink at Marta.

She had almost dug her nails into Nate's thigh when the kids-topic came up. The Agent tried to maintain a straight face but needed to grab Lynn's hand that was clawing into his thigh to get some release from the pain.

"Wait, but I can be the godmother?" Marta's jaw was on the floor now.

"Sure. But Oliver will be the godfather, so if you ever break up you will still have to deal with each other to make our kids happy. So get yourselves together," Nate answered this time.

"That can be arranged. I don't plan to get rid of her anyways," Oliver said and gave Marta a kiss. Nate took the time to lean over to Lynn and whisper in her ear:

"Sorry if that was a bit too much pressing forward with this topic. I know we haven't talked about it in detail."

"It's fine. I like the idea of settling down with you in a house with a pool and our kids splashing around the water until one of them cries and needs cuddles from their daddy."

"I love the sound of that." He gave her a kiss on the cheek.

"But maybe not in the next few months."

"No, maybe not. We have a whole life to have kids. No need to rush," he agreed with her. Lynn had only turned 30 that year and they had time to have kids. But just the fact that Nate thought about a future with her and considered having kids with her, made her heart skip a beat. This man was the best thing that happened to her ever. Lynn smiled at Nate who had jumped into another conversation with Oliver about the rivalry between Peter and Eliana.

Their past year had been a rollercoaster and Lynn almost lost him and her own life. But right now when Nate and she were sitting here and chatting, shooting each other smiles and side-eyes from time to time, Lynn realized that her life was perfect the way it was.

Because all the ups and downs had led them to this.

# Better half of me

**March 28th, 2023**

"What do you think about a picnic tonight? Just you and me and a beautiful sunset?" Nate whispered in her ear. He had approached Lynn from behind, wrapped his arms around her middle, and pulled her close.

"That sounds wonderful, honey," she giggled in response.

"I brought you French toast for breakfast. Just wanted to say hi to my very attractive girlfriend before I head down to the gym with Oliver."

"French toast? You're the best boyfriend ever!" Lynn exclaimed while turning around within his arms. She gave him an Eskimo kiss before connecting her lips with his.

"Try my best," he responded between kisses.

"You're doing good. Just keep going!" She smiled at him. Nate gave her a last kiss on her nose before he turned around and was about to leave the doctor's office, when Lynn called his name one more time. Nate froze in the doorframe, turned his upper body and head a little, and looked at Lynn.

"I love you."

"I love you more."

With a very present smirk on his face Nate finally left the med-bay and jogged downstairs to the gym.

That morning she took as much time as possible to enjoy every bite of her breakfast and still wasn't finished when Tia knocked on the door to check if she was ready to see her first patient.

"I'm coming." She shoved the last big bite in her mouth, stood from her chair and followed Tia into examination room 1.

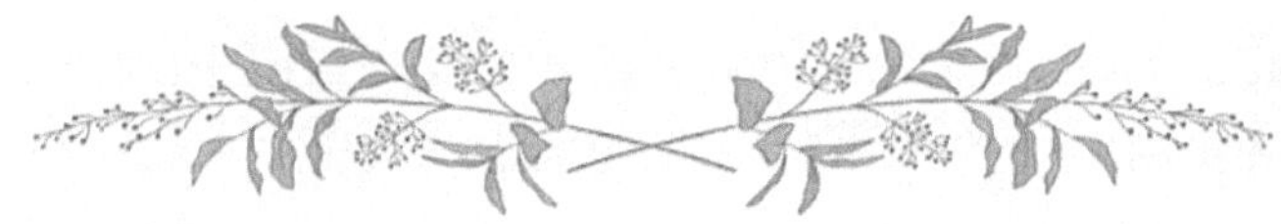

A few hours later Lynn was about to end her shift when she heard another knock on her doctor's office.

"Come on in," she shouted while hanging her white gown around the backrest of the office chair.

Her back was turned towards the door so she couldn't see the person entering her office. When she turned around she saw someone hiding behind a huge bouquet of wildflowers. Similar to the one she got while still being a patient in her own med-bay but it was twice the size of the other one.

"Wow. What did I do to deserve such a huge bouquet of flowers?"

"Being the best doctor in the world, looking hotter than sriracha, having the most beautiful smile in the world, giving the best cuddles. I can continue that list if you want me to," Nate answered with a little chuckle while holding the bouquet towards Lynn.

She carefully grabbed it out of his hands and finally saw the beautiful face of her boyfriend. He had shaved his beard, only a little stubble was left. His hair was cut as well and was now shorter but still long enough so that it curled a little at the end. He had some hair product in it because it looked extra fluffy today. All Lynn wanted to do was drive her fingers through it while plastering his face with kisses.

"I don't know if we even have a big enough vase for this," Lynn sighed but the moment she ended her sentence, Nate showed her his other hand that he had still hid behind his back.

It contained a big black vase that would definitely be big enough to contain the wildflowers.

"I know. That's why I bought one as well." He smiled at her.

"You're the best!"

Nate left the room to fill the vase with water and when he returned he placed it on Lynn's desk so that she could put the bouquet in it. The colorful wildflowers looked wonderful on the wooden desk and Lynn couldn't stop looking at it with a smile on her face.

"It's so beautiful," she whispered.

Suddenly she realized that she hadn't thanked Nate for the bouquet yet so she stepped around the desk to give her boyfriend a kiss. He welcomed her with his arms stretched out, grabbing her waist, and pulling her towards him impatiently.

"Thank you, honey," she mouthed on his lips before closing the gap between them.

"You're more than welcome. I know how much you love wildflowers."

"Yes, because..."

"...they're perfectly imperfect. I know, darling," Nate ended the sentence for her before kissing her nose.

"And because wildflowers can grow even in the most deadly and chaotic surroundings. They're so strong that they'll find a way to live even when all the circumstances tell them not to. I think that is beautiful," she smiled at him.

They stepped away from each other and Lynn took her time to eyeball her boyfriend from head to toe. He was wearing a long sleeve black dress shirt that hugged his muscular upper body perfectly. He also wore matching dress pants that showed off his thighs and definitely highlighted the small bulge around his hips as well. She wasn't sure if he realized what this did to her. Letting the heat between her legs appear just by checking him out.

"You look extremely handsome today, mister," she commented after her eyes went back to his head.

She could see him smirk. He had noticed how she was checking him out and that her eyes had stayed a little longer on his manhood.

"Always trying to impress my girlfriend."

"To be fair, you look good in anything." Lynn chuckled.

"Even naked?"

"Especially naked." They both laughed, before Lynn lowered her head to check her own clothes.

She realized that she was still wearing her navy-blue scrubs. Nate had seen her worried face expression, so he said,

"I've already picked out your outfit so quick stop at your room and then we need to go. It's already 5:30 and the sun will set before 7. And we have to eat first," Nate instructed while grabbing Lynn's hand and gently pulling her out of the med-bay.

The doctor couldn't stop smiling. She enjoyed seeing him spoil her so much. Ever since she was released from the med-bay he had been more than only supportive. He had been the best boyfriend ever and he had kept his promise and started seeing a therapist again.

With every session the betrayal was stored deeper in his brain, making him barely think about it anymore. He focused on the future, focused on being happy. It needed him to almost lose her for Nate to finally move on. Like Marta had screamed at him. She had been right. He needed that kick in the ass and he felt guilty that Lynn was always the one who had to suffer for it.

They entered Lynn's room and the moment she saw the yellow sundress laying on the bed she exclaimed a loud "ohhhhh".

The dress was almost floor length so that Lynn was able to move freely in it. It had a closed neckline, with some tiny buttons on front that went down to right over her breasts. Its color was almost like mustard. It had some cords around the waist so she could make it fit for her body, separating the dress in an upper and lower part.

"It's beautiful," she mouthed, grabbing the dress from the bed and holding it in front of her body while looking in the mirror.

"I hope you like the color. It's nothing usual, but I thought you would look amazing in it." Nate stepped behind her and placed a few tender kisses along her exposed neck.

"Let me get off my scrubs and change into it."

Lynn was excited to wear the dress. Excited to see if she looked as good as Nate expected her to do. She opened the buttons and shoved it over her head, tightening the cord around her waist when it sat in place. She started closing the buttons, but Nate stepped right in front of her and gently brushed her hands away. He started fastening the buttons, beginning right over her breasts.

"I have dejá vú," Lynn laughed, remembering the time she had injured her shoulder and Nate helped her to get dressed.

"Me too," Nate mouthed while he closed the last one. He placed his hands on Lynn's upper arms and gave her a quick kiss.

"I don't remember this from back then," she laughed.

"No, but I'm happy I can do it now. You look beautiful by the way."

Lynn turned around and watched herself in the mirror. The skirt was loosely dancing around her legs and the color of the dress matched perfectly with her slightly tanned skin.

"I really look beautiful," she said to herself. Nate had his hands on her waist now, hovered right behind her, and watched her eyes lit up the moment she saw herself in the mirror. He had hoped she would look good in the dress but now seeing her was even better. The dress was perfect.

"Just for the record, you also look good in everything and especially naked," he said against the skin of her neck, kissing along it tenderly.

"Just for the record, if you don't stop now we probably won't leave this room again," Lynn whispered, trying to cover the low moan that escaped her throat.

Nate stopped immediately and Lynn whined. That wasn't exactly what she wanted.

"That'd be a shame. I made mini burgers and veggie skewers for us."

Lynn turned around to face him, her eyes shining bright in anticipation of the food she was about to get.

"That sounds wonderful. Let's head out then!" she exclaimed.

"Hold on. You need shoes and a jacket. It's gonna get cold later," he said before holding black ankle boots in front of her.

Then he pointed to the black leather jacket that was laying on her bed.

"Oh sure. Thank you. These look great," Lynn said after she had slipped into the shoes and grabbed the jacket from the bed.

She wouldn't need it right now but he was right. It was the end of March and when the sun set it started to become too cool for sitting outside without a jacket. Maybe that was the reason why he wore a long-sleeved dress shirt too.

Nate took the jacket out of Lynn's hand to carry it before intertwining his fingers with hers. They left her room, made another quick stop in the kitchen to grab the basket with the food, and then finally went out of the building and towards the picnic spot they had visited a few times. They weren't able to drive anywhere else because Lynn was still on house arrest but they were happy to at least be outside of the building from time to time.

After arriving at their favorite spot Nate spread the blanket on the grass and Lynn placed the food containers on it. She saw that Nate had a bottle of champagne in the basket and wondered why the hell he'd bought such an expensive drink. Of course there was orange juice as well.

Nate collapsed onto the blanket and grabbed the first food container to open it. It contained a lot of mini burgers that had almost driven him nuts while making them. He'd had to prick a skewer through them so that they wouldn't fall apart while he was carrying the basket towards the woods.

Lynn licked her lips before grabbing one of them and taking a big bite. Nate watched her curiously, his hands shaking a little. He was obviously nervous so Lynn reached out her hand and grabbed one of his.

"They're delicious, don't worry."

Nate smiled at her before taking a bite of one as well. They were indeed delicious. Lynn tried each of the different burgers and praised him multiple times for the food he'd made. She also liked the vegetable skewers.

While they were enjoying their dinner the sun started to set. As they were surrounded by trees they weren't able to see the sun directly but the sky was colored in beautiful orange and pink colors. The light seeped through the trees, making it seem like Nate and Lynn were surrounded by a fairytale forest.

"Wow, look at the light!" Lynn exclaimed, turning her head around to memorize as much as possible from this special moment.

"Yeah, it's so beautiful."

Nate was unusually quiet and she still felt him trembling. Lynn was worried. Maybe Nate wasn't feeling good?

"If you want I can take a picture of you in this light? I bet the combination of your dress and the light looks wonderful in a picture," Nate suggested and Lynn smiled.

She barely took pictures of herself but this moment was so wonderful that she'd love to have a picture of it.

"Yes, sure," she said, standing from her sitting position and brushing the dirt off her dress.

"But let's take a selfie first!" Nate stepped next to her with his phone in one hand.

He wrapped one of his arms around her waist, opened the photo app, and extended the arm with the phone in front of them. After re-positioning themselves a few times to check for the best lighting they smiled into the phone and Nate took a few selfies with them smiling into the camera. Then he took a few with him kissing Lynn's cheek before they did a final round of them fully kissing.

Lynn grabbed the phone and scrolled through the pictures to check if they turned out to be good.

"We look so happy in these pictures," she chuckled.

"Because we *are* happy, darling," Nate answered before giving her another kiss.

He grabbed the phone again with still-shaking hands. Lynn raised an eyebrow at him. She considered asking him if he was alright but he didn't give her the chance.

"Now some pics of the beautiful woman in this beautiful light."

Lynn did a few poses, feeling more than uncomfortable while looking into the camera.

"Darling, you're doing great. No need to frown the entire time," Nate laughed.

"I'm just not used to this," Lynn protested, her head hanging low in frustration; she really didn't like to be in the spotlight.

"Okay, let's try a few from behind. You walk towards the trees over there and I'll stay right here," Nate instructed, pointing towards the trees he meant.

Lynn nodded, turned around, and took a few slow steps towards the trees. She was still uncomfortable, but being turned away from the camera helped.

"Maybe you could try to spin around or something. I saw that online," Nate suggested.

"Nate Sheppard, did you eventually sign up for Tik Tok?" Lynn laughed.

"Maybe," he answered, letting out a loud chuckle as well.

"Okay I'll try to do a few spins."

Nate struggled to focus on taking pictures because Lynn looked so beautiful in her dress. She was illuminated by the brightest pink and orange colors, making her look like a fairy.

"You look beautiful, darling."

"I could never be an influencer. I feel so uncomfortable just standing here and posing for a camera. It feels so damn weird." She frowned while coming closer to Nate.

"I know, but the pictures are amazing. Let's try one more, okay?"

"No, I'm fine. I bet you already took tons of pictures." She smiled, now standing right in front of him.

She leaned into him and gave him a peck on his lips.

"One more, okay?" he asked with puppy dog eyes.

Lynn didn't understand why it was so important for him but she agreed with a loud sigh.

"Just because you asked so nicely."

"I'll make it up to you later, I promise." He winked before instructing her once more.

He wanted Lynn to run towards the trees again and then suddenly turn around and look into the camera. Nate wanted to video it because he thought she would look amazing. Lynn grabbed the skirt of her dress and held it up a little so she wouldn't stumble while running.

She started running towards the trees and couldn't stop laughing. The wind brushed through her hair and the beautiful colors bathed her in their glory. After a few steps she spun around exactly as Nate had instructed her.

Instead of seeing him filming her as she expected he was on one knee, smiling widely at her. He held something out in front of him but as Lynn was several feet away, she couldn't see what exactly it was.

Her lips parted and she looked at him in shock.

Was this what it looked like?

With one foot in front of the other she made her way towards where Nate was patiently kneeling.

Her heart was beating faster with every step and her own hands began to tremble. The object in Nate's hands became more and more clear until she finally identified it as a black velvet box. Lynn raised her eyes to meet his ocean blue ones.

His eyes sparkled with more strength than she had ever seen before.

She covered her mouth with one hand as she stopped right in front of him, unable to say a word.

"Lynn," Nate started with a quiver in his voice.

She knew he was trying to stay as calm as possible but his hands were shaking and he shifted slightly on his knee.

"When I met you I was in a very dark place. After years and years of darkness I'd lost all hope that I'd ever have my old life back. That I'd ever be happy again. I wasn't able to smile, I wasn't able to deal with people and if it wasn't for work, I wasn't even able to truly live. I was barely hanging on, surviving day by day. I was haunted by the past and reminded every single day that I was a monster. That I'd killed people. And I was reminded every single day about the torture I'd been through. Every day I wished I'd died back in Iraq. So that I wouldn't have to go through that over and over again."

He saw tears fall Lynn's eyes and she stepped closer while extending her hand. Nate grabbed it with his free hand, shifting a little in his position.

"But then you came into my life and the sun rose again. My personal sunshine. You guided me out of the darkness and suddenly I had hope again. With so much passion and patience you managed to crack my shell, break down the walls around my heart, and silence the demons in my mind. I was able to smile, I was able to love. The first movie night when you fell asleep in my arms, I realized that this was exactly what I needed. That this is exactly what I'd always craved. Happiness. Warmth. Love." Nate smiled at the woman standing in front of him who couldn't stop crying.

He'd prepared a whole speech over the past week but now he was kneeling there and just listened to his heart while he chose his words. It was raw and unplanned but it felt right.

"Nate," she whispered but he gave her a sign that he wasn't done yet.

"I'm addicted to your company, your smile, your warmth, and your love. Every time you touch me a fire erupts on my skin and every time you kiss me it feels like heaven. A year ago my heart was frozen and I wasn't able to feel anything other than sadness but now my heart is full of love and you are the reason for it. You saved me, Lynn Summers. When I gave up you extended your hand and you offered help. And although I huffed at you and was a grumpy little idiot you forced me to grab your hand and you pulled me out of my rabbit hole. You gave me the life I always dreamed about." Nate took a deep breath.

"I've no idea why I deserve someone as wonderful as you. You are so smart, Lynn. I admire how amazing you are and I love to see with how much passion you live every single day. Helping others is your whole life and I can't stop smiling when I see you swirl around the med-bay. And you look adorable with your tongue sticking out when you're concentrating," he chuckled a little and Lynn did as well.

"Your eyes have the most wonderful color and I love how they're illuminated in the light every morning when you wake up next to me. How you always make sure to cuddle with me first thing in the morning and never leave the bed without kissing me and reminding me how much you love me. I mean, how could I forget? Your love is the fuel for my body. I enjoy every single second with you and even when we fought or during the time I was behaving like an asshole, I knew that you loved me. I felt it. Because we're connected on a different level. We're soulmates, Lynn Summers. We're meant for each other. I can't imagine a single day without you. It's not possible. My heart wouldn't take it. It would just stop beating. You are my comfort, my home, my safe place. I know as long as I have you, nothing can happen to me."

He let go of Lynn's hand for a moment, to brush away the tears that made his vision blurry.

"I know it's not even a year and I might sound crazy right now but you're the love of my life and nothing can change that. When I saw you lying in that hospital bed I realized how fast life can end and that I didn't have the chance to tell you in detail how much you changed me and how much you mean to me. I knew that if you pushed through it, I would go to your father and let him know that I would be by your side forever, if you want me. I know I can be an idiot sometimes, but I want to be your idiot. Always and forever."

With a smooth movement Nate opened the velvet box and revealed a golden ring with a sparkling diamond embedded on top. Lynn gasped and alternated her gaze between the ring and Nate's sapphire-colored eyes.

"Lynn Summers, will you let me be your idiot? Will you marry me?"

Nate hadn't even finished the last word when Lynn started to nod her head as fast as possible.

"Yes, Yes, hundred times yes!" she exclaimed, kneeling down in front of Nate and placing her palms on his cheeks. She had a wide smile on her face, which Nate copied immediately. Lynn pulled him close and connected her lips with his in the most passionate kiss they ever shared.

It was full of love.

It was the first kiss between fiancé and fiancée.

The first kiss of the rest of their life.

"I can't wait for you to be officially my idiot. I love you so much, you can't even imagine how much," she whispered.

Nate placed his palm on her chest, right above her heart.

"I can feel it and I love you even more," he responded before giving Lynn another kiss.

"Impossible," she answered in between kisses.

After a few more kisses Lynn leaned back on her feet, looking at Nate with sparkles in her eyes and a wide smile that would never fade again.

Nate grabbed the ring and slipped it on her left ring finger.

"The ring is beautiful. I love it. Thank you so much," she smiled widely.

Nate took the small pillow out of the velvet box and dug his finger deep into it. Then he pulled a golden necklace out of it, making Lynn raise an eyebrow at him.

"I know you can't wear it at work so I thought you might want to wear the ring around your neck instead. Then you still have it by your side all the time, even in the OR," Nate said and Lynn's eyes filled with tears once more.

"That's so thoughtful, Nate. Oh God, I love you so much," she whispered before wrapping her arms around his neck and hugging him tightly.

Nate managed to wrap his free arm around Lynn and hugged her back.

"Can we please stand? My knee's hurting," he whined in her ear.

Lynn gasped, jumped back on her feet, and pulled him upwards. Nate rubbed his knee with a grimace on his face before starting to laugh.

"Nobody told me proposing would be so uncomfortable!" he exclaimed, making Lynn start laughing as well.

"Noone said love is easy, honey," she answered before wrapping her arms around his waist.

"It's easy when I'm with you," Nate responded.

He placed a tender kiss on her nose before wiggling himself free from her embrace. He ran towards the blanket to open the bottle of champagne because this was a moment to celebrate.

Lynn stared at her ring again, moving it around on her finger while she took the few steps towards the blanket.

"Lynn Sheppard," she mumbled under her breath but Nate hadn't heard her.

"What did you say, darling?" he asked, holding two flutes with the sparkling wine inside.

"Lynn Sheppard sounds wonderful," she repeated, making Nate's face light up again.

"Are you sure? You don't have to give up Summers if you don't want to. I don't care about your last name as long as I'm with you."

"I'm sure. I want everyone to see that we're connected for life and I want our children to have the same last name we do," Lynn responded.

Nate reached out his flute to her and clinked their glasses.

"Cheers to the Sheppard family," he exclaimed.

"Cheers to us," Lynn responded and they both took a huge sip.

After months of fighting, hoping and praying, they were finally happy. Together they had beaten the demons in Nate's mind and heart. Today they were smiling at each other and knew that their future was bright.

They knew that no matter what demon might come, they would be able to defeat it.

Together.

Them.

Nate and Lynn Sheppard.

The End

If you still can't get enough of Nate and Lynn,
they will return once again with an extended epilogue:

*Defeated Demons*

Coming **November 2024.**

# Message

Trauma from your past can eat you alive over and over again,
but there comes the time where you finally have to let go.
You have to accept that the past is in the past.
You have to move on and look into the future,

Because you can't change your past but can create your future.

Think about it!
Before it's too late.

# Acknowledgments

Acknowledgments for a third book are actually way harder than for a debut, but here we go again.

Going into 2023 I was in a mental state of not believing in myself, not liking myself and not thinking I could ever come out of this rabbit hole.

And I wouldn't have if I hadn't had these people around me.

Am I a self-confident person now? Absolutely not.

But I found my passion, I found my smile again and I even started to be proud of things that I accomplished. Like publishing three freaking books!

**Ann,** again I wouldn't be able to do this without you. You're the best best friend someone could ask for. You helped me fight through the divorce and were the first one to read various versions of this book. I have tears in my eyes because I don't know how I will ever be able to give you the same amount of support that you gave me. There are so many more words I want to say to you, but I'll do that in person. Next Friday, on our regular movie night.

**Marta,** with every day you've become a bigger part of my daily life. I love our weird conversations and I hope nobody reads the chat, because they would send us to therapy right away. I can't wait for the biggest Martasaurus hug when you come to visit me and Nimbus next year. Or wait. When this book comes out, you're actually sitting next to me. Feels interception, man. Thank you for being my emotional support in every breakdown. Thank you for sending me tons of messages to make me feel better when I feel worthless, ugly, and not good enough. Thank you for crying with me and laughing with me. Te quiero.

**Becks**, thank you for dealing with my insecure ass. Thank you for stopping my rants about me being the worst author in the entire world and nobody will ever read one of my books. Thank you for finding the right balance between assuring me and slapping my face. I'm so happy that I found you. I'm sorry for all the commas you had to delete, all the "*I am*"s you had to turn into "*I'm*"s and all the show-not-tell moments that drove you nuts. I promise I've learned a lot in this editing process and I'm improving with every book. Only twenty books more and I might finally understand commas in English.

**Don & Mel Saladino**, thank you for saving my life. I know I did the first step on my own, but I wouldn't be sitting here without you holding my hand afterwards. Meeting you in Mexico was a booster for my recovery. When Don told me "It's good to be alive, isn't it?", one morning, something in my brain flipped and I was finally able to really move on in my healing process. Thank you for supporting me on this journey and encouraging me to chase my dreams. I'm a fucking published author, because you inspired me. Thank you.

Last but not least a huge thank you to Tia, Erica, Mihaela, Maja, Tracey, Jacky, Paloma, Fleur, Vanja, Harry, Shicara, the wonderful human beings at the SugarClub, my super supportive street team, and everybody who stood by my side and helped me survive the time of the divorce and everything that came with that.
I'm happy.
And this is all because of you.

# *About the author*

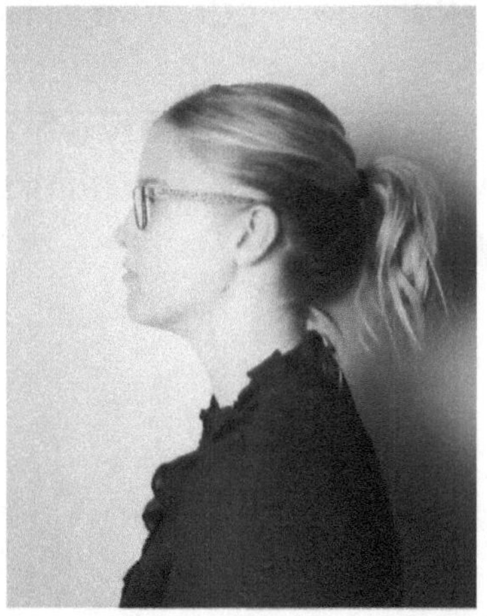

Jessica Girke is a 30-year-old German who loves to write Contemporary Romance books that include heavy topics like mental health issues.

Her structured job as financial analyst is a great contrast to the creativity that floods her brain while writing books and short stories.

In her free time she loves to work out, read while lying in a hammock in her garden, having movie nights with her best friend or cuddle her cat Nimbus.

jessicagirkeauthor

jessicagirke@gmail.com